T0301201

LILLIAN ARMFIELD

HOW AUSTRALIA'S FIRST FEMALE DETECTIVE TOOK ON TILLY DEVINE AND THE RAZOR GANGS AND CHANGED THE FACE OF THE FORCE

LEIGH STRAW

For Larry

hachette
AUSTRALIA

Published in Australia and New Zealand in 2018
by Hachette Australia
(an imprint of Hachette Australia Pty Limited)
Level 17, 207 Kent Street, Sydney NSW 2000
www.hachette.com.au

10 9 8 7 6 5 4 3 2 1

A catalogue record for this
book is available from the
National Library of Australia

NATIONAL
LIBRARY
OF AUSTRALIA

ISBN 978 0 7336 3810 7

Cover design by Luke Causby/Blue Cork
Cover photographs: Angel Place, photo by Sam Hood, Hood Collection, State Library of NSW,
PXE 789; photo of Lillian Armfield from author's collection
Typeset in 12/18.6 pt Sabon LT Pro by Bookhouse, Sydney
Printed and bound by Clays Ltd, Elcograf S.p.A

MIX
Paper from
responsible sources
FSC
www.fsc.org
FSC® C001695

The paper this book is printed on is certified against the
Forest Stewardship Council® Standards. McPherson's Printing
Group holds FSC® chain of custody certification SA-COC-005379.
FSC® promotes environmentally responsible, socially beneficial
and economically viable management of the world's forests.

Contents

Prologue

MAY SMITH PULLED A BRICK OUT OF THE WALL OF AN OUTHOUSE at the back of a shabby terrace on Terry Street, Surry Hills, and stuffed a few small packages in behind it. She knew the coming police raid wouldn't just be a routine search of a suspected drug house and she was hoping that the police would turn over the house instead of the old crapper at the back. May Smith, also known as 'Botany May', was a notorious Sydney cocaine dealer and, on this day, she was edgy and running out of time.

It was April 1928, the Roaring Twenties – the era of Scott and Zelda Fitzgerald, flappers and fast living for those who could afford it. The 'talkies' had extended the celebrity of movie stars, and Art Deco design was symbolic of the cultural edge of the period. It was an era for the person 'on the make', and gangsters and organised crime were on the rise. In Australia, a number of violent shootouts showed the police and public that gang violence wasn't limited to the movies or places like Chicago and New York. Criminal business was booming in Sydney's underworld and it drew crooks in from across Australia. The fatal shootout between Squizzy Taylor and Snowy Cutmore in St Kilda in October 1927 ended a violent criminal rivalry that spanned both Sydney and Melbourne. Australia heralded its own era of gang violence, organised crime and police crackdowns which drew the cities close to Prohibition.

Prostitution, sly grog (selling illicit alcohol from unlicensed premises) and cocaine were the mainstays of criminal business in Sydney. If you could work across all three criminal activities, you could rake in the money. Botany May had tried her hand at all of them. Now she was trying to edge out her competitors by increasing her supply but it was risky business and made her the target of police.

While the criminals were professionalising their businesses, the police were developing separate teams to target specific criminal activity. The Criminal Investigation Branch (CIB) now included a detective branch known as the Drug Squad, which was tasked with targeting drug traffickers in city-wide raids. Its investigations had singled out May Smith as one of the city's worst dealers. Her house was placed under watch and constables reported back, 'shocked to see the number of girls going in her place at night'. They were May's working girls.

Botany May was good at thwarting police raids by hiding drugs in the toilet or throwing them in an open fire but the police now knew where to look and were ready for her quick, last-minute scramble to lose the gear. May had to get craftier.

May wasn't the police's only concern, though. She also had thuggish associates – 'cockatoos' – who would be on the lookout for her and wouldn't hesitate to put the boot into a police officer. The raids had to be well planned and executed, so the detectives needed someone who could get them a result.

There, in the shadows of Terry Street, Special Sergeant Lillian Armfield was hunched down, doing what she did best: watching and waiting for a suspect to slip up. Lillian had joined the Women's Police to make a difference to the lives of young girls and women – to 'protect and serve' them on the streets – but she was also drawn to policing work for the same reasons as so many others who have followed since: the enjoyment of community work alongside the thrill of police chases and hunting for clues at crime scenes.

The job now facing Lillian Armfield was the opportunity to bring down May Smith's lucrative drug business, which was linked to various houses around Darlinghurst and Surry Hills. May preyed on drug-addicted prostitutes and convinced them to deal cocaine on the side for her, while she made a fortune from it. She paid her workers off in cocaine and kept them in a vicious cycle of prostitution and drug addiction, selling their bodies to buy more cocaine. Lillian saw firsthand the impact of this drug crisis around eastern Sydney. Women told her about their drug debts and being held to ransom by brothel-keepers wanting their cut from the sex and drugs. If Lillian was going to have any chance of fulfilling her duties and preventing more young women from entering into prostitution, she needed to take down people like May Smith.

Terry Street, bordered by Kippax, Foveaux and Elizabeth streets, was already on the police radar after numerous neighbourhood complaints about rowdy drug and sex customers. Sydney's poorest families jostled there for space among some of the city's most dangerous crooks in skinny terraces. The houses measured just under three metres across and sat on thirty-eight square metres of land. They were rundown places with small rooms rented out to different people. The walls were thin and the windows close to the street so police were regularly called out after wild parties and violent assaults.

May Smith had featured in an assault case on Terry Street several years earlier, in 1922. A brother and sister were apprehended on the street after a man had been robbed and violently assaulted. Esther, the sister, acted as a decoy for her brother. Her job was to lure men down lanes only to retreat once her brother approached and he would then rob the stranger. Appearing in court to give evidence against the siblings, May Smith – a 'slender young woman, wearing a neat, sensible summer costume' – told the courtroom she had been visiting friends nearby and saw the attack unfold. It was a rare occasion for May: she was the witness rather than the defendant.

By the late 1920s, May could no longer pass as a community-minded dressmaker. She was a notorious underworld crook and, while eastern Sydney locals would often support a crook over a cop, not all of May's neighbours appreciated the business she was in. When a neighbour came forward with evidence against May, Lillian grabbed the opportunity to use him as an informant, a 'fizgig'. The man told Lillian that May was hiding suspicious packages in her outhouse. This information was crucial to narrowing Lillian's surveillance efforts. Now all she had to do was wait for May to slip up.

Lillian kept close watch over May's house for days in the cooling weather of April 1928. Staving off moments of tiredness and boredom, she was desperate to catch May in direct possession of cocaine but she knew she couldn't blow her cover just for an arrest. As she kept close enough to catch sight of any movements near the outhouse, Lillian's eyes scanned the entire terrace while also watching for any sign of May's associates hanging about the place on lookout. There were eyes all around Surry Hills, watching and waiting for a police officer. She would risk being compromised if she watched May's house all day, so Lillian rotated her surveillance. Morning shifts were mixed in with lunchtime patrols and early evening shifts. She could be close but hidden in doorways or backyards. May's neighbours weren't all in support of her criminal business, as Lillian now knew from her fizgig. It was still dangerous work, though. Alone in the shadows, Lillian was putting herself at risk. May's associates could have attacked Lillian, in the cover of an alleyway, and few passers-by would have known or wanted to stop, fearing for their own lives.

May was a smart crook – the two didn't always go together in Lillian's mind – and was likely waiting for the cover of darkness to retrieve the drugs she had hidden in the outhouse. So Lillian waited in the shadows. Her ears pricked at any noise or movement from inside the house. There were moments, as with all surveillance jobs, when Lillian thought she might have missed May and lost the opportunity.

The real thrill of the job, when the adrenaline pumps to full capacity, is the moment a takedown is imminent. Lillian suddenly caught a glimpse of May heading into her backyard, moving towards the outhouse. Lillian elevated herself on some packing boxes to see over the wall, and held her breath as May, holding small packages against her body, hurried back inside the house. Lillian ran to her informant and told him to call the detectives. While Lillian banged at the front door of May's place, the informant hurried the other police officers into place over the phone: 'Miss Armfield's going to hold the fort till you blokes come, but you'd better make it snappy.'

Lillian Armfield thumped one more time on the front door, adrenaline surging through her body. This was the five per cent of her work when everything happened quickly and a crook was taken down. It was the exciting part, by comparison with the other ninety-five per cent of Lillian's days spent building investigations, watching houses, filling out forms and updating her police notebook. Her surveillance had paid off this time and Lillian was ready for May Smith.

Botany May opened the door. Lillian looked down and fixed her eyes closely on her. May was a good few inches shorter than Lillian but she knew how to look after herself with her fists. Her hair was matted and combed into a part close to her skull. The hairclips did little to keep the thick waves fixed in place. She scowled at Lillian and tried to make herself look bigger. Experienced crooks know to keep quiet and avoid saying anything that will incriminate them so May pulled her fur cape tight around her shoulders and waited for Lillian to speak.

Lillian stood up even taller, pushed her shoulders back and readied herself for the accusation. She told May she was there on the suspicion that May was concealing cocaine in her outhouse. In the ensuing moment of silence, the pair measured each other up. They were both in their forties but May looked a good decade or so older. The deep lines across her forehead and bags under her eyes told a hard story of years living in Sydney's crime streets. You didn't mess with someone like May, unless you had a backup team in place.

May took off to the kitchen. Lillian waited warily in the doorway, always suspicious of a criminal's movements. Her police training taught her to never turn her back on an offender. If she did, she would leave herself vulnerable and open to attack. Lillian had every right to be cautious. May was suddenly coming at her with a boiling hot flat-iron, screaming obscenities, ready to attack. It didn't matter how she planned to use the hot iron on Lillian, scalding or clobbering her with it, it would hurt like hell. Lillian bolted from Botany May and her flaming iron: 'I pulled up my skirts and ran for my life. As I turned the corner the iron bounced behind, but I didn't risk going back until I had reinforcements.'

There was little else Lillian could do. Female police officers couldn't officially carry a gun until 1979, some fifty years after Lillian's showdown with Botany May. Lillian had a gun much sooner than that but it was not regular issue and was only meant to be used in serious situations. Though she knew Botany May was tough, Lillian hadn't expected May to come at her with a regular household item like an iron. With nothing more than her police medallion and police card to identify her as an officer of the law, Lillian ran to her backup, Sergeant Small and a few other male officers, who were now nearby. If they were quick, they would be able to catch May still in possession of the drugs.

With the Drug Squad detectives by her side, Lillian headed back to Terry Street, readying herself for the arrest. Too preoccupied by chasing Lillian with the iron, May hadn't managed to get rid of the cocaine. When Lillian searched her, Botany May gave up and said: 'It is no use; here it is.' She handed over five packets of cocaine, whereupon she was hauled off to Central Police Station and charged with cocaine possession.

When May appeared in court soon after, Lillian was there. Dressed in her usual long skirt, blouse and with her hair short and crimped close to her head, Lillian adjusted the string of pearls – her trademark accessory – around her neck and waited. She was in court to represent the Women's Police and provide evidence, if needed, but she wasn't just from the Women's Police: she *was* the Women's Police. She had a small team of women working for her but everyone knew the Women's Police would not have been possible without Lillian Armfield.

Botany May – 'the most notorious retailer of cocaine in Sydney' according to the newspapers – was sentenced to twelve months' imprisonment unless she could pay the fine. She paid the fine rather than do the time. Botany May didn't learn her lesson, though. Less than a year later she was again found guilty of cocaine possession. This time she was sent away to Long Bay Prison for ten months with hard labour.

It was an important victory for Lillian Armfield. Reporters covering the first case in May 1928 wrote that it was Sergeant Small who had secured May's conviction, with the assistance of 'Policewoman Armfield'. By the end of the year, in the next case against May Smith, Drug Squad detectives were named in newspapers alongside 'Sergeant Armfield' and one of her female constables. They were increasingly looking like a team, 'hot on the trail' of drug dealers. In the *Police Gazette*, distributed to all police stations across New South Wales, May Smith's arrest was credited to Lillian and four male officers. Lillian was now included in wider investigations that previously were only the terrain of male detectives.

There will never be another Australian police officer like Lillian Armfield. Many women have followed her into the job but none have experienced it quite the same as Lillian did. Her policing career was of its time and shows us what it was like to police Sydney's underworlds in the early twentieth century. More than this, Lillian not only had to fight crime but also prove to the boys in blue that women could be there too. She was one of the first female police officers appointed in Australia – the first of two, in fact – and was the nation's first female police detective. Back when Lillian's work as a detective was not formally recognised by designation with the title 'detective', she paved the way for women to eventually become detectives in the Australian police forces. Lillian worked as a detective even without formal recognition for her work. There was no precedent so everything she did on the job was on her own initiative.

This is the story of gangsters and prostitutes, runaways and dodgy fortune-tellers, razor wars and the rise of organised crime as investigated by a policewoman who set the standard for women in the Australian police force. It's a story that starts with two convicts and a police constable.

1

Rogues, Coppers and the Asylum

AUSTRALIA'S FIRST FEMALE DETECTIVE WAS THE DESCENDANT of thieves. Lillian Armfield's great-great-grandfather, James Ruse, arrived in Sydney as a convict on board the First Fleet in January 1788. Just as his descendant Lillian would do over a century later, James made the best of the unexpected opportunity presented by a government 'experiment'.

James Ruse endured treacherous conditions at sea for over eight months in cramped, unhealthy transport ships alongside other men, women and children. The eleven tall ships of the First Fleet were filled with convicted felons, military men (some with their families), a small number of free settlers, and the colony's first governor, Arthur Phillip. When they finally reached their destination, everyone was desperate to fill their lungs with fresh air and take in the completely unexpected view awaiting them. It was new, raw and awe-inspiring. It was unlike anything the convicts had seen before.

There on the banks of what would be renamed Sydney Cove (now Circular Quay), they stared out at the newest outpost of the British Empire. The magnitude of this moment remains with us today: here were the first non-Indigenous people setting up a new life in the distant continent which would come to be known as Australia. Few, if any, on board the ships would have considered the legacy of their arrival. The immediate thoughts were of getting to shore and setting up places to live and sleep. Most simply hoped they would survive long enough to see a settlement created in this isolated outpost of Britain's ambitious empire. James Ruse was one such participant and witness to history.

In those first moments, too, off in shadows and progressing to the water to ward off the newcomers, Indigenous people were watching and waiting. The area was a 'discovery' for the British government and its people, but the traditional custodians, members of the Eora Nation, had lived for thousands of years along the shore and across the land. They were coastal people from around the harbour and upriver, and had sustained many generations. Their witnesses on the shore that day would pass on the stories of this first contact. In the days and weeks that followed, the local Dharug people of the western Hawkesbury further up the river were starting to hear stories too. The strangers looked as though they were there to stay.

In his early twenties, James Ruse had made the fateful decision to break into a house in his native Cornwall and steal two silver watches. He was initially sentenced to seven years' transportation to Africa but instead spent five years on a crowded hulk moored off the Plymouth shoreline, living with the ever-present temptation to escape back onto English soil, wondering about his fate.

The British government was trying to figure out what it would do with its overcrowded prisons and hulks, and the hundreds of prisoners, like James Ruse, sentenced to transportation. Previously, British convicts had been sent to the American colonies, but after the Americans won their independence from Britain in 1776, they no longer wanted the expelled criminals of their former ruler. It was an unwelcome dilemma for the politicians in Westminster. Africa was suggested as a location for a penal colony but the weather and distance proved too difficult for what was planned. Botany Bay entered the British imagination after Captain James Cook's explorations of the east coast of Australia in 1770. With Africa out of the picture, the government returned to Cook's findings, along with those of the botanist who had accompanied him on the trip, Joseph Banks. Prime Minister William Pitt and Home Secretary Lord Sydney devised a plan that would ease pressure on the prisons and extend British naval and trade power. The convict colony of New South Wales was thus conceived in the minds of British politicians and would begin with a British military force accompanying convicts across the high seas. The British viewed it as a grand experiment and one that would test even the most experienced military and government personnel: how do you create a respectable settlement from Britain's castoffs?

In those first weeks and months, as the convicts worked to create a settlement, James Ruse quickly adapted to his new life. There wasn't really any other option: he was a prisoner of the Crown and was at the disposal of the authorities. James worked from sunrise to sunset in a cotton shirt and trousers, his hands numb from hours of labour and his head thumping from the heat of the sun. Convicts were initially made to wear a waistcoat and jacket as well but the number collapsing from heatstroke forced the guards to rethink clothing requirements. Guards and convicts alike were unaccustomed to warm southern hemisphere days, which were in stark contrast to what they knew back home. The heat was debilitating and less clothing did little to battle fatigue. The authorities relented further, needing a productive workforce, and on hotter days, especially in the hot weeks of February, convicts were given an hour off during the day. Male convicts worked in small teams – chain gangs – and were put out to individual service as labourers. They built houses and government buildings, and laid the roads that would form the grid for Sydney Town. Female convicts cooked, cleaned and were sent out to work as domestics.

The Sydney settlement was a strict, brutal and sometimes bloodthirsty place, where discipline was maintained through violence. If a convict absconded, neglected their work or was charged with general misconduct they were punished with floggings using the torturous lash. Tied up to the punishment triangle, their backs were flayed with every strike from the lash. If the overseers judged them to be particularly insolent, the lash might have nails tacked to it, which ripped even further into the flesh. Women were spared the violence of floggings but could be made to work long hours with exhausting chores in the house or on the land.

The original inhabitants of this place watched on in amazement and horror. The Gadigal, the band of Eora people from the Sydney area, watched buildings take over vast tracts of their land and white people spread further and further out. The bloodied base at the bottom of the punishment triangles served as a metaphor for the new brand of justice being brought with the white people, first thought to be spirits. Interactions between the Indigenous people and the newcomers were a mixture of 'resistance, accommodation, violence and exploitation'.

James Ruse gave little thought to the fact he was arriving in someone else's land. He was consumed with his immediate future, which meant serving out the year he had left of his sentence and starting out on his own as a free man. The convicts knew very little about the Indigenous people of the area and were not privy to information from the government. Eventually, a newspaper was created for the settlement – the *Sydney Gazette* – but in those first weeks and months word-of-mouth carried information as did government broadsheets that were more receptive to colonial perspectives. If James knew anything of the Eora people, it would have been from speculation and conjecture. He might have seen small bands of people watching him, but fear and isolation combined to wedge a gap between the Indigenous and non-Indigenous communities.

Despite the penal nature of the settlement, it began to resemble a home. After a few months – and close to starvation as they awaited more supply ships – the convicts, free men and women, and members of the colonial establishment watched as the huts became small houses and businesses, and government buildings started to line the main streets. Above the main site of Sydney Town, another settlement grew along 'craggy rocks on the western slopes'. It was named The Rocks. A sense of community developed there among the convicts and ex-convicts as they persevered with the life dealt out to them. This was their new home and their children, who were born there in the years that followed, would know of no other place to call their own. For those children, Britain would be an imagined, foreign place of their parents' life story, different to their upbringing in Sydney Town.

Over the next few years, convict and free settler communities were established, and Sydney Town became a government and trading hub. Convicts continued to work long days and served out lengthy sentences but a decade after the tall ships entered the harbour, the Botany Bay hellhole of the British imagination was receding from view for the convicts continuing to arrive in their hundreds. One convict, William Noah, was welcomed on shore by the many residents of The Rocks in what he called a 'long & wished-for country'.

By July 1789, James Ruse had served his sentence and wanted land to set up as a farmer. He applied for a land grant and, while Governor Arthur Phillip was impressed with Ruse's industriousness, he still had to wait for official confirmation that the full sentence had been served. This would take months, given that the communication had to travel on board ship for months to England and back again with a reply. Recognising this, Governor Phillip allowed James Ruse to occupy an allotment out at Parramatta, over twenty kilometres from the Sydney Town site. James took up his acre and a half in November 1790 and became the first convict granted land in the colony.

Over a hundred years before Lillian Armfield was appointed as part of an 'experiment' in the police force, her great-great-grandfather was part of another experiment. Governor Phillip was keen to see if a former convict could reform and take up farming. If ex-convicts could reform, the colony might be able to attract more free settlers and turn its fortunes around. Potential immigrants in Britain were wary of selling up and moving to the other side of the world to what was still essentially a penal colony.

There was a lot resting on whether self-sufficient farming would be successful. The first years of the colony were particularly hard. Starvation threatened the small population several times and supply ships were few and far between in the harbour. Morale sank even lower when reports came in via the newspapers of ships wrecking along the coast and losing their cargo. It's no surprise, then, that the land James Ruse took up became known as 'Experiment Farm'.

Around the time he was trying to set up his own farm, James Ruse also fell in love. An Englishwoman, 21-year-old Elizabeth Perry, caught his eye one day as he was walking near his allotment. Elizabeth was working at Rose Hill and was a recent arrival in the colony, having disembarked from the *Lady Juliana* in June 1789. The *Lady Juliana*, with more than two hundred passengers, was part of the Second Fleet and was the first exclusively female convict ship. Some of the women were prostitutes from London, while others were thieves, receivers and shoplifters.

One of the convicts on board was eleven-year-old Mary Wade. She had been convicted of highway robbery – assaulting and stealing from another young girl on a roadway – and sentenced to death. This was commuted to transportation and she served some of her time on Norfolk Island. She had two children on the island and nineteen more when she came back to the mainland. At the time of her death in December 1852, Mary reportedly had more than three hundred descendants. Former Prime Minister Kevin Rudd is a descendant of Mary Wade.

Like her lover James Ruse, Elizabeth Perry was a convicted thief. She had stolen a number of items from a house in Middlesex and was sentenced to seven years' transportation. It wasn't simply a petty theft, however. Elizabeth had stolen a gown and petticoat, a cloak, a silk handkerchief, silk shoes, cloth shoes, two caps, a muslin neckcloth, four half-crowns and three shillings. It was a remarkable haul for a young woman and she was lucky to escape the death penalty.

James and Elizabeth married in 1790 and became model colonists for the government's social reform program. Convicts and ex-convicts often preferred to live in de facto relationships in the colony, much to the dismay of church leaders espousing the sanctity of marriage. Reverend Samuel Marsden was so concerned about the number of illegitimate births in Sydney, he created a 'Female Register' in which he listed overall numbers for married and unmarried convict and free women who did or did not have children. Of the 1832 children in the colony, and that Marsden noted in his register, close to half were illegitimate. James and Elizabeth Ruse were, however, staunch Catholics and married before having children.

The Ruses battled for months against famine and drought to make Experiment Farm self-sufficient, and the gamble paid off. James cultivated wheat, corn and turnips, and he set up a small kitchen garden. He ploughed his land carefully, watching the changing seasons, and improvising by burning off ground cover and fallen branches in cooler periods of the year. Fifteen months after setting up what he now called Ruse Farm, with its attractive brick house, James no longer needed provisions from the government store. He used a small team of convicts to help clear and maintain his land. In the space of only a couple of years, James had turned his life around. What had started out as a nightmare, of banishment to the other side of the world, was now an achievement of spirit.

Elizabeth Ruse also enjoyed a renewed sense of opportunity. She was the first female convict to be awarded full freedom and emancipated. Pardons were passed on to convicts who did not reoffend, could show great initiative and would contribute to the future of the settlement. Convicts could be issued with conditional or absolute pardons but the decision was contingent on their work and community connections. The success of the fledgling colony depended on everyone contributing economically and socially. Reoffending was dealt with harshly, as we know from the punishments, and emancipation offered convicts an opportunity to gain currency with the free settlers. By marrying James and helping him to maintain Ruse Farm, Elizabeth had shown herself worthy of full inclusion in the colony. The couple served their sentences, contributed to colonial expansion and filled the government stores with much-needed crops so that others could sustain their own families.

Unfortunately, the Ruses' success was also an opportunity for others to exploit. Around two-thirds of the convicts sent out through the transportation scheme were guilty of crimes of opportunity. James Ruse turned out hundreds of bushels of corn that were sold on to the government. The farm's convict workers saw this prosperity and some decided to abuse it. The farm was targeted on a number of occasions during the night, with convicts taking off with some of the crops. By October 1793, James and Elizabeth had had enough. They were ready to sell up and move on.

While the Ruses battled thievery and the shifting fortunes of the farm, people were talking about land opening up in the Hawkesbury region. In the minds of the convicts and colonists – already having confronted the isolation of Sydney Town – the Hawkesbury was even more remote and detached from the centre of the colony. However, it was clear that more land was needed to sustain the growing number of convicts regularly arriving from Britain. Their population would increase to 5000 by the turn of the century. Free settlers, convicts and ex-convicts were already cultivating the best land available in and around Sydney, and it couldn't sustain everyone. Two expeditions to the Hawkesbury in 1789 had indicated the land could be farmed and government stores bolstered by an increase in farming grants producing more food for the colony. The settlements around Parramatta and out along the Hawkesbury River were the first in a long stage of expansion that would see colonisation extend further into the inland areas once a new route was created through the Blue Mountains in the 1820s.

James and Elizabeth Ruse were among the first twenty-two settlers granted land along the western part of the Hawkesbury River. From 1794, the Ruse family was made up of five biological children and another two adopted children. Parents and children alike had to quickly clear the land and ensure there was a route back to Sydney for supplies and government assistance if needed. The survival of the first settler groups depended on initiative, perseverance and improvisation with the resources available to them on the land and around the river. Their tools were rudimentary at best, with few being able to afford proper farming equipment.

The Hawkesbury settlers lived in ramshackle huts in the first weeks until they cleared enough wattle and gathered soil, clay, sand and animal dung to make a wattle-and-daub composite to create house walls. The wattle strands were fixed in place by hand and the composite plastered over the top. It was gruelling, hard labour. The Ruse family most likely lived in a small two-bedroom hut with a fireplace and chimney in one of those rooms. Later structures included metal roofing and the addition of a kitchen. In those first months at the Hawkesbury, Elizabeth Ruse cooked over an open fire with wooden slats across the top. Eventually, an 'open range' was built and pots were suspended on brackets or hooks above the open fire.

The days were taken up clearing land, ploughing crops for sale to the government stores and maintaining small kitchen gardens for family meals. It was a formidable task and one that James and Elizabeth Ruse hoped would pay off, but the isolation was a deep psychological barrier. Aside from the intermittent arrival of boats and supplies via the river from Sydney, the Hawkesbury was a hard place to get to. A major road wasn't planned until the 1820s and a ferry point was created in 1829. The Ruse family lived near other families on their own thirty acres, but that was still a considerable distance on foot in the event of accidents or children getting lost in the bush or coming to grief in the surrounding water, one of the greatest fears of parents in the area. Beyond the farming acres gradually being cleared, homes were bordered by dense woods and the varying tidal flow of the Hawkesbury River. The winters were cold and wet, and storms threatened to pull apart any ramshackle huts or half-built brick homes. Hot and humid summers brought devastation in the form of thunderstorms and bushfires.

The farmers were also living on other people's land. The Dharug people's custodianship of their country stretched back thousands of years. Conflict was inevitable with the ensuing clash of cultures. The clearing of land for agriculture meant the newcomers were encroaching on Indigenous lands and access to food sources. In their ignorance of the longevity of Indigenous spirituality, history and connections to the land, the newcomers decimated sacred sites and restricted tribespeople from entering areas essential to men's and women's business. For the Dharug people, there was a sudden breakdown in culture and loss of land, with little compensation offered.

Kate Grenville's novel *The Secret River* famously brings this story to life in fiction, but it is based on fact. Grenville's great-great-great-grandfather Solomon Wiseman was an early settler at the Hawkesbury in the 1820s and would have probably known, or known of, the Ruse family. The novel's main protagonist, William Thornhill, is transported to New South Wales along with his wife, Sal, and their young children. Once in Sydney, Thornhill is given the opportunity to take up land along the Hawkesbury. What ensues through the narrative is a vivid insight into the realities of encounters between the original inhabitants and the newcomers. With settlers unwilling to give up their chance at freedom and the wealth that could be gained from the land, and Dharug people resisting the loss of their land and connection to country, violence broke out along the frontier.

Several battles took place – mostly using guerrilla tactics – between 1795 and 1802, with others in 1804 to 1805 and around 1815. The first battles featured the Aboriginal resistance leader Pemulwuy, who speared a convict in 1792 and began raiding farms around Parramatta and the Hawkesbury. Some of the settlers, including David Collins, a judge advocate, believed the raids were retaliation for the kidnapping of Aboriginal children and the clearing of land and sacred sites. Pemulwuy was outlawed in November 1801 and shot dead by a colonist in June 1802. His head was cut off and sent to England. Elders are still trying to locate his skull so it can be repatriated back to Pemulwuy's land and his spirit can finally rest.

This was the life facing the Ruse family from 1794. Dispossession, dispersal, conflict and war over the clearing and taking up of land that was already under the custodianship of the Indigenous inhabitants. The threat of raids by the Indigenous people was talked about between settlers, stories were shared from the newspapers, and a close watch was kept on the surrounding bush for any sightings of Pemulwuy and his raiding teams. There were now around four hundred settlers and their families cultivating farms that stretched thirty miles along the river.

In June 1804, according to the *Sydney Gazette*, some three hundred members of the Dharug people threw spears at Hawkesbury settlers. The settlers fired back and called for a military detachment to be sent to deal with the group. This violence came after settlers had shot and killed Dharug people close to farms. Dharug elders travelled to Parramatta to talk to the new governor, Philip Gidley King, to make the colonists understand that they had been driven from their land and desperately needed some places where they could live.

We don't know if James Ruse was ever a part of the conflicts but, even if he was not, it was clear by the middle of the 1810s that most of the Dharug people had been killed and the survivors had no other option but to escape further into the interior.

The dramatic arrival of the newcomers drastically changed the lives of the Indigenous people in Sydney and the surrounding areas. From 1788 to 1840 – when New South Wales ended transportation – 80,000 convicts arrived in the colony. By 1850 the non-Indigenous population of New South Wales had risen to around 200,000. Compare this with an estimated 770,000 Indigenous people across the Australian continent in 1788 which fell to 119,000 by 1900. It is a startling comparison.

As well as the deaths during the frontier wars, disease also ripped through Aboriginal communities, with smallpox – an introduced disease – killing hundreds in Sydney and along the Hawkesbury. Entire families died of the disease, and communities lost elders and with them irreplaceable knowledge.

It was here along the troubled waters of the Hawkesbury that Lillian Armfield's great-grandmother, Elizabeth Ruse, was born in 1794. Elizabeth and her siblings grew up during some of the most dramatic years of Australian history and, along with growing awareness of frontier conflict, they had to show resilience and adaptability. In later years, these two traits would carry into Elizabeth's great-granddaughter. Elizabeth Ruse was fifteen in 1809 when floods forced her family to move to a grant at Bankstown and from there she witnessed her father's changing fortunes. Governor Macquarie granted him a hundred acres at Riverstone but census records indicate he probably only had forty-five acres at Windsor. Times were tough and the Ruses were forced to remortgage on a number of occasions.

When the debts increased, James Ruse resorted to drastic action. According to one family story, he arranged for his daughter Elizabeth to be married off to sixty-year-old John Wells in 1812 so James could pay off a debt. The story is supported by an 1812 marriage certificate for the pair. Elizabeth was eighteen when she married Wells but, according to family, the marriage was never consummated. It's not clear how many years Elizabeth carried on the pretence of the marriage but sometime into it she met her second husband.

He was a local police constable and, in him, Elizabeth saw an opportunity for a better life.

Edward Hobday Armfield was brought out to New South Wales from Scotland to work on a shale mine for kerosene. He took up work as a policeman in Windsor, one of the five major towns around the Hawkesbury. Before the police force was amalgamated in 1862, police constables were usually convicts handpicked by the governor for the job or ex-convicts who had earned a pardon, although by the time Edward Armfield joined the police, a more organised Police Foot Patrol had been established. Free settlers were preferred and answered to the local district magistrate.

Edward Armfield seems to have come into Elizabeth Ruse's life not long after she married John Wells. In 1813 he and Elizabeth had their first child together, Rebecca, followed by George in 1815 and Ann in 1817. However, there is some interesting personal information recorded for the children. Rebecca's parents are listed as John Armfield and Elizabeth Ruse. George's father is Edward Armfield but his mother is Mary Ruse (Elizabeth's sister). Ann's parents are listed as Edward Armfield and Elizabeth Wells. John Wells did not die until 1820 and it could well be that Elizabeth Ruse lived as his wife until the birth of Rebecca. Listing incorrect parents may have saved some controversy, particularly when Elizabeth was raised in a Catholic family. The birth certificate parentage certainly doesn't fit with Armfield family history, which has Edward and Elizabeth as parents to Rebecca and George. Family history records Edward and Elizabeth marrying in 1822, the same year their child Joseph was born, and both he and his five siblings were identified on their birth certificates as being the children of Edward and Elizabeth.

Elizabeth's parents, James and Elizabeth Ruse, died within a year of each other in 1836 and 1837, after over forty years of marriage. They were buried in the same plot in St John's Cemetery, Campbelltown. On his headstone, James Ruse was remembered as a member of the First Fleet and a settler who sowed the first grain in the colony. Ruse wasn't the first to sow grain but he certainly was unique in establishing the first sustainable farm. In their lifetime, James and Elizabeth saw Sydney and New South Wales continue to expand with free settlers arriving by the thousands each year. British colonisation of the Australian continent continued with colonies established in Van Diemen's Land in 1803, the Swan River in Western Australia in 1829 and South Australia in 1836. What had started with a few hundred convicts, including James Ruse and Elizabeth Perry, quickly developed into a rolling frontier of colonial expansionism.

The convicts' daughter and the police constable created the next link in Lillian Armfield's story. Elizabeth and Edward Armfield's son George was Lillian's grandfather. He married Ellen Izard in 1850 in Sutton Forrest in the Southern Highlands of New South Wales. Ellen was a Hawkesbury local and she and George had six children, with one dying as an infant. Their son George Henry Armfield married Elizabeth Wright in Berrima in 1882. George and Elizabeth moved to Mittagong shortly after, and it was here and around Berrima that they had eight children. Their first child, George, died at birth, as did their last two children, Henry and an unnamed male infant. Lillian May Armfield was born in Mittagong on 3 December 1884. She was the eldest of the surviving children, who included Percival, James, Muriel and Ruby.

So much of the tenacity and perseverance of Lillian's convict forebears passed down to Lillian and developed in her the character and resolve that would later allow her to make the best of her own unexpected, unique contribution to Australian history.

•

Mittagong, or Mitta as the locals call it, was a popular stopping place in the late nineteenth century for travellers heading south from Sydney. They were joined by workers looking for opportunities in the mines, in the iron foundries, and in timber mills. The centre of Mittagong, typified by the aptly named Main Street, was the picture of rural decorum when Lillian Armfield was growing up: a long, wide, clean street lined with hotels and shops. The town is nestled between three mountains and magnificent waterfalls on the edge of the Southern Highlands. Mittagong has been home to many characters over the years, including its first non-Indigenous resident, William Chalker, a former convict who became the town's chief constable. The irony wasn't lost on the locals.

Born with the Southern Highlands surrounding her, Lillian Armfield grew up in a rich, resilient and scenic part of rural Australia. The famous Heidelberg School artists of the late nineteenth century were painting just outside of Melbourne but inspiration for their paintings can be seen in other places around the country, like Mittagong. The Australian landscapes they depicted, particularly summer scenes, are iconic in their vision of washed-out blue skies meeting dry, golden land continuing over sweeping hills and mountains with gum trees holding prime position, and sheep huddled under their canopy for some shade. There are ballads, melodies and poetry in all the eye can see. Eucalypts line road tracks and tower over the landscape as a testament to the raw resilience of the Australian environment. And then in the blink of an eye, it seems, the season changes and green shoots come up out of the ground overnight and, within a few days, the ground gets ready for autumn and cooler weather. The rivers fill with rainwater and the soil dampens and flows along the crevices of the land.

Adaptable, tough, imposing, resilient and beautiful: the Southern Highlands permeated Lillian's character, physique and looks. She grew to a height of almost five feet eight inches (172 centimetres), with light brown eyes, a fair complexion and brown hair. Though she didn't take nonsense from anyone and, according to family, could look intimidating, Lillian was gentle, caring and genuinely wanted to help others. Her toughness was matched with a wry sense of humour and a smile that won over many in the town as she developed from a gangly child into an impressive young woman.

The Armfield children grew up with the belief that there were different domestic roles for boys and girls, as was expected at the time. Manual training work was offered to the boys – Percival and James worked in labouring with their father – and Lillian and her sisters learned household chores and skills. Elizabeth Armfield also believed her daughters should be educated so they could contribute to the world outside of the home. The sisters were taught to read and write and knew some mathematics so that, from a young age, Lillian learned girls were just as capable as boys. This was Lillian's world for many years. The Armfields were a close-knit family with parents who raised the self-worth of their daughters and gave them the confidence to seek their own direction in life.

It was a very interesting time in which to come of age as a young woman. From the 1880s, the first wave of feminism focused on women's suffrage and civic representation, in an effort to extend women's voices into the public world of politics. A women's rights activist, Rose Scott, set up meetings in her Sydney home from 1882 and was instrumental in the creation of the Womanhood Suffrage League in 1891. The first women's suffrage society had been established earlier in Melbourne in 1884, and by 1902 women aged twenty-one and over could vote in state and federal elections. But it wasn't unmitigated freedom and, as Lillian would soon learn, women could push the boundaries and seek different directions to social norms, but there remained a large gap in exactly what this supposed equality meant. Voting and running for office was one thing; being accepted into what were seen as traditional male working roles outside of politics was another thing entirely.

At the same time Lillian was being educated by her mother, young girls and women were turning their attention to the literary world and opening up the imaginations and possibilities for their female readers. Stella Franklin, a young country girl from Talbingo on the edge of the Snowy Mountains, started writing a story for her teenage friends which became an Australian classic. In the story, *My Brilliant Career*, Sybylla Melvyn agonises over whether to marry or remain single and become a writer. Sybylla's quandary was a real one for young women at the time who wanted a professional career. The story would be picked up again in the late 1970s as a film starring a young Judy Davis and a fresh-faced new talent from New Zealand, Sam Neill. The director, Gillian Armstrong, knew that a colonial woman's story would speak to young women of the second wave of feminism.

Lillian Armfield doesn't seem to have wrestled as much as Sybylla with whether or not to take up a professional career. Already confident from her upbringing, where daughters were educated and respected, and where country life demanded resilience irrespective of gender, Lillian considered some of the new possibilities opening up for young women. Her family allowed her to decide on whether to stay close to home or explore her opportunities further afield. Lillian chose a career in the city and travelled to Sydney in 1907 to where her family's Australian story had started so many years before. It was quite a remarkable decision given that Lillian's brothers and her sister Ruby remained in country New South Wales in Lillian's early years in Sydney. Muriel, the sister Lillian was closest to, moved to Sydney in the early years of Lillian's police work.

We don't know how much of the Ruse story was passed down to Lillian – though her family today know the story well enough – but it's likely she kept any mention of convict ancestors out of her applications for work. These days, convicts have been popularised and celebrated to such an extent that finding one in the family tree is no longer a marker of shame. Back in the early twentieth century, having a convict in the family was the perennial skeleton in the closet. The convict period was treated like a blot on Australia's colonial story. It became 'Australia's birthstain', and state governments were willing to cover up and destroy convict records. Readying herself for a respectable, professional job in the city, Lillian revealed only what was necessary to get a job. She was the daughter and granddaughter of labourers from the Southern Highlands.

Lillian's first job in Sydney was as a nurse at Callan Park Asylum in Lilyfield. Callan Park was a formidable place with large prison-like sandstone buildings. There were thirty buildings for the poor and mentally ill, and some criminal patients who were shut away from the rest of society as 'lunatics'. When it opened in 1878, Callan Park contained a hospital ward and rooms, along with a recreation room and church. Patients were encouraged to exercise to improve their mental health and attend regular church services to learn moral lessons that were meant to help with their re-entry, if possible, into society. This was especially true for young women placed in the asylum after prostitution offences. Male patients worked in carpentry, tailoring and blacksmithery, while female patients worked in the kitchen and laundry.

The buildings could accommodate over seven hundred patients but the complex was soon overcrowded. In the late nineteenth century there were 636 men and 318 women receiving treatment at the asylum. There were attempts to improve care, medical assistance and overcrowding by the early decades of the twentieth century but Callan Park remained a feared place for those coming to the attention of the state welfare authorities. An inquiry into the asylum was launched much later, in 1948, after a *Sun* reporter made allegations about the mistreatment of male patients. He had talked to a number of attendants who wanted an inquiry into the actions of other staff who were known to beat patients into submission and assault them for no apparent reason.

In 1907, 23-year-old Lillian Armfield was appointed to look after female patients. Later, reflecting on her work before joining the police, Lillian would tell newspaper reporters she had to maintain a strong, often unrelenting, disciplinary approach to 'dealing with difficult cases' at Callan Park. She had to put on a tough demeanour to be taken seriously by the female patients, some of whom were older or had seen more of life in the city than Lillian.

One of her jobs was to observe, supervise and control the city's 'wayward girls' who had been sent to the asylum either by their families or the police. They were usually picked up on the streets and charged as vagrants if they could not provide the officers with details of their work or residence. Some of the women were prostitutes, while others were associated with 'dangerous types' and gangs. Others simply didn't conform to society's expectations of respectability and were sent to the asylum for moral reprogramming. Unmarried pregnant women could also find themselves sent to the asylum or a similar institution right up to the 1970s.

The work at Callan Park was challenging. Lillian was responsible for the care of individuals admitted as mental health patients, some of whom were there against their will. 'Controlling' them could mean restraining patients and administering drugs to placate them. In 1900, one former patient described the nurses as 'mechanical' and 'inhumane'. This was before Lillian started there, but the strict disciplinary culture had not changed. Lillian would have taken her orders from the older nurses training her and, because of this, would have followed their approach to asylum care.

We don't know what the patients had to say about Lillian – asylum voices are rare in our historical records – and she revealed very little about her work at Callan Park. However, if her future policing reputation is anything to gauge it by, she would have been tough, disciplined and strict but she also would have attempted to look after the women and girls under her care, trying to understand the circumstances that had brought them to the asylum. Lillian wasn't without compassion. She wanted to help women and didn't believe all wayward girls were inherently bad, as defined by society's standards.

Like the other nurses employed at Callan Park, Lillian lived in the housing facilities set aside for female staff. While it meant she lived and worked in the asylum every day, the arrangement provided her with employment and housing security. Although the city was very different to the world Lillian had known back in Mittagong, she developed a love of the beach and wandering the inner-city streets.

The Callan Park grounds are beautiful, running down to Iron Cove, a bay on the Parramatta River. During her time working at the asylum, Lillian was only a few kilometres from where her Ruse and Armfield family members had created their new lives on the banks of the Parramatta decades beforehand.

Though she was fast becoming a Sydney professional, Lillian also enjoyed time away from the city to visit family back in Mittagong and other towns in the Southern Highlands. One family photograph from around 1910, taken when Lillian was visiting from Sydney, is revealing for what we can see of her as a young woman. The Armfields pose together in their back garden surrounded by native bushes and shrubbery. They all have similar eyes and mouths, and while they are trying to look serious for the shot, Lillian's younger sisters, Muriel and Ruby, give away the hint of a smile. They don't look to be a wealthy family but they have put some effort into wearing fine clothing and presenting themselves well. Lillian's sisters are wearing dresses that would not look out of place in the home or in domestic work. Lillian is seated in the centre of the photograph, flanked by her parents and with her siblings standing behind. Her hair is parted in the middle and she is wearing a blouse, jacket and long skirt. She is a professional woman of the early twentieth century.

Little did Lillian know that in less than five years, her career would take another turn and place her in a unique position within Australia's history.

2

Special Constable 65

AUSTRALIAN POLICING BEGAN WITH THE RUM CORPS ROWDIES of the late eighteenth century. They were Royal Navy marines who arrived aboard the Second Fleet in 1790, and while they were far from being a professional outfit, Governor Phillip needed to police the penal colony. The first night watch was made up entirely of 'well-behaved' convicts, each armed with a baton and a keen sense of irony at being given the job of policing their fellow convicts. By the nineteenth century, there were a number of police units around the New South Wales colony before another governor, Lachlan Macquarie, introduced ranks from 1811. Governor Macquarie wanted free men in the job rather than ex-convicts. He wasn't convinced former felons could ever be entirely trusted. By 1862, the colony had a professional police service and a decade later there were over seventy police stations manned by over eight hundred male officers. Ex-cons could get a job in the police but not law-abiding women.

Women were still waiting for their chance fifty years after the professionalisation of the New South Wales Police Force. The opportunity came after the activism and campaigning of other women. The first wave of feminism and the female suffrage movement of the late nineteenth century placed women at the centre of social change. Australia was the second country to give women the vote but, as our Antipodean neighbours are apt to point out, New Zealand beat us to it in 1893. By 1911, all Australian states allowed women to vote in state elections. Edith Cowan was the first woman elected to an Australian parliament and served one term in the Western Australian Legislative Assembly from 1921.

Social equality campaigns also extended to police work. In the US, women began assisting with police work in 1891 but Alice Stebbins Wells, hired in Los Angeles in 1910, was the first female officer with arrest powers. In Britain, the Women's Police Service was founded in 1914 and was staffed by volunteers, mainly responsible for protecting young women in public and assisting female prisoners. Women's groups in Australia looked on with interest. Here was an opportunity to highlight sexism within one of the most prominent professions in the country.

Campaigns for the introduction of female constables in New South Wales were based around the need for the police to improve relations with young street girls and offer ways to prevent female offenders from getting caught in a cycle of institutionalisation and incarceration. Women's groups argued reactive policing was failing young women and little care was taken to support women released from prison. Female victims and witnesses would also be better assisted if they could talk to female officers, particularly in the case of sexual assaults. 'Indecent assault on a girl under the age of 16 years' was a common charge against male offenders appearing in Darlinghurst Gaol from 1913 to 1914, during strident campaigns for police reform. An indecent assault conviction usually carried with it a sentence of twelve to eighteen months in prison but women's rights campaigners wanted greater prevention of assaults by a police force targeting it as a serious crime. If this were to happen, women had to be at the forefront of preventative work and this meant employing female police officers.

The case for establishing a women's police force in New South Wales was helped by the outbreak of war. Australia's commitment to fighting in World War I from August 1914 depleted the ranks of male police officers. If they wanted to enlist in the war, policemen had to give up their jobs.

Two hundred and twenty NSW police officers served in the war, including Constable Henry Chadban. Henry enlisted in Liverpool, New South Wales, in May 1915 and was sent to the Gallipoli peninsula where Australia had witnessed its 'baptism of fire' only weeks beforehand. Chadban was wounded in fighting in August and was hospitalised with a fractured skull. Back in Sydney, the newly appointed

Inspector-General of Police, James Mitchell, was keeping a close eye on the casualty lists. He came across a mention of Henry Chadban as wounded in action and wrote to the AIF Military Headquarters in Melbourne. Soon after, he received the devastating news that Chadban had died of his wounds in the military hospital in Malta on 13 August 1915. There would be another forty-five letters like this.

After years of agitation by women's groups, and with a dearth of male recruits due to the war, the state government finally decided to push ahead with the introduction of the Women's Police. Two positions were advertised in the newly formed Women's Police in June 1915. Inspector-General Mitchell offered his full support to the appointments and readied himself for the media attention they would bring. Mitchell was a hard-working, no-nonsense policeman originally from Aberdeenshire in Scotland. After emigrating to New South Wales, he spent ten years working his way up the ranks at various country and city police stations. A career policeman, he had taken a leave of absence in 1904 to explore new methods of crime detection being introduced in Britain and the United States. He was appointed superintendent in 1908 and continued up the ranks until he was appointed inspector-general in 1915.

Inspector-General Mitchell was clear in the newspaper notices about what the police were looking for from female applicants. Women had to be under thirty, with a 'fair education' and 'of good character and address'. They also needed to be 'capable of enduring hardship and fatigue in the execution of their duty'. Mitchell had a model in mind for his first female officers and preferred women with a nursing background or experience working in asylums. Handling difficult patients and inmates and working long, gruelling hours would ready them for shift work, foot patrols and lengthy investigations.

Newspaper publications and government gazettes offered their support to the new policing career open to women. It came, however, with a clear message that women had a particular use within the police service. *Freeman's Journal* declared women would do a better job than men but not in all criminal investigations. The female officers were there to police other women. There would also be no threat to men's jobs as women had a place in the force which was useful, but not equal to the work of men:

> Were she to have a sort of roving commission as a redresser of wrongs, and meddle too much with matters which are more appropriately now left, wholly in the hands of men, the woman policeman might become a questionable gain to the public. At any rate, she is worth a trial, and her appearance on the scene may be greeted with all good wishes.

Tucked away on a break from her work at Callan Park Asylum, Lillian Armfield came across one of the notices for the Women's Police in the newspaper. After eight years at the asylum, working long hours and witnessing the increasingly harsh treatment being offered to patients, Lillian was ready for a new professional challenge. The discovery of the police notice would change her life. Like her great-grandfather,

Edward Armfield, Lillian wanted to be a police constable. She filled out the application, gathered her references, and mailed it off for consideration.

Over four hundred other women also applied for the two advertised policing positions. They came from across New South Wales, South Australia, Victoria and New Zealand, leaving little doubt that growing numbers of women were looking for professional careers. But it wasn't just a new professional opportunity. The applicants also had to show they were up to the challenge of being the first women in a hitherto all-male police force, most of whom were reticent about following the progressive examples of the United States and Great Britain.

From this cast of many, two women were appointed in July 1915. Reporters clambered to get their first look at the pair as they met with the press, joined by their superiors. Australia's first female constables – with 'strong personality and commanding appearance' – were trailblazers who paved the way for many other women. As they sat there, staring out at the reporters and waiting for the first questions, the magnitude of what they were doing was not lost on the new officers. They were already professional women and were ready for this new challenge.

Maude Rhodes was introduced as Special Constable 64 and she brought with her an impressive resumé. English by birth, she had studied and worked in London, and one of her early jobs had been looking after young girls in state care. On one occasion, she chaperoned over fifty young women on a voyage from England to New Zealand. After moving to New South Wales, Maude became an inspector for the State Children Relief Department.

Rhodes wanted to see 'policewomen scattered all over Australia' and paid the same wages as men for the same work. She was committed to working closely with the various women's organisations. This was an important part of the early public relations campaign around the Women's Police. Inspector-General Mitchell knew he had to maintain the support of the women's groups but also include them in future planning within the force.

Lillian Armfield – Special Constable 65 – was the next appointee to meet the reporters. This time they took even more notice. Described in the newspaper articles that followed as 'tall and well-built', Lillian impressed the reporters with what they called 'a smile that will surely help her to win her way into the hearts of the women with whom she will have to deal'. Lillian was a year older than the cut-off age of thirty, but her experience working as a nurse at the Hospital for the Insane at Callan Park had put her ahead of other applicants. Nurse Armfield was well suited to becoming Special Constable Armfield.

Lillian handled the reporters' questions calmly and thoughtfully, telling them she was ready for the task ahead but knew it wouldn't be easy. She didn't say it publicly at the time but later recalled knowing there would be women who wouldn't want her protection and would see her as merely a puppet of a male police force targeting the very poor in working-class communities. She wasn't fazed, however. Lillian's tough resolve was obvious from this first interview: 'I am expecting plenty of trouble, for women are found difficult to handle by their own sex, and will probably be more likely to resent interference from me than from a policeman.'

The press conference was a public relations campaign in which the police were parading their prize female recruits. Neither Lillian nor Maude was daunted by it, though, partly because they had already endured being shown off to their police superiors earlier. Recollections from other female recruits later help us imagine what this would have been like for Lillian and Maude. Peg Fisher applied for a position in the Women's Police in the mid-1940s and had to meet with Commissioner William MacKay. She was joined in his office by other policemen – commanders and superintendents – who walked around, checking her out: 'I'm standing in the middle of the room and they're giving me the once-over . . . looking me over from every angle. I felt like a prize cow at the Easter Show.' While they discussed her in a corner of the room, Peg asked, jokingly, if she was going to get a blue ribbon. She got the job.

It would have been even harder for Lillian and Maude walking into Central Police Station in July 1915. All eyes in the station would have been on the pair as they entered what had been a completely male space up to that point. You can almost hear the front doors creaking back into place in the silence of the moment as the policemen stopped their work and looked both women up and down. Lillian and Maude were aware of the many pairs of eyes taking in their physical appearance. With her fair looks and strong build, Lillian attracted longer stares than Maude. She always dressed well, usually in a blouse and skirt, and with a string of pearls around her neck. She was ready.

Male officers were known to make quips about the work women were meant to do at the stations. According to some of the women who followed in Lillian's footsteps later, remarks about the arrival of the tea ladies or mention of where the mops were kept were common jokes on the first days on the job. The male officers were outwardly friendly to Lillian in those first days, she would later reveal, but they were very quick to point out that they did the real work. Lillian and Maude were given an office at the back of the building, away from the front of station business.

But their business was often every bit front of station. Having led relatively unassuming working lives before their entry into the force, Lillian and Maude were now in the public realm and their work was discussed everywhere from government offices to the back rooms of police stations, and at women's group meetings. Lillian knew, from her first days in the police, she would face ongoing public commentary about the work of the Women's Police: 'I had plenty of reminders . . . that policewomen were still on trial in the public mind.' There were no precedents, no one already paving the way. Australia's first policewomen were also the first appointed in the Commonwealth.

The work of the Women's Police was crafted in a very specific manner. Female special constables were employed primarily to look after the welfare of girls and women. It was a considerable job with duties including: keeping children off the streets; working with schools to prevent truancy; reading the various daily newspapers 'to put detectives on the track of those who are apparently endeavouring to decoy young girls by advertisement or by any other means'; patrolling the railway stations and wharves looking for runaway or lost girls, as well as regular patrols around slum neighbourhoods looking for drunken women and neglected children. This was enough in itself but the Women's Police were also required to keep a watch over brothels and wine shops attracting vulnerable young women into their business, patrol public parks each evening and enforce 'the rules concerning pedestrian traffic'.

Inspector-General James Mitchell, seldom one for mincing his words with the press, or anyone for that matter, was clear about the intentions behind the appointments of Special Constables Armfield and Rhodes. Female officers were the frontline of preventative measures to reduce the numbers of young women decoyed into prostitution, charged with public drunkenness, or assaulted late at night in parks. Their main beat was the poor neighbourhoods of eastern Sydney around Woolloomooloo, Darlinghurst, Surry Hills and Paddington. One of the benefits of putting women on the streets in police work was that they could go undercover in the brothels and darkened alleyways where streetwalkers worked, and hopefully get the girls to inform on their brothel bosses. This was something male officers could not do. Young girls and women on the streets were less inclined to talk to male officers and felt they could relate better to other women.

Both Lillian and Maude signed an indemnity agreeing that the police department was not responsible for their safety and welfare. The force's duty of care to female officers was severely limited and there was no compensation for injuries sustained on the job. Neither Lillian nor Maude was supplied with a uniform, instead they were expected to wear civilian clothing which they paid for themselves. They were visibly different to male police officers. Furthermore, Lillian and Maude had no baton or gun to defend themselves. They were completely unarmed and had no powers to arrest anyone. Female officers were expected to question girls and women and, if required, take them to a station for further questioning. Only their male colleagues could arrest and charge offenders. Out on the streets, as Lillian would realise in the coming months and years, this was often unmanageable. She could try to detain a person but had to wait for her male colleagues to arrive and make the arrest. It made her vulnerable on the streets when crooks realised she couldn't arrest them. The public were told the work of the Women's Police was low risk, hence the absence of weapons, but Lillian's investigations would soon show otherwise.

While the Women's Police were introduced to protect and police girls and women around inner and eastern Sydney, it wasn't that straightforward. Few jobs were more difficult for women in the early twentieth century than working in the Women's Police. It wasn't just that Lillian Armfield was a woman working in a male-dominated world; she worked around streets where girls and women were threatened by or directly involved in drug and human trafficking, prostitution, gang warfare, murder, abortions, kidnappings and rape. It's a far cry from the trendy cafés, shops and night spots eastern Sydney is known for today. From Devonshire, Kippax, Foveaux, Albion, Crown and Riley streets to Oxford, Palmer, Bourke and William streets and around the main streets of Kings Cross, Lillian patrolled areas ridden with crime and a natural distrust of the police. From houses to laneways, shops and market stalls, to nightclubs, wharves and beaches, the landscape of crime was a vast one for the special constables.

Outside of the obvious risks on the streets of Sydney, the work of the Women's Police, mainly focusing on girls and women, developed along the general lines of policing work. Lillian's training was minimal by comparison to what was offered to male officers. Unlike her male colleagues, Lillian did not go through the police academy. Her training ran concurrent with her first year on the job. She learned the law, became familiar with court proceedings, was taught fingerprinting techniques and given some self-defence training.

An essential part of policing, now and in the early twentieth century, involves 'area familiarisation' – officer knowledge of local areas. Like many police officers, Lillian and Maude regularly went out on foot patrol, closely working their local areas and getting to know the residents, at-risk youth, likely offenders, and known criminals. Lillian learned to walk the streets and fit in, all the while keeping a close eye on the people and places around her, familiarising herself with the streets of eastern Sydney. As one newspaper reporter would later write, after spending an evening on one of Lillian's patrols: 'Miss Armfield never forgets a voice or a face.'

Police observation was a key part of Lillian Armfield's work. During her foot patrols she catalogued suspicious activity and incidents in her police notebook and used this information to build up her knowledge of criminal neighbourhoods. She also familiarised herself with inner-city areas and came to know the locals well, beyond the criminal elements. This observation work was complemented with a collection of written information for intelligence files.

Lillian Armfield also made some innovative contributions to the Women's Police. She introduced the 'dawn patrol', which combined regular foot patrols with close surveillance of life on the inner streets of Sydney. Every morning at five, Lillian and Maude patrolled the inner-city streets looking for girls or women in danger, living rough, or wanted on warrant. They were early morning street-sweepers, but of a different kind. These dawn patrols would influence women's policing for decades to come.

Another important aspect of policing work in the early twentieth century – which still holds true today – is the time spent waiting with complainants, offenders or victims at the police station. While waiting for paperwork to be filled out and signed, or an arrest to be processed, Lillian talked to and got to know offenders and victims better. It was another way in which she built up a relationship with the girls and women she policed around eastern Sydney. In the early years, she usually had to pry information out of them, but once she established a rapport with known criminals and gained their respect – many recognised Lillian was, like them, battling against a male-dominated world – they would open up to her. Some of them became her informants.

This is what it was like to be a police officer in the first half of the twentieth century. Before the digital age, police investigative work was based on reading police gazettes, newspapers, newspaper clippings of arrest and court cases, and collating information from other officer notebooks. Police station occurrence books and charge books also provided important information on occurrences where police attended and charges against individuals, listing their personal details and the offence committed. There were also the many files relating to major investigations.

Police work has changed dramatically since Lillian was in the job. High-tech policing is now an everyday reality for officers across the country, immersed in the digital age with a variety of technological developments assisting in identifying and cataloguing offenders. The recording of information includes the wider use of intelligence-led policing and human intelligence sources, and patrol cars kitted out with Automatic Number Plate Recognition, video recording, radio communication and a mobile data terminal. Communication systems are encrypted and officers in the patrol cars can check licence, car histories and locations, and run identity checks that can reveal offences, warnings and outstanding warrants. Each Australian state and territory uses a variety of criminal databases that assist officers in investigating crimes and providing information for evidence-based policing teams to map crime and criminals.

Although the public relations campaign said policing women was low risk, it was dangerous work.

Lillian and Maude faced their first serious assault on the job in August 1917. During one of their city patrols, they came across a young woman acting inappropriately with soldiers who were home on leave from the war. Lillian confronted the woman, tried to apprehend her, and was hit along with Maude, who had jumped in to help. The woman bolted after the attack. Two warrants for her arrest were issued but it was a long shot as Lillian and Maude didn't know her name. With only a physical description and the woman's known association with soldiers to identify her, in a large city like Sydney all bets were on the young woman staying clear until the dust settled.

It wasn't the last time Lillian would be physically threatened on the job.

Lillian's work took place around neighbourhoods where rival youth gangs were involved in street battles against each other and were known to threaten, rob and assault people passing by. Eastern Sydney also witnessed the rise of organised crime – funded by drugs, prostitution and sly grog – with streets, houses and businesses linked to crime bosses. The criminals were making a mockery of the police force and the inspector-general had to field rising criticism from the government, newspapers and locals around eastern Sydney.

The issues of the *New South Wales Police Gazette* covering the years up to the late 1920s reveal the gravity of the spike in crime. In the years from 1916 to 1920 the *Gazette,* which contained details of crimes committed, numbered between 600 and 800 pages. By 1928, as Sydney was in the grip of the crime wave known as the Razor Wars, the *Gazette*s numbered over 1100 pages. Gang, gun, knife and general assaults dominated along with warrants issued for known criminals involved in serious crime relating to drugs, sly grog and prostitution.

Police officers accepted their work was risky and knew some of the dangers they might regularly face on the job. The 1924 Annual Report for the NSW Police Department – cataloguing cases, crime types and crime trends – lists a number of offences under the title of 'Dangers and risks incidental to the performance of police duties'. One of the main charges was assault on a police officer.

The risks were very real and in the years to come Lillian would face off with drug dealers and other violent men and women who were ready to take on a police officer trying to haul them down to the station.

Lillian knew if anyone followed her home to her rented bedsit at the end of a shift, she would have to protect herself. With most of her family living out in the country, Lillian lived alone and was likely to continue doing so. Female police officers were barred from marrying and having children.

If Lillian wanted to have a family she would have to leave the force.

In the years to follow, Lillian would see the worst of what people could do to themselves and each other, but she always remained committed to her policing work because she knew she was making a difference. She knew that the Women's Police was a worthwhile 'experiment' and could become a legitimate and respected part of the overall police service. Lillian set out to ensure women were pervasive in policing work and could handle all types of crime. On this she had to lead the way. It started with her daily 'dawn patrols' around the city looking for runaway girls.

3

Runaway Girls

WHEN LILLIAN AND MAUDE BEGAN THEIR WORK IN THE NSW Police Force in 1915, World War I was raging in Europe and the Middle East, and Australian troops experienced warfare on a mass scale for the first time as they went ashore at Gallipoli on 25 April. Far-off places like Egypt, the Dardanelles and Turkey came to life for ordinary Australians as they read about the latest campaigns in the newspapers. Every day the casualty lists told their own story of what the Australians were going through. The *Sydney Morning Herald* included a regular series on 'Australian Heroes', with photographs of troops who had been wounded or killed at the front.

For one family in Orange, in the central west of country New South Wales, events much closer to home were far more pressing in July 1915. Their young daughter was missing and they suspected she had made her way down to Sydney. The girl's parents phoned Central Police Station and officers acted quickly on the information. The girl's description was sent to all city stations and a photograph was distributed and then pinned up in Central Police Station. She was a long way from home, some three hundred kilometres, and had never been to the city before. With a population of over 700,000, Sydney was the nation's largest city and a stark contrast to the girl's home town of Orange with fewer than 10,000 people. A country runaway could easily get lost in Sydney, which is what the girl from Orange was banking on.

Detective Sergeant Tom Mankey called Lillian Armfield into his office. He handed her the photograph of the teenager and watched as she studied the image, memorising the girl's face. Mankey didn't think it would take much to find the girl, given she was 'a very pretty kid' and would stand out in the crowds. Lillian was less convinced. The girl's blonde hair and beautiful looks would bring her the worst attention from Sydney's pimps, prostitutes and drug runners. Everything about the girl sent alarm bells ringing for Lillian. She was a young, naive easy target.

Lillian handed the photograph back to Mankey and listened as he gave her his orders. He wanted the girl found as soon as possible, telling Lillian to patrol the inner-city streets and keep a lookout for the girl from Orange. Lillian needed to 'get hold of her quick' and 'snaffle her' before, as Mankey pointed out, she had 'time to change from that blue frock with the polka dots'. If she changed her dress, she would be almost impossible to find. Lillian also had to act quickly before the young girl found somewhere to stay and hide.

It was no easy task looking for a runaway in a large, bustling metropolis like Sydney. Cars, carts, trams and horse-drawn carriages jostled about trying to avoid each other and the throngs of pedestrians along the main street. George Street was packed with buildings lining the pathways, with the dome of the Queen Victoria Building prominent further along the street. Down at Circular Quay, while there was as yet no Harbour Bridge (it would be completed in March 1932) or the modern-day Opera House, it was a hive of activity.

Lillian Armfield was well acquainted with these tourist areas of Sydney, but it was eastern Sydney she needed to patrol and know like the back of her hand: from Woolloomooloo on the waterfront, south to Darlinghurst and down to Surry Hills and Redfern, then back up to Paddington and towards the coast. These were the streets where tourists dared not tread and where her job would daily come alive as she watched for anything that seemed out of place, especially runaway girls.

In the overcrowded and poverty-stricken streets of eastern Sydney, the air was thick with smoke from the factories and smelled of hops from the breweries and a mixture of seawater and fish odours from the waterfront. The streets were lined with sand and dust and congealed food scraps in the gutters from people cleaning out their household rubbish. The electrical cables running up to the power lines drooped lower than they should have and drainage pipes were dented from years of fists and feet banging against them. Maybe a few heads too.

Here in the poorest of Sydney neighbourhoods, families were making do as best they could. They crammed into terrace houses with other renters – single people, families and elderly folk – where poor sanitation and rising damp were put up with as much as the rotting floorboards, rodents and cockroaches. It was here in Surry Hills that the writer Ruth Park toured the streets for her daily serial which became the 1948 book *The Harp in the South*. She placed her main characters – the Darcy family – in 'a cranky brown house, with a blistered green door, and a step worn into dimples and hollows that collected the rain in little pools . . .'

The eastern Sydney streets were also a children's playground with working-class tykes making the most of what the area offered. Barefooted kids chased each other around in billycarts. The kid who could survive the race to the bottom of the hilly streets became a local legend. Others, less successful and more inclined to come off the cart in dramatic fashion, wore the bruises, scrapes and dents across their bodies like trophies from a battle. If they gathered about long enough, the youngsters would sometimes get the offcut meat bits the butcher didn't need or rejected product from bakeries such as rolls that had failed the rising dough test. For so many of the kids, coming from very poor families, any extra food was a godsend.

The wealthy had long since given up on the eastern Sydney neighbourhoods, choosing instead to rent out their terrace houses. Landlords could expect a regular rental turnaround from poor workers and their families looking to live close to the factories and wharves. However, most houses were showing dramatic wear and tear by the early years of the twentieth century. They were developed in 'undrained, unlevelled, unshaped ways' and overcrowding was a serious problem. Houses were built close to laneways, taking up as much vacant land as possible. Rickety wooden fences lined the streets, unsuccessfully hiding the outside toilets where privacy meant hoping no one would pass by when nature called. The weatherboard houses, with their rotting wood planks, could hardly weather anything, let alone torrential rain in winter and the humid heat of summer.

The City of Sydney faced a serious housing crisis by the 1910s. One deputation meeting with the premier in 1912 highlighted two major problems: a lack of appropriate housing accommodation and high rents. Not much had changed a few years later. In 1918 it was estimated that anywhere from between 150,000 to 200,000 people were living in 25,000 houses in the eastern suburbs. At least six to eight people lived in each house but town planners believed another 500,000 people could be accommodated. This meant, on average, each house could contain up to twenty people. This was less of an issue in the middle-class houses of three or four storeys, but the working-class terraces of two storeys and cottages of only one level were full beyond capacity. In the poorest parts of eastern Sydney there could be three or four families and a couple of single occupiers all living in one terrace and sharing the kitchen, bathroom and backyard toilet.

Lillian Armfield often toured some of the worst slum areas looking for runaways like the girl from Orange. Most girls who ran away from home had a few pennies in their pockets and little thought as to how they would pay for their new life in the city. Slum accommodation was all they could afford.

One of the places on Lillian's list to check for the runaway from Orange was Frog Hollow, an infamous slum which the police described as a breeding ground for some of Sydney's worst criminals. Located on the western side of Riley Street, Surry Hills, Frog Hollow was full of decrepit housing structures. The slum was on a sheer cliff, which added to its unstable nature. Nine metres lower than the surrounding buildings, Frog Hollow could be accessed from three different places, which meant anyone escaping from police, including runaways, had a number of exits.

Frog Hollow was demolished by 1930 along with a number of similar structures, but better housing was slow in coming up. When better houses were built the improved conditions meant higher rents, which were often beyond the wages of workers in the area. The very poor had little option but to move in with friends and relatives and share whatever space was available.

There was a clear distinction between male and female crime, particularly in the minds of the church, policing and state authorities. Poor boys hanging around the inner-city streets progressed from petty street crimes to more serious and organised crime first by joining gangs and then by working for the crime bosses.

Darcy Dugan, one of Sydney's most notorious bank robbers and escape artists, started out as a teenager stealing from city stores and selling knock-off makeup to young women around eastern Sydney. He quickly came to the attention of brothel madam Tilly Devine when the prostitutes working for her mentioned the cheap makeup they were getting from Darcy. Tilly gave him a place to stay when he was on the run from the law but in return he had to help with her criminal business, either as a drug runner or by protecting her workers.

One of the ways the police tried to curb youth crime was by sending petty offenders to the Metropolitan Boys' Shelter on Albion Street in Surry Hills. Boys were given some education in the shelter and regularly exercised in the yard, giving them something to do away from the notorious crime streets of eastern Sydney. In the cold, dark and authoritarian space of the shelter, away from family and cut off from their friends on the outside, some boys became hardened against a society that had outcast them.

George Tarlington came to the attention of police officers when he was singing down at Central Station in 1924. When officers couldn't get in touch with his family – his parents and siblings who were at home in Redfern – George was packed off to the Albion Street shelter. He spent the evening in a dormitory sleeping alongside many other boys in beds lined next to each other. George's parents collected him from the shelter the next day but his father was furious he had been picked up by the police and sent to Albion Street. His night in the police station and then the shelter meant the police would be looking more closely at the Tarlington family and George's father, a working-class shoe repairer with an ingrained mistrust of police officers, didn't appreciate the extra attention. The night in the shelter didn't deter young George, however, and he would find himself in and out of homes and shelters as he escalated from shoplifting to more serious criminal connections in the 1930s.

Girls were not treated the same as boys. There was little acknowledgement or acceptance that girls could enter into a life of crime. The prevailing idea was females were weaker and more vulnerable and because of this were lured into criminal underworlds through sex and prostitution. Lillian's work focused on runaways as being in danger rather than dangerous. A runaway like the girl from Orange could give herself a new name, get work in a shop and afford to pay rent in a dilapidated terrace with other young women in similar circumstances. But what the young girls didn't reckon on was the terrace house being a front for prostitution. It was Lillian's job to ensure young girls were not lured into prostitution and crime.

The young girls' sexuality was considered to be another danger. Girls wandering the streets were stereotypically labelled as promiscuous. They were stopped by police or charity workers and quizzed about their family support and where they were living. If they hadn't already been lured into the world of prostitution, they were in danger of it. A *Seduction Punishment Bill* had been introduced into the New South Wales Legislative Assembly in 1887 to make seduction a crime. It aimed to protect the chastity of young, unmarried women but wasn't passed. Though concern for young women had led to the writing of the bill, it was too heavy-handed and authoritarian in how it proposed to deal with young women and sex.

The *Catholic Press* newspaper was particularly worried about young girls ignoring the advice of the churches regarding threats to their innocence on the streets. It warned its readers in September 1915 of strangers and brothel madams in the business of corrupting young women. The *Press* warned against young girls getting into a carriage or cab with a stranger. If they did, they might be lured into a strange house, which would then be revealed as a brothel. For their own good, young women were advised to stay off the streets at night and carry identification in their purses.

One fear of the time was young girls and women being decoyed into sexual slavery. It was called white slavery – the enslavement of white people by non-white people – and Chinese men were targeted in public campaigns about the trade. Following on from Federation in 1901 and the introduction of restrictive immigration policies, non-white residents in Australia were treated with suspicion by the authorities. White women involved in prostitution provided social reformers with an opportunity to raise fears about foreigners and the Chinese 'other' within Australian society. White slavery debates 'reinforced the idea that foreigners had designs on the purity of young girls'.

The reality, however, was quite different. While there were Chinese men who lured young women into opium dens and prostitution, Sydney's most notorious brothels were run by non-Chinese men and women. In one case, in March 1921, Mary Boyd, a well-known sly-grogger and brothel owner, was charged with luring three young women into her brothel. The prosecuting police officer told the court Boyd was known to decoy girls into her house where she 'fills them up with beer and then makes prostitutes of them'.

Newspaper stories about white slavery, sometimes sensationalised, were the cause of one man's desperate effort to find his runaway wife in 1913. The couple were new immigrants in Sydney and had found some work when suddenly the young woman went missing. Unable to find any trace of his wife, the husband's worry increased when he started reading about white slavery in the newspapers. In his mind, his wife had been kidnapped and sold into sex. He gave up work and used all his savings to scour the city and surrounding towns for her. She was found in a country town, working as a hotel servant. Rather than being lured into sexual slavery, the young bride had been whisked away from the city by women in the employment office who offered their help after hearing about her abusive husband. This was no case of white slavery: it was an abusive husband trying to track down his wife.

Whatever was going through Lillian's mind at the time – trying to protect the young girl from Orange from prostitution, white slavery or living in a criminal hovel – she continued to scour the streets, checking the slums and terrace houses, looking for her.

Suddenly, at the lower end of Surry Hills, Lillian spotted a young girl matching the description of the runaway from Orange. She closed in quickly and grabbed the girl, who scratched and wriggled against Lillian's firm hold. This was where Lillian's experience restraining asylum patients helped in her police work. She was also a lot broader and taller than the teenager and she knew how to use her physique to full effect. While the girl squirmed, Lillian reminded her she had a family looking for her and the streets of Sydney were no place for a young girl.

Lillian looked for the quickest way back to Central Police Station but was halted by a menacing crowd drawing near. In only a few minutes, two hundred people surrounded her. On these crime-ridden streets, given the choice, locals preferred crooks to cops and they didn't mind using their fists to show it. They'd rather see a girl left to her own devices on the streets than be taken away by the police. They resented a policewoman thinking she was in charge of other people's kids. The girl could end up being sent to a girls' shelter and from there the dreaded girls' home out at Parramatta. Some of the women crowded close to the girl would have already been through the hell of institutionalisation.

As Lillian clung on to the young girl, still looking for a way to haul her to the main station, someone from the rear of the crowd threw a bottle at Lillian. It smashed against a wall and a shard of glass cut the side of Lillian's face. With her heart racing, blood hot on her cheek, and still trying to hold on to the young girl, who was now afraid of the mob, Constable Armfield looked over the top of the crowd for help. The women in the crowd were furious and were ready to rush at her but they were held back by the men around them. It wasn't to protect Lillian; it was so the women wouldn't end up on an assault charge and gaol time. Familiar faces looked out at Lillian from the crowd. In only a short amount of time on the job, she was getting to know the criminal notables of eastern Sydney.

Surrounded by the throng of angry locals and trying to keep her young charge safe, Lillian had nothing more than her handbag and fists to protect herself. It seemed ludicrous to Lillian that she couldn't carry a weapon like her male colleagues did. If she was going to stand half a chance on these crime-ridden streets she needed to defend herself. She clutched her handbag, ready to swing it if someone got too close.

Suddenly, a police whistle sounded from the back of the crowd. Two male uniformed officers ploughed their way through the crowd, quickly dispersing it. Either news of the mob had travelled back to the station or the constables were nearby and heard the commotion. Whatever the case, while Lillian had wanted to do the job alone, she was grateful for the assistance.

The young girl was taken to the children's shelter while her parents made their way to the city to collect her.

Sydney's runaway girls were often from country areas and had little idea of what to expect in the city. They fantasised about an independent life with new friends and adventures. When they stepped off the train and tried to find their way in the city, reality hit. They faced a large, unforgiving city that preyed on their naivety or lack of family and financial support. So many of the girls, as Lillian would find in the years ahead, were conned into working as prostitutes. Now that the girl from Orange was going to be reunited with her parents, Lillian was relieved there was one less girl on the streets.

Years later, as she reflected back on her career, Lillian would tell this story without naming the girl. She only talked about her as a girl from Orange. Often this was to protect the identities of young girls and women she had investigated who were still alive and had not come back into contact with the law.

As they did with the girl from Orange, the police worked closely with the families of missing girls, often placing notices in newspapers. One notice placed in the *Sunday Times* in January 1915 tells the story of one family's desperate bid to find their loved one. Lettie Smith, a fourteen-year-old girl from Gundagai, was on her way to visit her sister in Surry Hills when she failed to show up. Lettie's family were worried she had left the train before getting to Sydney or had become lost once reaching the city. Her distraught sister wandered the inner-city streets looking for Lettie. She was increasingly aware that she was also risking her own safety as she began asking locals questions near brothels and underworld haunts. Police officers found Lettie soon after and her family were notified. Interestingly, a notice in a Gundagai newspaper in February reported Lettie underwent an appendicitis operation at Glebe children's hospital.

Lillian Armfield started her police work in the months after Lettie went missing and was found but her story resonated. It was Lillian's job to ensure other young girls like Lettie Smith were reunited with their families. She developed a list of known runaways, with details of their physical descriptions and photographs given to police by families. Lillian needed to ensure she would be able to identify the girls on the streets. The face was one of the most important identifiers because while girls could change their clothes or cut and dye their hair, their general facial features remained the same. Their eyes would remain the same colour and their freckles were hard to cover with makeup.

Sadly, Lettie's life did not play out well after she was returned to her family in Gundagai. She married Robert Manning in 1920 but died nine years later aged twenty-nine. The inquest into Lettie's death was a major story in the local newspapers when it was revealed Lettie might have died from complications following a botched abortion. Without clear evidence of this, the coroner could only deliver a finding that Lettie died from septicaemia 'following on a mishap', but the implications were clear. Lettie had seen a local woman who was known to perform abortions. In this sad case of the death of a former runaway, Lillian realised there was only so much she could do after finding girls and young women on the streets. Once returned to their families, especially further out in the country, they were beyond Lillian's responsibility. She did, however, try and check in on the welfare of young women who remained in the city and, for years after they had come into contact with Lillian as runaways, some were happy to share tales about their new lives, for better or worse. Lillian worked hard to gain their trust so that she would be seen as a person they could approach if they ever needed help.

Runaway girls weren't necessarily homeless; they were usually living in places with criminals or were consorting with known crooks on the streets. Young girls were often lured into terrace accommodation with promises of cheap rent and easy work, except this often meant seeing to the needs of men who visited. For a girl living on the streets and unable to get work, which so often happened to runaways in the city, the terrace houses became sinister places. Lillian offered the girls clothes, access to work and some money to get them away from the criminal haunts. As she later told a newspaper reporter: 'You'd be surprised the number of girls who come to the city without knowing anyone or where to go to live or get a job.' They had usually had a quarrel with their parents and taken off to the city, with little thought for how they would support themselves. Lillian reached an important conclusion about the girls she was tasked with finding: 'it was my experience that very few girls are bad beyond redemption'.

Prevention was also a key part of Lillian's patrols of Central Railway Station. As she told a *Sun* reporter in 1938:

Policewomen meet trains coming in from the country, and also ships whenever there is time and other duties permit. In this way we are able to avert many undesirable things happening to girls and young women, so many of these city-seekers are just youngsters who have had a quarrel at home and have run away.

Along with Maude Rhodes, Lillian patrolled Sydney's main railway station and found many runaway girls before they were lost to the inner-city streets. With improvements in transport – trains more regularly running to and from country towns to the city – runaways had a quicker and more readily available means of escape. What they weren't expecting was policewomen waiting for them in Sydney.

Lillian would often stand and watch the trains arrive, focusing on the ones coming in from country towns. Crooks and brothel owners also frequented Central Railway Station looking for impressionable young women. They would offer accommodation and work, and from there get teenagers and young women involved in prostitution and crime.

After she was released from prison in 1919 – going down for five years for 'sticking to a man' – infamous Sydney crime figure Kate Leigh wandered around Central Station looking to lure young girls and women into her criminal businesses. Leigh offered new arrivals to the city a place to stay and ready work, telling runaway girls that they needed her protection.

It's interesting that she was essentially saying the same thing as Lillian but with very different intentions. Kate Leigh's protection often meant avoiding hefty rental payments by helping out in her criminal trifecta of sly grog, cocaine and prostitution.

Lillian did her best to get to the girls before crooks like Kate Leigh. Her general method of greeting new arrivals in the city followed a few key steps. She tried to be the first person to greet young women off the trains, or ferries depending on where they were coming from. If they didn't want assistance from the police, and their families hadn't listed them as missing, Lillian told them the safest places to stay, usually where she had the ear of the landlord. Lillian would then make regular visits to the landlord to check on the new arrivals. Any runaways she missed would be tracked through her methodical search of hotels and boarding houses near the station and through the city.

Tracking down runaways in boarding houses was how Lillian came across two teenage girls who had run away from their homes in Wellington in country New South Wales. The police were alerted to the missing pair when family contacted Central Police Station asking about their whereabouts. In the weeks before their arrival in the city, the girls travelled to various country towns but quickly moved on when their adventures were noted by curious locals. Within a day of being in Sydney they met Lillian Howell. She was perched on her top step, watching them walk along Hunter Street in the city. Howell convinced the girls to come into her house and then offered them a place to stay. She told them work wouldn't be an issue. The girls were told they could make at least a pound from going to another room with male visitors. Out of that pound they were to give Howell eight shillings. This would work out well for all involved, Lillian Howell told the girls, if they promised not to sit at the window looking out on the street.

A little while later, Lillian Armfield was passing by. The girls had forgotten their promise to the owner of the house and were spotted by Lillian as they sat at the window. The terrace was already listed as a house of ill-fame – a brothel – and police watched known prostitutes come and go. Constable Armfield befriended the girls one day and wondered why they were so done up with makeup, just to sit at a window: 'The girls were not bad girls really, and I doubt they would have admitted to the shocking instructions of the woman who ran the employment office and so-called residential. She was nothing but a procuress . . .'

Lillian Howell was arrested in June 1924 and charged with running a house of ill-fame. In court, the girls were questioned about how they had made a living before and after coming to the city. They told of travelling to various country towns where they entertained men and were paid for an 'immoral purpose'. When they got to the city, Lillian Howell convinced them to work for her at the boarding house looking after male visitors. Yet, despite the police evidence against Howell, she was acquitted. Interestingly, Lillian Armfield later told journalist Vince Kelly that Howell 'jumped her bail and left the city'. Had her memory confused events or was this how Lillian wanted the case remembered?

The usual process when runaways were located was to take them to Central Police Station while parents or carers were notified. The station was in a good location for policing the inner-city streets. Located on a large block between Liverpool, George and Pitt streets, it was in the middle of the main streets connecting out and leading to Central Railway Station, Circular Quay and the eastern Sydney thoroughfares. Like the other city police stations, it was laid out so most of the business took place on the ground level. The officers' room and charge room were located at the front of the station, with the muster and storerooms towards the back and leading onto the cells. The prisoners' yard at the back of the station was secured with high walls and barbed wire on top and was closely supervised by police officers.

Lillian and Maude would bring their runaway girls into the front part of the station where they would be processed at the front desk. They might then be transferred to one of the officers' rooms or the muster room to await news on their family's movements and plans for their overnight care. Some parents had to travel hundreds of kilometres from country areas to the city, so male and female police officers worked out how to provide the runaways with somewhere to stay. Lillian often found them a room in a reputable boarding house but if the wait dragged out or family didn't arrive, Lillian was forced to place runaways into state care.

The Metropolitan Girls' Shelter on Avon Street, Glebe, was one of the main places where girls were sent after family could not be located, or if they had absconded from police care and were found on the streets associating with known criminals. The girls were commonly placed there while waiting to appear in court on charges of idle and disorderly or vagrancy. The shelter was used as a last resort by Lillian and members of the Women's Police.

The Glebe shelter had a notorious reputation in inner Sydney. Christina Green (nee Riley) was thirteen when she was sent there. As a young Wiradjuri woman who had been taken from her family and placed into state care from the age of three, Christina had already seen too much of care before going to the girls' shelter. To a thirteen-year-old, the building was cold, haunting and more like a prison: 'there was hardly any sunlight at all and only one small section in the court yard outside where all you could see was the cold sandstone walls standing tall, and only seeing a small spot of the sky above, and inside nothing but the solid doors with heavy padlocks and cold cement floors'. It was a depressing, soul-destroying place where young girls like Christina contemplated suicide.

Lillian Armfield was there to police young women and ensure they remained on the right side of the law but she was not without compassion. She tried to keep girls out of the shelter, doing her best to contact family or, if they were older, find them work and a place to stay. Even for Lillian, who was often strict about what she expected of those of her own sex, the Glebe shelter was not her preference for getting girls off the streets. She knew, as did police in general, that it could lead to their being sent to an even harder institution like Parramatta Girls' Home.

Try as she might, Lillian couldn't keep an eye on all newcomers to the city. She and Maude Rhodes placed regular notices in the *Police Gazette*s so that officers at different stations across Sydney could be on alert for missing girls. A typical 'Missing Friends' notice in the *Police Gazette* read like the following one from August 1918:

> Missing, from her home, Myrtle-avenue, Bankstown, during the last three months, and not since heard of, Bessie Moreland or Hook, 17 1/2 years of age, 4 feet 6 inches high, stout build, brown hair and eyes; wearing a red skirt and navy-blue knitted coat. Information to Special Constables Armfield and Rhodes, No. 1 Station, Sydney.

Some runaway girls were in fact trying to get back to their families. Lillian worked in the Women's Police at a time when young Aboriginal girls were taken from their families and placed into state care. From 1900 to the 1970s, between one in three and one in ten Aboriginal and Torres Strait Islander children aged sixteen and under were forcibly taken from their families if they were legally categorised as 'half-caste': having one Indigenous and one non-Indigenous parent. State authorities, supported by a non-Indigenous chief protector, placed Indigenous children in institutional, adoptive and foster care, with little or no consultation with their families. The belief was that Indigenous children of mixed descent could be assimilated into the wider white society. The consequences of these practices were devastating and continue to affect the mental, physical and overall wellbeing of members of the Stolen Generations.

In the midst of all this, Lillian found runaway Indigenous girls and sent them back to institutions. Young Indigenous absconders couldn't be returned to their families because they were 'half-caste' children. These kids didn't need to be wandering the streets or committing crimes to be removed from families and placed into state care. While young Indigenous people had similar experiences in state care to non-Indigenous children, most were there simply because they were Indigenous.

When Lillian Armfield told the press she wanted to do her best to help young girls and protect them from harm in the city, she was talking about non-Indigenous girls. It was beyond Lillian's powers to then look for the family of Indigenous children. Policing young Indigenous girls meant returning them to the notice of the chief protector and his government department. In one case, Esther Estler was arrested by Lillian Armfield and Maude Rhodes in September 1916 for 'absconding'. She was 'returned to the custody of the Aborigines Board', which had full power over her. Any methods Lillian had to help young girls on the streets were not to be applied to Indigenous girls. The release of the *Bringing Them Home* report in 1997 which documented the stories of children taken away from communities, some of whom were abused in institutions, finally brought about greater recognition for the devastating impacts of child removal. It came, sadly, many years after Esther Estler absconded and was sent back into the custody of the Aborigines Board.

Lillian and Maude worked together closely on cases relating to girls and young women. As the only female constables they relied on each other in their investigations, in accumulating their knowledge about girls and women on the streets and in providing protection for each other around the city. However, we can't assume that just because they were appointed at the same time and worked together, they got along. There was a clear rift in their partnership by 1918 and a power imbalance favouring Lillian's role in the Women's Police. Perhaps it was because she had worked for eight years in Callan Park Asylum, but Lillian thought of herself as the more senior officer to Maude Rhodes. It was Lillian who was running the show and featured in any publicised cases for the newspapers. Maude was mentioned but Lillian was the face of the Women's Police.

The story handed down in policing circles is that Maude failed to take an order from Lillian about a job down at Central Railway Station late in 1919. Lillian made a complaint, portraying herself as her superior officer, and Maude was discharged from the force. She left early in 1920 and returned to her work in the Children's Department. Maude had seen the tough, unrelenting side of Lillian: she had high expectations of the women who worked with her. Policewomen who followed after Maude's departure recalled how Lillian expected long hours and complete dedication to the job, regardless of their personal life. It suited Lillian, particularly in her younger years with her family back in Mittagong and Berrima, but it wasn't appreciated by other special constables who looked for a better work–life balance.

This strict, tough exterior was how Lillian coped with being a female officer in the heavily masculine world of policing. She was already visibly different working as a constable in her civilian clothes around male constables wearing uniforms. When she was eventually issued with an item of uniform it was a handbag. Few officers took her seriously in the beginning, believing the Women's Police were a flash in the pan, or at least only good enough to police other women. While she wandered the streets looking for lost girls, Lillian's male colleagues reminded her they were doing real police work. She developed a thick skin and learned the best way to get ahead in the job was to keep her head down, fulfil the duties required of her work and continue to convince the inspector-general that the policing experiment with female officers had been worth the gamble.

It wasn't an easy job and Lillian also faced growing criticism from outside the force. Lillian's earliest supporters in the women's organisations were now closely watching how she policed young girls and women. She was still very much on trial in their eyes too.

The Women's Progressive Association (WPA) was particularly outspoken about the force's double standards. Young women were apprehended in brothels, whether soliciting or not, but their male clients were left largely unpunished. If Lillian thought she had champions in the WPA, she was sorely mistaken. Annie Golding, the association's president, believed the Women's Police were stigmatising young women more than solving the issue of double standards: 'The intention was not to brand them as criminals by putting the stigma of jail on them, but to prevent their lapse into that stage by other means, such as judicious advice, putting them on probation in their homes under parents or near relatives.' Another suggestion made by a women's campaigner writing to the *Sydney Morning Herald* asked for hostels to be opened specifically for girls coming to the city. In these establishments girls 'full of ambition and the joy of living' could enjoy the independence they craved but would also have to attend technical or teaching colleges.

Things got a lot worse when Lillian found herself at the centre of another case featuring a teenage girl charged with being idle and disorderly. The young girl had been living with her married sister in Newtown when Lillian came across her in a park one day. They sat and talked on a bench and Lillian quizzed the girl about her work. Lillian was particularly worried about the girl's dishevelled appearance and filthy hair. In the mind of a police officer at the time, this led to concerns about her lifestyle. Lillian took the girl to Central Police Station and when she appeared before the court shortly after, her hair had been cropped. The girl asked the magistrate to send her to a religious home for six months. There's no way of knowing if the police encouraged her to say this to avoid a hefty fine or imprisonment but when the story hit the newspapers, there was a public outcry from the women's organisations. The girl's sister and brother-in-law claimed they could look after her and the Women's Police, namely Lillian Armfield, were referred to as 'convicting agents'.

The cropping of the girl's hair was particularly offensive to women's rights campaigners. It was an indignity for young women and had been used for many years to ready female offenders for either time in prison or institutionalisation in a girls' home. Yet what the critics failed to understand was that Lillian had nothing to do with the hair cropping. Officials from the Justice Department were responsible. Once a young woman was processed at a police station and awaiting a court appearance, her hair could be cropped to tidy her appearance in court. It was heavy-handed no doubt, but it wasn't a direct action of the Women's Police.

Lillian Armfield came close to resigning from the police force after the media storm around the hair-cropping incident and another case of idle and disorderly. It wasn't because she felt she couldn't do the job. She thought she was doing Inspector-General Mitchell a favour by lessening the criticism of the introduction of the Women's Police. She was reminded in her conversation with Mitchell that her main job was to preserve law and order. As Lillian would later say, 'That's just the way I feel about my work.' From her very first days as a special constable, Lillian was also instructed to avoid publicity: 'it was only when we appeared in court that the public learnt about our work, and then only about those specific cases in which we gave evidence'.

It was hard to avoid publicity. The Women's Police were under pressure to meet all the demands of the women's campaigners who watched cases closely in the courts and as they were reported in the newspapers. Special constables also had to ensure they were improving the welfare of girls and women. This was criticised when women were sent off to institutions or sentenced to time in prison. However, while protection and welfare were key duties of the female officers, they were police all the same. They still had to police crime and punish offenders breaking the law.

Amid the backlash over the hair-cropping incident and the bad publicity for the work of the Women's Police, Lillian met with Inspector-General James Mitchell and offered to resign from the job. Mitchell laughed and told her he was having none of it. He'd been through enough controversies in the police to know most of them blew over and the hair-cropping case was a minor incident. Lillian pushed him on the point and Mitchell became serious. He wasn't afraid of controversy; he'd worked his way up policing the hard streets of Aberdeen and he wasn't about to wilt. People will always be critical of the police, he told Lillian, but officers should never lose sight of the importance of their work. His officers had to push on with 'the most important job in the whole community, preserving law and order'.

In 1920, Mitchell made a public appeal for parents to look after their children. There was only so much the police could do to look after runaways; parents had to ensure they watched their children more closely. Let's remember this was back in 1920. Even today, police are still pleading with parents to keep an eye on their kids. When children are acting up and mucking about on the streets – sometimes committing petty crimes that lend themselves to experimentation with more serious crime – police will start by looking at their home lives. This is what James Mitchell did back in the 1920s, down-playing any threat from white slavery, and telling the press:

> People may rest assured that there is no evidence here of the white slave trade . . . It is purely a lack of parental care that accounts for children absenting themselves from their homes. If those children were not allowed to employ so much of their time at picture shows and other places where they come into contact with strangers those things would not happen. Much more stringency should be exercised by parents.

Lillian knew she couldn't help everyone and her interference sometimes made a bad situation worse. In one case, she attempted to legitimise the relationship between a young woman and her lover but it backfired. Lillian convinced the young woman to marry her Chinese lover so that their children wouldn't be stigmatised as illegitimate. They married but the husband resented the involvement of the Women's Police and blamed his young wife. They split up, he took off, and the wife started drinking heavily. Lillian then had to place their young children into state care. The case deeply affected her: 'A bit of the road to hell could certainly be paved with my good intentions.'

Missing girls during the war years were one thing but the inter-war years of the 1920s posed an even greater challenge for Lillian and the work of the Women's Police. It was the era of the flapper with her shorter dresses, short hair and bold makeup. The intent was to break with traditional dress and social roles. Many flappers dressed in what was seen as a more sexual manner, emphasising their feminine looks and body shape to gain attention. Dresses were lighter, brighter and sometimes backless. Some dresses also represented androgynous identities, where the straight-down flow of the garment flattened the chest and the dropping of the waist hid hips. Pushing traditional gender roles in which women were expected to be demure and not express their opinions publicly, young flappers smoked, drank alcohol, swore and were vocal about sexual inequality.

Newspapers and church leaders worried that the flapper identity was only one step away from young women being led into Sydney's underworlds of drugs and prostitution. Public commentary focused on the vulnerability of girls but Lillian Armfield learned another important lesson during her first years on the job. She knew some young women chose a life of crime. While women's campaigners may have only seen girls in need of moral reprogramming who were being dealt with heavy-handedly by the Women's Police, Lillian watched the streets closely and saw an interesting trend. By the first years of the 1920s, a growing number of young women were starting to play a more active, powerful role in the rise of organised crime. Some of them started out as runaways.

Not all runaways wanted the protection of Women's Police and some were certainly very capable of creating a new life in the city, albeit through crime. They were flappers but they were also finding new ways of being and opportunities within Sydney's underworlds. Nellie Cameron was one such woman and would grab Lillian's attention during the Razor Wars of the late 1920s. Nellie defied any attempts on the part of Women's Police to reform her: she embraced a modern identity that had allowed her to run away from home and find work and a new place for herself in the city. She would become one of the most powerful runaways in eastern Sydney, making a name for herself in the criminal underworlds of prostitution and drugs, and she would come to know Lillian Armfield well.

Every year, Lillian rescued hundreds of girls from the streets of Sydney. Her dawn patrol and surveillance of trains and inner-city accommodation turned up many of the young girls reported missing. She would later tell a reporter that the key to success was 'working with womanly sympathy' but the complexities of life on the streets also showed her she needed to be tough. Some of the young women were, according to Lillian, 'real trimmers' and couldn't just be sent back to their parents. When Lillian's guidance failed, she had to resort to charging them with vagrancy or putting them into state care as neglected children.

The cases that most deeply affected Lillian were the ones in which girls ran away from home to hide a pregnancy. In an effort to bear the burden of shame alone – knowing there would be little help from the young man involved – they took off to Sydney and took matters into their own hands. One of the saddest parts of Lillian's job involved visiting hospitals and looking for runaway girls found in laneways after botched abortions. Midwives and nurses offered their services for the 'problems' of pregnancy but there were also a number of poorly trained pseudo-medical people purporting to be able to perform an abortion. They usually ran their businesses at the back of rundown terraces with poor sanitation and nowhere for girls and young women to recover.

The *Poisons Act* of 1905 had tried to address the rise in backyard abortions by making ergot of rye, an abortifacient, available only by prescription. The *Private Hospitals Act* three years later also stipulated that all patients needed to be registered and births and deaths recorded. The *Police Offences Act* of the same year also restricted advertisements relating to abortion, though they would not have named it as such. Prosecuting abortion was hard for the police: it sometimes took a deposition from a dying young woman and reports from neighbours who were unhappy at the practice going on so close to their homes. However, it was often difficult to prosecute abortion if a patient was unwilling to testify and the police could not prove under warrant that a premises was used for the practice. Abortionists, driven underground, were quick to hide any medical implements and hurried patients out onto the streets afterwards.

There were only ever a dozen or so arrests for abortion recorded each year in Sydney in the early twentieth century but Lillian Armfield claimed to have investigated hundreds of cases where an abortion ended a young girl's life. Lillian and other police officers sometimes turned up to a hastily arranged party at a house where an abortionist claimed they were with friends and had no idea who the dead girl was lying in the street near the house. Backyard abortions were horrific and affected both male and female police officers. As well as finding a dying or dead young woman, the police sometimes discovered the discarded foetus nearby.

Lillian could never have continued on in the job without the firm conviction that she was making a difference. As she walked through the corridors of the hospitals and discovered runaways who had died at the hands of an abortionist, she could have easily found it all too much and given up. But she knew, too, in those same corridors, in wards tucked away from prying eyes, there were also young girls who had survived. It was Lillian's job to convince them that one bad turn did not have to define their lives. The Women's Police were there to remind young and vulnerable girls that second chances were possible, if they accepted help: 'One of my most difficult tasks was to try to convince girls like these who had taken the wrong turning, that it was never too late – or too soon – to get back on the right track.' Sometimes all it took was convincing the girls someone was looking out for them and would be there when they needed help. At their most vulnerable, feeling embarrassed and lost in a hospital bed and recovering from the trauma of a backyard abortion, Lillian showed young girls the sympathy they so desperately needed. The tall, tough female officer was equally the kind woman with the pearl necklace who sat with and listened to girls and young women while they recovered in hospital.

It was this human connection to her work and a commitment to making a difference in the community that kept Lillian in the job. Doing her work 'behind the scenes and unnoticed by the public' in these first years, Lillian was proving herself worthy of her appointment to the Women's Police. As so many others would come to see in the years that followed, Inspector-General James Mitchell was a good judge of character and ability. In recruiting Lillian Armfield in 1915, Mitchell saw the potential in her country upbringing and the tough resolve that had supported her well through years of work in the asylum. He knew Lillian had the makings of a fine police officer.

In her duty to protect vulnerable girls and women, Lillian also had to investigate other crimes and criminals around eastern Sydney. While searching for missing or wayward teenagers and young women continued to be a part of her work, Lillian's other major cases from 1915 involved raiding fraudulent fortune-tellers. Working in the shadows of inner and eastern Sydney, she earned herself a reputation as one of the city's most effective investigators.

4

Fortune-teller Frauds

FORTUNE-TELLERS HAD BEEN PLYING THEIR TRADE ACROSS THE Australian cities from the late nineteenth century but business really took off into the twentieth century. In Sydney, fortune-tellers and clairvoyants mainly worked from the back rooms of their houses but increasingly they were branching out beyond home visits. Some were going door to door and working in market stalls and small shops. Their work developed in a variety of forms from the most common practice of card and palm readings to crystal-gazing, reading tea leaves or the less common reading of heads, faces, fingernails and personal objects. Communication with the spirit world was also an important part of the work of clairvoyants, differentiating them from fortune-tellers. Though conversing with the spirits sometimes came into telling fortunes, it was less common than the other forms.

These days we tend to view fortune-telling and clairvoyance as relatively harmless services where clients engage with future predictions and spiritualism anywhere from psychic events to hen's parties, but back in the early twentieth century fortune-telling was prohibited under the *New South Wales Police Offences (Amendment) Act* of 1908. Based on older English Elizabethan laws, which coupled fortune-telling and witchcraft as superstitions and troublesome to the community, the NSW criminalisation of fortune-telling was based on the belief that it was not a professional or serious practice and was more about ripping people off. Fortune-tellers were also stereotyped as associating with thieves and criminal gangs. Fraudulent fortune-tellers were suspected of coaxing information out of clients that could be sold on to thieves who would use it to break into homes or workplaces. Clients might, for example, give information about work hours and forthcoming holidays that would leave their business or home vacant. Most of Sydney's popular fortune-tellers also worked around the city and the eastern neighbourhoods associated with criminal underworlds, which further raised police suspicions.

Susie Simmons experienced the police crackdowns firsthand in 1909. She was charged with unlawfully pretending to tell a fortune after an undercover police officer had attended Susie's house on Campbell Street, Glebe, with a companion and offered to pay to have his fortune told. During the session, Susie conversed with spirits and people she claimed were dead family members of the officer, telling him he was going to receive bad news. Susie's lawyer told the magistrate his client would plead guilty but Susie stood up and protested: 'I cannot plead guilty to pretence in this matter. It is reality to me . . . If other persons have not seen a spirit, they cannot say I have not seen one, and when I say I have your Worship cannot contradict me.' He did, however, and sentenced Susie to one month's hard labour in prison, but it was suspended under the *First Offenders Act* and sureties of good behaviour for twelve months.

Fortune-telling was generally accepted by the police and public when it was conducted in private or was not interfering with general day-to-day community life. If customers were happy, there didn't seem to be any point in making a complaint. It came to the attention of the police when a fraud was reported. 'Pretence' was a major issue in cases against fraudulent fortune-tellers. Often referred to as 'charlatans' in the newspapers, fortune-tellers were investigated when they appeared to be acting professionally but were really conning people out of their money with false predictions.

Though police had been investigating fortune-tellers for a number of years before Lillian Armfield's appointment, the work of the Women's Police was directly connected to fortune-telling cases. Fortune-telling was predominantly a female industry; eighty-two per cent of all defendants appearing on fortune-telling charges from 1900 to 1918 were women. The work could earn women up to ten pounds a week, much more than what traditional women's work in domestic service paid. It could also be quick money. A stall at the markets on a busy day could attract customers who would not normally go to a fortune-teller's house or accept the business from door-knocking. While predominantly fortune-tellers were women, so were their clients. Working-class teenage girls and women were notable among the fortune-telling clientele. Young single women wanted to know about their future love lives and older women usually consulted fortune-tellers when at their most unhappy in a marriage. The Women's Police were essential, as officers needed to work closely with the female clients making complaints, who usually preferred to talk to female officers.

Lillian Armfield's job was twofold: she was required to investigate 'charlatans' and see them through to prosecution in the courts, while also protecting their customers. For Lillian, this meant working with women who were often socially and economically vulnerable.

One case reported in the newspapers in 1902 highlighted the vulnerability of people seeking out fortune-tellers. A young girl from North Sydney took her life after seeing a fortune-teller. Her family did not know which fortune-teller she had seen, only that it had greatly upset her. The *Catholic Press* was particularly scathing in reporting the cause of the young girl's death:

> Sensible, but perhaps not very reflective, people are disposed to treat those miserable charlatans who live on the weak minded and credulous by means of palmistry and clairvoyance

with good-natured contempt and toleration. This attitude is wrong. The contemptible creatures who thus batten on the foolish should be stamped out in the most determined fashion, not so much because their occupation is on a lower scale than mendicancy, as that they are responsible for much crime and unhappiness.

Some young women, such as this one in North Sydney, found it hard to deal with what had been predicted for them.

Women were also stereotyped as easy prey for fortune-tellers. A woman's mind was said to have a 'natural curiosity' for knowing the future. Newspaper reporters claimed that because women were more likely to engage in gossip – a favourite pastime of theirs, apparently – this made them an easy target for wanting to know what was going to happen around them in the near future. In other sexist discussions of the time, women were depicted as unable to control their emotions so would give away too much in their body language to fortune-tellers looking for cues for the information they would supply. This supposed vulnerability is what brought Lillian into the investigations, along with the high number of women seeing fortune-tellers.

Police crackdowns on fortune-telling coincided with the war years. Prosecutions increased during World War I, particularly in 1917 when a circular from the prime minister's office alerted police to community concerns that family members of servicemen, keen to know the fate of their loved ones at the Front, were being taken advantage of. The *Sun* newspaper declared in May 1917: 'Fortune-tellers are preying upon the wives and relatives of soldiers at the front.' Inspector Mitchell announced that all police stations in New South Wales were taking action to apprehend and arrest any fortune-tellers causing distress to servicemen's families. He reminded fortune-tellers that they would be prosecuted and could face up to six months in prison. Mitchell had had enough. Already sceptical of fortune-telling, he was adamant men and women were cashing in on wartime grief.

Australian families had been through a harrowing eighteen months by the start of 1917. The ANZAC landing at Gallipoli in April 1915 was a disaster and while the military authorities tried to convince the public otherwise, letters from soldiers spoke of the reality of war.

The war that Australians had believed would be over by the Christmas of 1914 raged on for another four years. By the end of 1917 – Australia's worst year of the war – more than 76,000 Australians had been killed or wounded, or were missing on the Western Front. In fact, two-thirds of all Australian deaths in the war were suffered in 1917, in the 'middle of a long war of attrition'.

By the war's end, of the 330,000 Australian men who enlisted and served, close to 60,000 never returned home. One in two Australian servicemen had been killed, wounded, gassed or taken prisoner. Australians suffered just under five per cent of all Allied casualties but the war dead were over fourteen per cent of all Australian men who had enlisted from

August 1914. A staggering twenty million men were injured in the war across all fighting nations.

With the prime minister's directive empowering the police further, and with increased support for her work, Lillian Armfield stepped up her investigations into Sydney's fortune-tellers. Lillian's main goal was to drive the fortune-telling business out of inner Sydney and show women how easily they could be duped. There was also some personal motivation behind it. Lillian's brother, James, was among the many Australians doing their bit for their country.

James Armfield enlisted at Goulburn in May 1916 and was quickly promoted to corporal. He was wounded fighting in France in May 1918 with a gunshot wound to his left foot. George and Elizabeth Armfield received a telegram a month later telling them James was in hospital and more news would follow. The next formal notification from the military came in January 1919 when notice was sent alerting the Armfields that James was returning safe to Australia. His service record, however, notes the war injury as debilitating enough to have him identified as an 'Invalid'. Lillian and her family knew through personal experience the pain of waiting on news. This made her even more opposed to fortune-tellers making money off the worried families of servicemen.

The Women's Police were given the work of investigating fortune-tellers because it was assumed to be less risky than other police work. The general idea in policing circles was that fortune-tellers posed less physical danger because mostly they were women. Yet Lillian's experience on Sydney's streets had taught her otherwise. She knew how violent some women could be and, as she would later reflect, violent women were as much a part of her job as their male counterparts. Both men and women didn't like being duped in their own game of deception. Male fortune-tellers made up eighteen per cent of defendants prosecuted for fortune-telling in New South Wales from 1900 to 1918 and married couples were not uncommon. Ethel and Walter Reip were convicted of fortune-telling when their house in Glebe came to the attention of police officers. Walter stood out the front of the house while Ethel conducted her work inside. He also made the appointments and collected the payments. Walter worked as his wife's 'cockatoo', the person looking out for police approaching. Generally, however, people involved in fortune-telling and communicating with spirits were very low on the list of violent offenders.

When women started coming forward with stories of being ripped off by fortune-tellers, Lillian used her edge on her male colleagues in being able to prosecute them. Lillian's casework began with notices in newspapers. She scanned the local papers every day looking for advertisements for fortune-tellers. Knowing 'fortune-teller' adverts would catch the attention of police scanning the papers, fortune-tellers had started advertising their work under titles like 'palmist' and 'clairvoyant'.

A suspicious notice or advertisement in a local newspaper, or a notice stuck to a shopfront, would alert Lillian to a house of interest and she would add it to her regular street patrols. She would take a quick, first look at the house on her patrol and then set up closer surveillance in the shadows of a nearby laneway or around the corner from a suspicious house. She knew she needed to work in the shadows to get results.

Undercover work became an essential part of police investigations from the early twentieth century. A probationary constable, Frank Fahy, was handpicked from Paddington Station in 1920 to shadow the underworld. He was recommended to the Sydney Criminal Investigation Branch (CIB) because he didn't look like a police officer. He also had an excellent working knowledge of some of Sydney's most dangerous places and neighbourhoods, and the city's leading crooks. Fahy was Australia's first official undercover cop and only a few select officers, usually high up in the force, knew about his dangerous and secretive work.

For thirty years, Fahy devised a variety of ways to spy on criminals and bring his colleagues in to make their arrests. He often posed as a vagrant, sleeping rough and wandering the slum streets, all while he waited for his chance to catch the crooks red-handed. He created a periscope device that allowed him to look undetected into rooms from a few floors down. He also attached a box to the frame of a motorcycle so that he could hide inside and take photographs through a hole he had drilled in the side. The letters on the box convinced passers-by he was a lawnmower repairman.

Undercover work is high-risk policing but Lillian was able to use her plain-clothes look to full effect. Watching people coming and going from the front and back entrances of the terrace house, Lillian noted any suspicious activity in her notebook. Without seeing the precise activities taking place inside a house, she had to rely on her gut instinct about the people entering and leaving the premises. A higher number of women attending raised her suspicions, as did evidence of them experiencing either a heightened state of happiness or anxiety upon leaving, depending on the fortune they had been told. When a potential client left the house, Lillian sprang into action. She stopped the woman further along the street or as she turned around a corner, and asked her about her business at the house. As she did with girls and young women on the streets, Lillian befriended the fortune-teller clients, telling them she was concerned about their welfare.

Female informers were another important part of Lillian's casework. She knew the problems associated with using informers – there was always a tension between the informer wanting to help and at the same time gaining something from a prosecution – but usually the women informing on fortune-tellers were genuinely aggrieved and wanted the police involved. Lillian also used her powers of persuasion and asked young, honest women she knew in inner Sydney to assist with her work. She would send them into the house of a suspected fortune-teller and ask for a full rundown of events afterwards. Female informers assisted in at least a third of prosecutions across Australia in the first two decades of the twentieth century.

In one case given publicity in the newspapers in 1918, a female informer, Miss Miller, assisted Lillian's investigation into a house at 28 Flinders Street, Darlinghurst. It's unclear whether Miss Miller felt aggrieved by the business or was acting as a concerned local, but either way she alerted Lillian to Henry Harold Eldridge's house. Lillian acted swiftly on the information and posed as a potential client outside of Eldridge's house. His undoing came when he gave Lillian a piece of paper that she was to sign for his 'protection'. Fortune-tellers often tried to evade arrest by issuing cards like this to clients stating they were not in the business of telling fortunes and anything predicted was left to the customer to believe or not.

The card of one fortune-teller, Mr Johnson, was given to Lillian during one of her undercover investigations. It read:

> Notice to Clients. Mr R. A. Johnson hereby gives notice to all who wish to consult him that he does not profess to be able to tell fortunes, and has no intention or desire to deceive or impose on anyone. Any client is at liberty to believe or not his statements as to prediction etc., and anyone who consults him must do so upon the understanding that he does not profess to be able to tell fortunes, or has any intention to deceive or impose upon anyone, or to obtain money by false pretences.

Mr Johnson's customers also had to honour a pledge stating they had read the notice and agreed to pay a fee for prediction statements. Mr Johnson was clearly trying to avoid charges being laid against him for deception through fortune-telling. However, because he was overstating the point that he was not telling fortunes and did not want to deceive anyone,

Lillian left his premises and notified her male colleagues (who had the power of arrest), and Johnson was charged and later convicted.

Lillian Armfield's investigations netted considerable returns for the police. She raided half a dozen fortune-tellers each month in her first years in the job, and it was all down to the development of her own detective and surveillance methods. She wasn't trained in how to be a detective, work undercover or conduct surveillance, but Lillian watched, listened and learned in her daily work around Central Station and on visits to other police stations. She asked questions about detective work and how to stake out houses under suspicion of criminal activity.

Lillian's undercover work investigating fortune-telling was not without its dangers. She patrolled back streets – where there were regular reports of thefts, violence and gang incidents – alone, or with another unarmed female officer. Lillian gained entry into the house or shop of a stranger with little idea of what was in the other rooms and how the person might act. She hoped they really were telling fortunes and not luring young women in to be assaulted or robbed. In a house, amassing her evidence against the fortune-teller, Lillian had to be sure that other officers knew where she was and would come to her assistance if she was away too long. With most of the leading fortune-telling businesses located in the inner-city and inner-eastern suburbs, officers at Central Police Station expected her back in good time.

Despite the chance of her real identity being revealed, Lillian never felt the need to take on an elaborate assumed identity. When a reporter queried her about her methods in 1918, telling her she must need disguises, Lillian said there was only really a need for different hats: 'It may not make any difference in a man but it alters a woman a good deal.' With her selection of small and large hats in different colours, Lillian masked her face, keeping it low and under the hat, coming across as a shy woman looking to have her fortune told but not wanting to bring any attention to herself. She was a smart operator and as the years passed on the job, she knew exactly how to get fortune-tellers to play into her hands.

A key part of this undercover work was that Lillian did not make the arrests. This had a lot to do with her duties as a female officer. She could investigate major crimes but had to report back to a male officer who would then go in and make the arrest. With no gun or handcuffs, Lillian couldn't make proper, contained arrests anyway. These limits on her police powers could also be used to her advantage. Sending in male officers to make the arrests allowed Lillian to remain undetected. Furthermore, fortune-tellers expected male officers to stake out their businesses. They certainly didn't expect the fair-headed, gentle-looking woman with a country twang to be a police officer.

Special Constable Armfield didn't carry a gun or baton but the greatest weapon in her investigations was her police note-book. Notebooks are still an important tool of police work. All police, regardless of their rank, are expected to record particulars of incidents while on duty. The notebook was Lillian's resource for future reference and she could use her notes as evidence in court. She started each day with a new entry, marked with the dates and times of incidents. Lillian recorded details of goings-on around premises and houses where a suspected fortune-teller worked. She recorded statements from informants before and after they went into premises. Complete details of incidents had to be written down with surnames underlined.

Lillian was expected to complete a notebook entry right after having visited a fortune-telling business. We can imagine her hurrying back to the station to request her male colleagues make an arrest, and while they were off apprehending the suspect, she would sit at her desk and fill out the notebook entry. Male officers would take a statement from the suspect and the details recorded would be compared with those from Lillian. In all of her investigations, not just fortune-telling incidents, the police notebook allowed Lillian to cross-check incidents, make connections between names and places, and demonstrate the work she conducted each day. Over the course of her career, Lillian would fill at least two large notebooks.

For a few weeks in the middle of 1921, Lillian watched a house in Redfern after intelligence was given to her that a fortune-teller was doing business there. She was given money by a sergeant at Redfern Police Station and, accompanied by a young woman – allowing her to look less suspicious – she visited the house. The rumours on the streets and details coming in from informants were that the owner, Alfred Peter

Ferguson, was running a fortune-telling business from a back room. Lillian and her friend knocked on the back door, posing as women desperate to have their fortunes told, and Ferguson took them inside. He asked them to sit at a table while he readied himself for his work. He went into a trance, 'flung his arms about, and told her she would marry a red-headed engineer in six months'. Ferguson told Lillian an elderly man was soon going to die and leave her money. Using the cash, she would travel either to Brisbane or New Zealand. Lillian left and alerted her colleagues at Redfern, and they returned to make the arrest. Alfred Ferguson was charged at Redfern Police Court in August 1921 with pretending to tell Lillian's fortune. It was Ferguson's second conviction on charges relating to fortune-telling and clairvoyance, and he was sent to prison for three months.

Lillian Armfield seemed perfect fodder for fortune-tellers who thought a single woman needed to be told that love was on the horizon. In fact, if the predictions of fortune-tellers had been right, Lillian would never have been short of attention from male suitors. Collectively, fortune-tellers and clairvoyants told her over the years there were more than 600 dark-haired men waiting to marry her along with 256 blonds and sixty-five bald men. By Lillian's reckoning, she should have been married 933 times. While she recounted this later to a journalist, it was tinged with some bitterness against the business. This type of prediction never sat well with Lillian. She wasn't looking for a lover; rather she was looking to arrest the men and women making the claims.

While Lillian could handle being duped by a fortune-teller – all in the name of her job – other women continued to take the advice to heart and it sometimes proved fatal. Twenty-five-year-old Bessie May Campbell Blackett was engaged to be married to a young man, Thomas Steer, from Queensland. They had known each other for years and Thomas was working hard cutting cane to make enough to buy them a house. Working as a domestic in Pyrmont, Bessie consulted a fortune-teller who told her Thomas was seeing another woman and would never marry her. It was all too much for Bessie. She poisoned herself with strychnine in Hyde Park on 23 February 1927. A young constable found her slumped on a bench and, despite an ambulance being called, she died soon after. Thomas Steer had to front an inquest and, overcome by Bessie's death, pleaded with the coroner that he had 'never wavered in his allegiance' to his fiancée. One life was lost and another devastated. Lillian sat in on the inquest, infuriated she didn't know who the fortune-teller was. All the police had was a statement from the woman Bessie worked for, to the effect that Bessie had confided in her.

Bessie's death hardened Lillian further against fortune-tellers and clairvoyants and was a reminder of the vulnerability of young women seeking them out.

It didn't matter if some people believed fortune-tellers had the ability to forecast the future; fortune-telling was an offence and Lillian was there to police it. She could use her discretionary powers in how she dealt with offenders – whether or not to report them – but the more she investigated fortune-tellers, the less she felt inclined to do so. Her stance on the business was always clear. She regarded fortune-tellers as among the worst crooks she investigated: 'I have met every type of criminal in the list but to me the professional fortune-teller is the most despicable of all. Men and women who tell fortunes for profit are all charlatans. There are no exceptions.'

We have to wonder, too, at how frustrating it was for Lillian to regularly be told about her love life and the many men who would make her happy. If she wanted to marry she would have to give up the job she loved, as female officers had to be single. There was never any mention of any lovers before she worked in the asylum or the Women's Police. Though Lillian worked closely with and shared a mutual respect with a number of male detectives, her family recall her distrust of men. Lillian's nephew recalls his mother, Lillian's sister Muriel, talking about the distrust being caused by an assault, but not much more is now known. It could also be that Lillian was more inclined not to trust men based on her work protecting girls and women from male crime and violence. To then be told by fortune-tellers that she would soon marry no doubt irritated Lillian.

Despite this, she also saw the funny side of this work, showing the humour that got her through any number of tough cases. She told a reporter in 1931: 'none of them has ever been clever enough to tell that I was a policewoman and there to get them fined for an illegal occupation'.

Lillian's investigations into Sydney's fortune-tellers and clairvoyants were some of her most popular cases reported in the newspapers. She won recognition for them in February 1918 when the *Sun* ran a lengthy article on her work. Maude Rhodes, still in the job then, is mentioned but it was Lillian who inspired the poetic piece under the headlines and featured in the story:

> P.C. Sixty-five!
> Fortune-tellers know her when the summonses arrive.
> She kept on prosecuting till the craft was nearly dead,
> And the dark, mysterious ladies scattered curses on her head:
> When I asked them, 'What's the trouble?' they unanimously said —
> 'It's P.C. Sixty-five!'

The *Sun* reporter was glowing in his praise for Lillian's work, saying fortune-tellers 'dread the mention of her name'. When Lillian was on the 'warpath' they knew their 'turn will come'.

According to the papers, Lillian became the 'terror of the fortune-tellers', and was a force to be reckoned with. The fortune-tellers were in 'daily and deadly fear of Miss Armfield'.

It was good press for Lillian and the work of the Women's Police but the publicity was also problematic. This was clear to the *Sun* reporter. Lillian didn't want to talk too much about her work and tried to sound convincing when claiming it was largely uneventful. It was a humble approach not out of character with her personality but there was an important message too in her silence about her wider work and methods. Lillian was wary of the press knowing too much about police work and giving away too much to crooks reading the newspapers.

Giving away too much to reporters is a perennial problem in policing. In their efforts to find criminals and secure prosecutions, police will often appeal to the public through the media. Reporters also want convictions in their duty to the wider community but sensational, titillating stories sell more newspapers.

Crime reporter Bill Jenkings got his first gig with the *Daily Mirror* in 1944 and was a regular visitor to the CIB offices. The police hierarchy knew they could make a good alliance with Jenkings if they fed him information and gave him the odd scoop on major crimes ahead of official statements. But Jenkings knew the police hierarchy would also tear him to shreds if he overstepped the mark. Ray Kelly, one of the most notorious detectives in the NSW Police, hauled Jenkings into the CIB one day, determined to find out who Jenkings was using as an informant for the stories he was writing about organised crime. Kelly had joined the force in 1929 and knew Lillian Armfield, though their careers were quite different. While Lillian worked by the rule book, Ray Kelly bent the rules to get results. Jenkings stood firm and didn't give up his informant.

The release of too much information about Lillian's work in her first years on the job could also have compromised future investigations and increased her vulnerability on the streets. Lillian's detailed physical description was never given in the newspaper stories – protecting her identity – but the publicity drew attention to her undercover work. Fortune-tellers were warier of their female clients, asking for identification before engaging their business – as Lillian found in a number of cases – and were on the lookout for a woman who could hold her own and fit in with the police. What worked in Lillian's favour is that, while she was the main investigating officer, Maude Rhodes worked the same streets. They alternated their daily routines and investigated separate premises.

Lillian used these favourable newspaper reports to highlight the need for more female officers. Praise for the Women's Police in the local papers – 'policewomen are doing good work' according to the *Sun* – helped her to petition the police hierarchy for an increase to her staff. Now the nation's leading 'woman sleuth', Lillian argued for more assistance in her major cases. When Maude left the job late in 1919, Lillian was adamant that she couldn't do the work alone.

A new female constable was appointed to the Women's Police in 1919. Mary Paulett was recruited to assist Lillian with the general work of the Women's Police but especially the fortune-telling investigations. The Paulett name was well known in the NSW Police Force and Mary no doubt came from a policing background. After Maude's departure, there were still only two female officers left to handle all of the investigations. Lillian knew she needed more officers to give the Women's Police an opportunity for ongoing success.

Inspector-General Mitchell agreed Maude needed to be replaced but the end of the war stalled Lillian's campaign for more female officers. Close to 300,000 Australian men had survived the war and were arriving back home in 1919, having done their bit for their country. Their resettlement into society became a priority for the various state governments. Former police officers were among the returned soldiers and were looking to reapply for their jobs. There was also an increase in applications from new recruits who, through their experience of military life and skills in using weapons, now considered policing as a career.

Even without the mass repatriation of ex-servicemen, Lillian was never in a strong position to argue for a drastic increase in female numbers. Men continued to be the target of police recruitments for decades to come. What she did, however, was to argue her strengths. Women were essential to policing women, and more special constables wouldn't be competing with their male colleagues. The Women's Police provided an additional service. The road to equality would be slow but Lillian understood that a gradual increase in the size and scope of the Women's Police was better than nothing. The culture of policing could be changed but a sudden and rapid approach would never succeed. Instead, it would increase resistance and heighten anxieties about women taking men's work.

Lillian persisted with her campaign for further appointments throughout the 1920s and eventually had a small team of women working under her. By the 1930s, Lillian worked with eight other female officers. However, this would come on the back of the violence of the Razor Wars and the rise of female organised crime figures.

Lillian didn't know this as she watched Maude Rhodes leave the job for good late in 1919, so all she could do was hope her efforts would be noticed. In less than five years, Lillian's work had resulted in successful investigations into runaways and fortune-tellers. She had built a rapport with girls, young women and their families living around her main eastern Sydney patrols. She made the work of the Women's Police her own and started to change the culture of policing.

Lillian's ground-breaking work investigating the fortune-telling rackets paved the way for her involvement in more serious investigations involving male detectives. Though there was enough work to keep her busy investigating runaways and fraudulent fortune-tellers, her ambitions went higher than the general duties of a female officer. Lillian wanted to get involved more broadly in police investigations, including drug raids and homicide cases. When the opportunity arose, it was, unfortunately, in one of the worst ways possible for a police officer: investigating the death of one of their own.

5

Centennial Park Shooting

POLICE WORK CAN BE LIFE-THREATENING. MAINTAINING LAW
and order on the streets, highways and waterways and in
communities across the nation puts police officers at risk from
motor vehicle or motorcycle accidents, assaults, stabbings,
and shootings. There have been terrible incidents through
the years when the dangers associated with working in the
police force went beyond what the old annual reports used
to refer to as risks that were incidental to the job.

The first recorded death of a police officer in Australia
was in 1803 when Constable Joseph Luker, an ex-convict, was
killed while patrolling Back Row East, in the centre of Sydney
near Phillip, Hunter and Macquarie streets. Luker was investigating reports of a robbery near a brothel when he was set
upon by a group of men. He was brutally beaten to death

and his weapon, a cutlass, was found embedded in his skull. Two other constables, Luker's colleagues, were charged with his murder but were found not guilty. Joseph Samuel and John Russell were also charged with stealing and murder but Russell was acquitted. Samuel went down in history as the man who could not be hanged. After three failed attempts at hanging, his sentence was commuted to life imprisonment. Since Luker's death in 1803, over 700 police officers across the country have lost their lives either directly in the line of duty or from injuries sustained while on duty.

A few months after Lillian was appointed to the Women's Police, Sergeant William Bowan of Dungog Station, in the Hunter region of New South Wales, died from internal injuries sustained when he tried to detain a mentally ill man. In September of the same year, another officer was shot dead by members of the Industrial Workers of the World who objected to the officer's arrest of one of their members the previous day. In November 1919, Constable Joseph Hush and another constable went out to Roseville to investigate a robbery. The officers accepted a lift from a lorry driver to take them back to Chatswood Station. A tyre blew out on the vehicle and both constables were trapped underneath. Constable Hush died at Royal North Shore Hospital.

There were also police deaths close to where Lillian grew up in the Southern Highlands. In 1921, officers in Bowral attended a house after reports of shots. The owner, Major Le Barte, had already killed his wife and when Constable

Frederick Mitchell crept in along the floor from the back door, he was also shot dead.

In January 1921, the risks associated with police work were brought even closer to home for Lillian and other officers in Sydney. The case would devastate the policing community and have wider repercussions for Lillian's role in future investigations.

•

Park assaults were one of the main reasons the women's groups had pushed for the introduction of female officers. They wanted the Women's Police to ensure the safety of girls by way of regular patrols of the city parks. Fears about the welfare of young women in parks had been heightened by a number of prominent cases, including one in May 1912 where a teenage girl in Harris Park was threatened by a man who claimed he would kill her if she didn't stop screaming. The man was scared off by someone walking by but the girl was left shaken and physically affected by the attack. A number of assaults were reported in Sydney parks afterwards, provoking a women's deputation to order a meeting with the Mayor of Sydney in July 1915. They were pleased with the introduction of the Women's Police but also wanted female rangers to assist female constables to protect young women in the city parks, especially at night. The mayor reassured the women's campaigners that the Women's Police would patrol city parks to protect girls and women. Lillian and Maude were already offering their assistance in walking women home from work in the evening and ensuring the safety of all girls and women going on walks through the parks. It would, however, be a difficult task to police all the major parks regularly with only two female officers available. Serious assaults still happened, despite the best efforts of the female constables. In June 1920, a young woman was molested while walking through Mosman Park when a man leaped out of the bushes at her.

Sydney's main parks, including Hyde, Centennial and Moore, were becoming feared places where both men and women were targeted. There was an alarming increase to the number of reports of assaults and stealing being lodged at Central and Darlinghurst Police stations in the years following Lillian's appointment in 1915. A number of organised thieving groups were also turning their attention to assaulting young lovers in the main parks. Distracted in their romantic efforts, the couples were easy fodder for thieves lurking in the bushes.

Gangs were a problem in Sydney from the late nineteenth century with the rise of what were called the 'push gangs'. Mainly made up of young men, who were called larrikins and street rowdies, push gangs roamed the streets mugging people and making a nuisance. Some of the most notorious gangs lived and operated in inner and eastern Sydney, including the Rocks Push, Surry Hills' Forty Thieves, and the Big Seven in East Sydney. There was a religious divide to the gangs – Protestant and Catholic – and young boys would often fight it out in the streets over religions that had been fought over for centuries. Gang street battles – over religion, money, stolen goods and territory – were common in Surry Hills from the 1880s.

One of the most infamous cases of gang violence and assault was the Mount Rennie rape case of 1886. A sixteen-year-old domestic servant, Mary Jane Hicks, was molested by a taxi driver and managed to escape, but was set upon by a crowd of youths waiting nearby. They were members of the notorious Waterloo Push Gang. Mary's deposition in court is harrowing reading. After she escaped the cab, a twenty-year-old man came to her assistance and offered to show her to the tram line. He convinced Mary to sit down and rest in a bush area, and she then saw more young men approaching. They hurriedly cleared some scrub, threw Mary down onto it, and assaulted her. Her tights were ripped off and her dress was torn to pieces. She lost consciousness and when she came around, the gang members were running off after a member of the public discovered them with Mary and alerted the police. The officers found Mary dazed and seated against a tree.

Eleven members of the gang were charged with assaulting Mary and two confessed to having sex with her, claiming it was consensual. Mary Hicks had to stand in court and provide details of the assault: 'I have never cohabited with men of questionable character; up to the time of the occurrence at Moore Park on Thursday last I had maintained purity of person.' As if she hadn't already been through enough, Mary had to state in court that she had not previously had sex. The Mount Rennie case highlights one of the deep-seated problems with rape cases through the years: all too often the victim has to prove their integrity and lack of provocation.

Of the eleven gang members originally charged, nine stood trial and four were hanged for their crimes. Only one of them died instantly. The hangman misjudged their heights and three of the condemned were left dangling for minutes, slowly strangled to death. For Mary Hicks, it might have been further evidence of justice for the rape.

Gangs operated through violence, protection and coercion – all the hallmarks of more serious crime – and organised crime figures often looked to youth gangs for teenagers keen to make some quick money. They were hired as drug runners and 'cockatoos' at brothels and sly-grog shops. There were also 'basher gangs' in the city, dubbed as such by police watching their thieving tactics. Organised into packs, the gangs operated with a leader picking out a victim and then giving the signal – tipping his hat – for the other gang members to move in when the coast was clear. The gang would bash the victim until he gave up money or any possessions on his body. Victims were often left bloodied and naked in the street. Central Railway Station was a hotspot for attacks, with gang members targeting early-morning and late-night commuters when there were fewer people about the platforms.

Undercover policeman Frank Fahy was given the task of identifying the main gang groups and tailing them to houses across the inner city, which were later raided by other officers. And Lillian Armfield no doubt alerted her fellow officers to gang activities, given her duties included watching Central

Station for missing girls. She would have been alerted too to the possibility they could be victims of the basher gangs.

While the police often focused on male gang members, street gangs also often used a 'female decoy'. Popularised as the thieves' woman, the decoy played a key role in gang activities by luring men into dark alleyways where the male members of the gang attacked them. Female decoys were named and shamed in the press as companions of thieves and undesirables, and depicted as preying on supposedly unsuspecting men. In November 1920, a young man was ambushed by eight or nine men as he walked through Moore Park with a female companion. He was assaulted and robbed and, interestingly, the young woman he was with disappeared. Thomas Preston was probably the victim of a female decoy.

Youth gangs were not the only ones to watch out for around the streets of Sydney. Thieving gangs operating with older male members were becoming a serious problem in the city parks by the start of the 1920s. They combined assault and theft with perving on young couples. The gangs were well-coordinated, and the member of one gang had perfected using long rods to steal handbags from women sitting on benches with their male companions.

Lillian Armfield had no time for the park gangs – referring to them as 'human scum' – and, like other police officers, she wanted the parks rid of the gangs. Through her investigations and patrols of the parks, Lillian realised most of the older gang members were married with families but suffered from what she referred to as a 'mental kink' which led them to 'sneak through parks at night to gloat over embracing couples'. In her efforts to protect young women in parks, and under pressure from women's groups to eradicate assaults, Lillian placed the 'peeping Tom' high on her list of offenders.

The police came under fire from the press and public to end park theft and violence. Where once it had been that parks were off limits later in the evening, thieving gangs began striking at all times of the day. 'Daysiders' and 'Nightworkers', as they were known about the underworld streets, split their shifts around the parks, preying upon unsuspecting members of the public. The park thieves worked in small teams and a code of silence prevented police from talking to any of them to garner information about recent thefts. There were about 100 of these criminal shift workers operating around Centennial Park in the eastern suburbs of Sydney. With close to 200 hectares of park space and bordered by main thoroughfares taking trams about the city, the park offered its own protection and escape for thieves. It was also a huge area for the police to patrol.

With the rise in park assaults, robberies and perving, the police were forced to increase their foot patrols, hoping to prevent further incidents. Twenty-nine-year-old Constable Frederick Wolgast was one of a number of police conducting foot patrols around Centennial Park, reporting back on suspicious activity and developing case files on known offenders around the area. Wolgast was a well-liked member of the force who had joined in 1912. He worked at Darlinghurst Station for a time before heading out to Berry on the South

Coast. He then transferred to Mittagong in 1916 and worked in other country areas before returning to the city to work at Paddington Station. He was engaged to be married and ready to settle down, combining family life with an impressive policing career.

During one of his foot patrols in Centennial Park, Constable Wolgast was alerted to a robbery. Witnesses would later tell police they saw two men near a young couple minutes beforehand. One of the men started crawling along the ground towards the couple and, when a bag was snatched, the young man with the woman, John Kennedy, yelled out for the thief to stop. Kennedy gave chase, along with another witness, who stumbled and fell a few yards ahead. Kennedy chased the offender 500 yards before Constable Wolgast jumped out of bushes nearby and took up the chase. The thief turned in another direction, trying to lose the police officer, but was unsuccessful. Constable Wolgast was not giving up but things took a deadly turn when the man stopped and turned to face Wolgast. He waited until the young constable was closer, pulled out a revolver, and shot him in the chest. Constable Wolgast didn't have a chance to return fire. The bullet passed through his lung and lodged in his right shoulderblade. He collapsed to the ground, telling horrified bystanders he was shot. Kennedy hurried over and grabbed Wolgast's gun, firing off three shots at the offender, but missed.

A small crowd gathered around Frederick Wolgast, trying to assist him and call for help. His ashen appearance and laboured breathing signalled the worst. He was rushed to

St Vincent's Hospital, Darlinghurst, with his family notified soon after. Constable Wolgast provided police with a deposition attesting to the events of the evening. At the end of it he said: 'I think I am going to get over this. There is only one thing troubles me, and that is the pain here.' He pointed to his chest and then signed the deposition. He died two days later at St Vincent's, with his distraught family at his bedside.

The news carried quickly to the city stations where officers were already conducting round-the-clock investigations. James Mitchell immediately knew what had happened by the look and demeanour of the officers bringing the news to him. Having delivered bad news to families over many years in the job, he recognised the calm solemnness of the moment. His officers were now working a murder investigation and were determined to find the killer.

Frederick Wolgast was farewelled with a public funeral and full police honours. The police band led his cortege along Oxford Street on its way to his burial in Waverley Cemetery. It was followed by hundreds of police officers on horses and on foot, including detectives and senior officers representing every station in the metropolitan area, and Inspector-General Mitchell in full uniform. Mitchell told the newspapers the murder was felt personally by everyone across the force. The police had lost one of their own and flags flew at half-mast in all stations. Wolgast's mother, sisters, brothers and distraught fiancée walked solemnly with the police guard.

James Mitchell took the loss of a fellow officer hard and told metropolitan officers they needed to launch a full, thorough investigation into the gangs operating around Centennial Park. It would mean long work hours and amassing intelligence from across the city on known gang members working out of the parks. The police also launched an undercover investigation at Centennial Park. Everyone was on alert for any information that would help find Wolgast's murderer.

Lillian Armfield handled many of the calls coming into Central Station from concerned members of the public. Even the crooks were appalled by the murder and wanted to help out, despite the fact that, according to Lillian, they 'normally would sooner have done a long term in jail than assist us to track down a criminal'.

In order to catch the killer, the police also needed to put pressure on his fellow gang members and force them to reveal his whereabouts. In Lillian's words, 'we made plans to catch one of his associates if we couldn't catch him, and learn what we could from possible betrayal'. The gang knew the full force of the police was going to be levelled at them and, if they were smart, self-preservation would matter more than protecting a murderer.

Lillian also took part in the undercover investigation at Centennial Park. Like her boss, James Mitchell, and fellow officers, she was eager to help in any way she could. In a major investigation such as this one, beyond the duties of the Women's Police, Lillian normally would have been expected to work in the background. On this case, however, she was able to show her male colleagues she could be an important part of serious crime investigations.

The police hatched a plan to use the cover of a young couple walking or sitting in the park to lure in the gang members. To do this, the undercover officers needed to look like a legitimate couple. Lillian offered her assistance, saying she was as good as anyone to patrol with a male officer, but Mitchell was worried it would be too risky for an unarmed policewoman. Instead, Lillian was given the task of making male officers look like young women. The disguise had to be convincing in order to lure out the killer's acquaintances. With the aid of wigs and women's clothing and accessories, the male officers were dressed to design by Lillian and coached about walking like women and making their appearance seem authentic.

Undercover patrols continued for a number of shifts until one evening the officers struck it lucky. A thief attempted to rob the young couple and was surprised to find they were police officers. In his haste to avoid a hefty charge, he gave up the name of Constable Wolgast's killer. Charles Wynne Speechley was arrested soon after in Cabramatta and charged with vagrancy. When he was taken back to Central Police Station, he was placed in a line-up that included thirteen other men. Closely scrutinised by police and four of his known associates, Speechley was identified as the murderer and form-ally charged.

Charles Speechley created a sensation when he appeared in court. Over 150 people packed into the public viewing gallery, 'riveted' by the case, according to the local newspapers reporting on the inquest and trial. Speechley was seated near Detective Tom Wickham, Lillian Armfield's close police colleague, and sat calmly, nodding to people he recognised. Speechley was thirty-one years of age but looked at least a decade older, with white hair and prominent stubble. There were deep lines under his eyes; whether these were from the worry of an innocent man or a murderer in fear of a conviction was what the jury had to decide.

Speechley was well known around the city parks, especially Centennial Park, and had loitered about there for up to six years stealing bags and terrorising couples. His friends had seen him with a revolver and he'd told them he wasn't afraid to use it. This was not incriminating evidence but when it was revealed the stolen bag taken from the couple and a revolver had been found by police at Speechley's brother-in-law's house, the case seemed tight enough for a guilty verdict.

Charles Speechley denied the charges, pleading that he was not guilty of the murder. He claimed to have spent the afternoon and evening with his wife at a picture show and then enjoying supper afterwards. This alibi was supported by Speechley's wife but the jury was not convinced. Charles Speechley was found guilty of the murder of Constable Wolgast and sentenced to life imprisonment, from which he was released in September 1941. It was an important win for the police force but a terrible reminder of the risks they faced in their work.

Lillian won recognition from Inspector-General Mitchell and detectives at CIB for her role in the investigation. From handling phone calls and public testimonies, to setting up part of the undercover work, she proved herself valuable in the force beyond the required duties of the Women's Police. In her work with the CIB detectives, her colleagues were noticing the impact the tall, hard-working woman from Mittagong was having on policing in the city through, in their words, her 'courage and sound good sense'.

The boundaries of the Women's Police were becoming blurred as Lillian crossed into more serious criminal invest-igations and began regularly assisting the male detectives. Ambition would push her even further. Lillian would never have made it through these first tough years in the job had she not been ambitious. By the 1920s she was ready to take it one step further. Lillian Armfield wanted to be a detective.

Timing is everything and, just as Lillian was setting her sights on detective work, Sydney's crime scene was experien-cing a dramatic change. Criminal empires were on the rise and, by the middle of the 1920s, Sydney was a heartland of organised crime.

Suddenly, the work of the Women's Police was far less straightforward than what Lillian had been recruited to do. She read the crime reports coming in through the station, watched the motley crew of crooks making regular appear-ances at court and kept up with the sensational stories being reported in the press. One thing stood out: an increasing number of women were involved in the organised crime groups and they worked for two female bosses. In the back streets and shops, houses and dens of eastern Sydney, two powerful criminal entrepreneurs were amassing great wealth from sly grog, prostitution and drugs. They maintained their syndicates through intimidation, coercion and violence. Tilly Devine ('The Queen of Woolloomooloo') and Kate Leigh ('The Dope Queen') were striking their own blow to the inequality of the sexes, albeit through crime.

Lillian knew there was only so much the Vice Squad and the Drug Squad were able to do in prosecuting Devine and Leigh. Female prostitutes and drug addicts were more likely to provide insider information on the brothels and drug trade to female officers. Along with this, female constables were the only officers allowed to search female offenders. The detectives were now looking to Lillian for help.

It started with Lillian familiarising herself with a key method of detection introduced into the detectives' branch. The Rogues Gallery were two albums of mug shots put together by CIB detectives so they would be able to visually identify some of Sydney's most notorious crooks. The albums were also known as the Special Photograph books. Sydney's leading undercover man, Frank Fahy, was said to have secured his job after he successfully identified the faces of men and women catalogued in the Rogues Gallery.

Mug shots changed policing methods. From around the middle of the nineteenth century, police departments all over the world began compiling mug shots of criminals. One of Australia's most famous early mug shots is of Ned Kelly in 1871. By the turn of the twentieth century, police photographers were employed more widely and were regular visitors to the various lock-ups. All Sydney detectives were required to know the faces of the crooks featured in the Rogues Gallery.

Lillian memorised the mug shots of female offenders from the *Police Gazette*s and Special Photograph books – loaned to her from the detectives – and combined this with her investigative work. Observing, cataloguing, and building her case files on girls and women in Sydney, Lillian was proving invaluable in the police.

Lillian's investigative work would now take her into the dark, dangerous and life-threatening underworld of Sydney's organised crime scene. She moved out to Sandridge Street, Bondi, to keep her distance from the crime streets of Darlinghurst and Surry Hills. It was also important to Lillian to keep her private life very private. Her family visited her in the city, including her sister, Muriel, to whom she remained very close throughout her life. Muriel moved with her husband and young family to southern Sydney not long after Lillian joined the police. In the years that followed, the sisters kept close to each other, and Lillian became a beloved auntie checking in on her nieces and nephews.

Lillian realised she might pay a high price for her ambitions in detective work. Kate Leigh and Tilly Devine used standover tactics to maintain their criminal empires and Devine wasn't afraid to assault a female officer who crossed her. Lillian Armfield's work now included investigating Sydney's prostitution underworlds and the madams, workers and clients who were maintaining the business. Lillian needed to restrict prostitution around eastern Sydney and prevent other young women from entering into the work.

In the depths of Sydney's underworlds there were also far worse characters than Tilly Devine and Kate Leigh. One of them was George 'The Midnight Raper' Wallace, nicknamed as such for his attacks on prostitutes. It was now Lillian's job to ensure gangsters like Wallace stayed away from eastern Sydney's streetwalkers. To do so, Lillian put herself right in the path of one of Sydney's most violent sex predators.

Portrait of the Armfield family, taken around 1910 when Lillian was visiting them from Sydney. Lillian is seated in the centre, flanked by her parents and with her siblings (left to right: Muriel, Percival, James, Ruby) standing behind.
(Photo courtesy Norm O'Brien)

Surry Hills terraces at 73–77 Foveaux Street. Lillian patrolled streets like these from her appointment in July 1915. *(City of Sydney Archives SRC21953)*

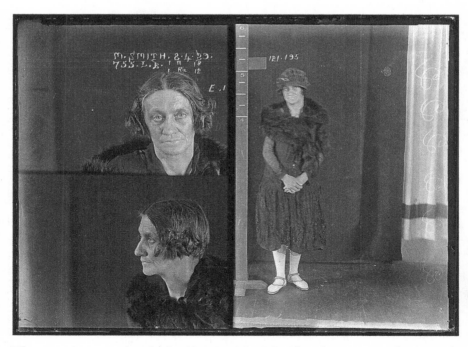

The notorious cocaine dealer 'Botany May' Smith, who attempted to assault Lillian with a red-hot flat-iron during a police stakeout of her terrace in Surry Hills, in April 1929 *(NSW Police Forensic Photography Archive, Justice & Police Museum)*

Nellie Cameron, the pretty girl of the underworld – lover of leading gangsters including Guido Calletti, leader of the Darlinghurst Push. Nellie was one of Tilly Devine's working girls. These police mugshots were taken in 1930. *(NSW Police Forensic Photography Archive, Justice & Police Museum)*

Guido Calletti, 1930. Calletti was a notorious criminal, leader of the Darlinghurst Push street gang and lover of both Nellie Cameron and Mary Markham (also known as 'Pretty Dulcie' and 'The Angel of Death'). He was gunned down by a gangster rival in August 1939. *(NSW Police Forensic Photography Archive, Justice & Police Museum)*

Sydney crime queen, Kate Leigh, mugshots taken in 1930. She amassed a fortune and a fearsome reputation from cocaine, prostitution and sly-grog sales. *(NSW Police Forensic Photography Archive, Justice & Police Museum)*

Tilly (Matilda) Devine, seen here with her husband, Jim, circa 1930. Tilly was Kate Leigh's criminal rival and just as notorious. *(Fairfax Photos FXT166896)*

The Devines' house in the Sydney beachside suburb of Maroubra. In July 1929 the violence of Sydney's Razor Wars spilled over to Maroubra when Jim Devine shot a member of Kate Leigh's gang outside his home. *(Fairfax Photos FXT28442)*

Photo of the Women's Police working in the Criminal Investigation Branch, Sydney, 1938: Lillian Armfield (sitting at rear of photo), Mrs Jeffrey, Miss Rosser, Mrs Burton, Mrs Ledger, Mrs Mitchell, Mrs Croke, Mrs Mooney. *(Justice & Police Museum JP87/148)*

NOW WE KNOW WHAT POLICEWOMEN DO

SGT. LILLIAN ARMFIELD DISCUSSES THE WORK

THE women police. One thinks of Amazons. A few minutes with Sergeant Lillian Armfield, their chief, explodes that myth.

Behind those penetrating brown eyes, beyond that kindly smile, you find the realist. A woman of great prudence, student of human nature—"And all day to study it," she says—here is an equable blend of driving force and quiet tolerance. Balance is her outstanding quality. A cottage by the sea is her Ultima Thule. What prompted her to become a policewoman?

"I DID several things after I left my home in the Moss Vale district. as a young girl. I was nursing in a mental hospital—excellent place to study human nature!—when, in July, 1915, the New South Wales Government advertised for women police, I answered the advertisement and so did another of our nurses. That's all."

And the training?

"Well, we had a year's intensive training, but from the beginning we were put onto the work, and two detectives went round with us. There were only the two of us then. Now there are eight, and preference is always given to the widows of policemen.

"The women police were primarily established to search women under arrest and for interrogating women and children in cases where they would feel more at ease if a policeman were not present. The National Council of Women was keen on the movement."

The scope of the work of these policewomen to-day gives them a roving commission.

"We are free to go anywhere and make what investigations we think wise. We are likely to be called out at any hour of the night. Normally we work eight hours a day, with one day off each week and twenty-eight days holiday in the year. We cover the city and the country. If a policewoman is wanted for a female investigation in the country, one goes from the central staff in Sydney."

Is she never afraid?

"Never. I never have any trouble. It is suggested that a revolver is an aid to courage.

"We carry no weapons. A warrant card explains who we are. Handcuffs! Oh, no, we never handcuff a woman. I try hard never to send a woman to gaol. Kindness and tact do so much. We don't put women in the cells. We bring them here to headquarters. If they are young and first offenders, I send for their people or their friends and they talk it over in a quiet room, and usually we find a better way out than gaol. In domestic quarrels the police do not make arrests, but if you can encourage 'troubled people to meet and advise them things aren't half so bad as they seem at first."

What about hysterical women, charged and arrested?

Sergeant Armfield has a method for these. "Authority with kindness. They always come without any fuss. You talk quietly and they come. They know it will be better in the long run. I have no difficulty in convincing them of that."

Are women more philosophical about arrest and the aftermath of their crimes than men?

"Definitely, I think so." When it comes to the point they accept the inevitable day of reckoning in Miss Armfield's opinion. They are more fatalistic than the men.

Enlarging on the scope of the policewomen's work, she explains that her work is not merely to police but to protect.

"Policewomen meet trains coming in from the country, and also ships whenever there is time and other duties permit. In this way we are able to avert many undesirable things happening to girls and young women. So many of these city-seekers are just youngsters who have had a quarrel at home and have run away.

"They usually have very little or no money. We bring them to my rooms here at headquarters, and send for their people and let them have it out. I keep them here as long as possible if their people can't come at once, and usually we take up a Kentucky amongst ourselves—policemen and policewomen—to get them food and beds. We try to find them jobs. If it comes to the worst I arrange for them to be taken into the Girls' Shelter at Glebe. That institution is conducted by the Welfare Department for children and girls, who are homeless or waiting to come up before the courts. If these country girls have already taken a retrograde step, then all we can do is try to save them from another."

Are they grateful? Or do they want to forget?

"Dear, no! They come back. Nearly all of them. Some come to see me after they have married. They bring me their babies to admire. I think a week never passes without some letter from somewhere—it might be another State—from the girls who have passed through these rooms in some sort of trouble, and are now happy and secure."

Realist uppermost, Miss Armfield acknowledges that there are some girls who are naturally bad, and do not respond to a helping hand. They choose a loose life for preference. But for those in whom the gleam still shines, she and her comrades in "the force" are willing to take risks. Frequently they made human salvage visits to houses of ill repute. On this work two policewomen go together, protected by two plain clothes detectives. Practically everywhere else they dispense with male aid.

"We get all help and kindness from the men police, but we feel we can go where they go, and we do." Without batons either!

And how about male arrests?

Sergeant Lillian grows reticent. "I have made them at times," she admits.

One such case, at least, made police history in New South Wales. Two young men were wanted for a sex crime. They had a lampshade shop in Sydney. They advertised for girls to make lampshades. Miss Armfield went to the shop, ostensibly to apply for a position. When the two men appeared she arrested them both and held them in custody, single-handed, while Inspector Thornley, then Detective Thornley, who was waiting in the background, went for other detectives. Long-term sentences followed the arrests.

Now, about that day off each week? What might Sergeant Lillian do with her spare time?

"Oh, I don't know," she muses, and suddenly one becomes conscious of pearl ear-rings above the tailored suit; of a feminine wave in her crisp short hair. "There is always so much to do at home, isn't there? Stockings to darn, and all that."

She swims for her exercise, and walks.

"And we get lots of walking." She wears thick brogues for every day service, 'but no routine uniform is required by the policewoman. "We have a free choice in our clothes, and often I must wear quite smart things going to certain social gatherings where I seek information."

The policewomen do not live in barracks. In this, also, they enjoy free choice of residence. "So long as it is quite respectable," says Sergeant Lillian Armfield, head of the women police.

"And when the yearly holiday comes, I dearly love an ocean cruise. But, ultimately, remember, I shall go into retirement in a cottage by the sea."

Article about Lillian published in the *Sun* newspaper on 18 August 1938; a studio portrait of Lillian, taken circa 1930. She wears her trademark string of pearls. (*Photo courtesy Norm O'Brien*)

SILHOUETTE WILL CHANGE

From Our Special Representative

LONDON, Wednesday.

Autumn fashions will show a less accentuated bosomline and hint at a lower waistline and a narrow-shouldered look reminiscent of the early 1900's which is 'in tune with the general silhouette shown in the new hairdressing, Miss Jean Guest told the Drapers' Summer School.

Favorite colors will be plum with lime green or dull gold, burgundy with stained glass blue or coral pink, fuchsia with glowing blue.

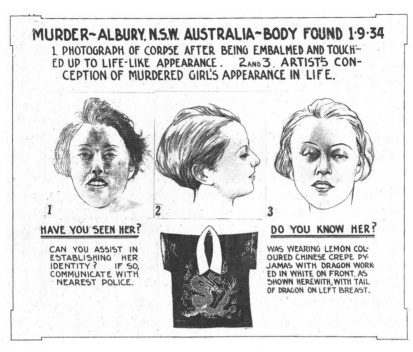

MURDER~ALBURY, N.S.W. AUSTRALIA~BODY FOUND 1·9·34

1. PHOTOGRAPH OF CORPSE AFTER BEING EMBALMED AND TOUCH-
ED UP TO LIFE-LIKE APPEARANCE. 2 AND 3. ARTISTS CON-
CEPTION OF MURDERED GIRL'S APPEARANCE IN LIFE.

1

2

3

HAVE YOU SEEN HER?

CAN YOU ASSIST IN ESTABLISHING HER IDENTITY? IF SO, COMMUNICATE WITH NEAREST POLICE.

DO YOU KNOW HER?

WAS WEARING LEMON COL-OURED CHINESE CREPE PY-JAMAS WITH DRAGON WORK-ED IN WHITE ON FRONT, AS SHOWN HEREWITH, WITH TAIL OF DRAGON ON LEFT BREAST.

Police reconstruction of the Pyjama Girl's probable appearance. The information and a death mask were displayed in many public places for over a decade. The body was also on display, preserved in formalin, for many years. *(Fairfax Photos FXJ198275)*

Lillian at the wheel of her car, date unknown. *(Photo courtesy Norm O'Brien)*

Lillian and her sisters Muriel (left) and Ruby (middle). This photo was taken after Lillian's retirement in 1949. *(Photo courtesy Norm O'Brien)*

Lillian's colleagues in the Women's Police treated her to an annual birthday harbour cruise for many years after her retirement. *(Photo courtesy Norm O'Brien)*

6

Policing Sydney's Prostitutes 'From Dusk till Dawn'

LILLIAN'S POLICE INVESTIGATIVE WORK TOOK HER INTO THE red-light areas of inner and eastern Sydney. Prostitutes soliciting on the streets favoured George, Pitt, Castlereagh, Elizabeth, Liverpool, Phillip and King streets in the city centre but police crackdowns there moved women to the alleyways and street corners around Woolloomooloo, Darlinghurst and Surry Hills. While soliciting continued in the city, more of the work moved into Lillian's main patrol areas, particularly from the 1920s. She could now add prostitutes to her growing list of women under investigation.

Sydney's vice reputation dates back to the arrival of the first female convicts in 1788. Prostitution doesn't seem to have existed before the arrival of the first Europeans – there's no evidence of it across Indigenous societies pre-1788 – making the sex business another commodity introduced with the newcomers. When the Second Fleet arrived in Sydney in 1788, the naval lieutenant Ralph Clark made a statement that would echo down the years: 'My God, not more of those damned whores!' Not all of the first female convicts were prostitutes prior to their transportation to the NSW colony but Clark's indignation created the stereotype of the female felon as a prostitute. One of those Second Fleet women, as we now know, was Lillian Armfield's great-great-grandmother, Elizabeth Perry; she was a convicted thief, not a prostitute.

In the first decades of the colony, Sydney's prostitutes worked from their homes in and around The Rocks. Streetwalking was also prevalent through the town, and by 1859 local politicians and members of the police toured the streets to investigate prostitution and offer some solutions. This was part of a wider investigation into the state of the working classes in Sydney. In what he referred to as 'scenes of vice', local politician J.H. Palmer reported on the poor living conditions of women in the brothels lining a lane from Kent to Sussex Street. There were women soliciting in Hyde Park and the Domain, as well as along the alleyways running off the main streets.

The gold rushes were partly to blame for the increase in soliciting. Women were left behind in the city while partners and husbands went off prospecting. Some women were reduced to selling sex to keep their families and pay the rent. There were other women, however, who saw prostitution as a new career. Church and charity workers revealed tales of young women who didn't want to see prostitution outlawed because they would be restricted from working in their profession legally.

By the turn of the twentieth century around two thousand prostitutes were believed to be working the streets of Sydney. For the Sydney Rescue Work Society, prostitutes were 'leading a life of shame and degradation' and living in 'sinister houses around Campbell, Palmer, and Riley Streets'. Churches referred to the inner-city streets as 'Darkest Sydney'. Social reformers campaigned the government to better regulate prostitution and a deputation from the Public Morals Association met with the government's chief secretary in March 1905 to discuss immorality in the city. The chief secretary offered his support but said the reasons for an increase in prostitution and the number of brothels were complex and that government legislation was needed to tackle the deeper social issues leading to immorality. As the newspapers reported, the issues included 'poverty, drink, betrayal, lack of opportunities for proper employment, lack of home training, lack of religion. Large cities, too, were one of the world's curses.'

Lillian Armfield first met some of Sydney's prostitutes through her work at Callan Park Asylum. A number of the female patients – 'common prostitutes' – had been picked up off the streets by the police. They were usually repeat offenders arrested on soliciting or idle and disorderly charges. Prison, the police expected, would only harden streetwalkers further and introduce them to other women in similar circumstances. This might remove the stigma of their work, which was exactly what the police wanted to highlight. Callan Park provided police with a place to keep streetwalkers out of the public eye and deter their activities.

Families sent their daughters away to the asylum when they were wandering the streets and associating with known prostitutes. Religious and domestic lessons were supposed to correct the error of these young women's ways but some would not be swayed, even when stricter methods of drugging and solitary confinement were introduced.

It's difficult to know the extent of Lillian's work at Callan Park as she talked more about her police work than she did her nursing duties. However, from what little she did say, it seems her contact with young women sent away as moral deviants encouraged her towards prevention over incarceration. If she could keep an eye on vulnerable girls on the streets and in housing around inner and eastern Sydney, she might be able to prevent them from turning to prostitution.

Lillian knew from speaking to young women that some entered into prostitution because they could earn more money from it than a regular job. Some did it to pay the rent while others were lured into prostitution with hopes of a better lifestyle. With more money to spend, young women could enjoy luxuries from clothing to makeup and nights out at clubs. Even in the nineteenth century the newspapers were reporting on this phenomenon:

A very large proportion of the unfortunates who infest the streets of Sydney at night, and who may be seen flaunting about elaborately dressed, and apparently joyous and happy, are very young girls, natives of the colony. In numerous cases those girls are induced to follow this course of life from seeing nothing but the fair side of the picture. They see girls whom they formerly knew in service dashing about at theatres and other places of amusement, expensively dressed, with all the airs and appearance of fashionable ladies . . .

Lillian knew, however, that very few of the young women working as prostitutes would achieve this.

By the time Lillian joined the police, there had been some major changes to the policing of prostitution. While brothels had been operating since the middle of the nineteenth century, in a relatively small capacity, by the turn of the twentieth century they were being targeted as sites of moral deviance. The NSW Police Force began lobbying for changes to the law to curb prostitution and brothel-keeping. Police wanted soliciting to be punished with up to six months in prison. Men living off prostitution and landlords of houses of ill-repute were to face up to twelve months' imprisonment. Brothel-keeping, police argued, should be punished with twelve months' imprisonment. The *Police Offences (Amendment) Act* enacted in 1908 criminalised street prostitution. Police were increasingly successful in driving most women off the streets, but regulation of prostitution also turned it into a 'deviant underworld'.

Lillian Armfield was given the task of policing the 'deviant underworlds'. Sometimes she worked with a plain-clothes policeman to catch women soliciting on the streets. Lillian, or another policewoman, walked along inner-city streets with a plain-clothes male officer, posing as a couple. As Lillian later recalled, 'We were used as decoys . . . the street-women didn't give us more than a casual glance.' That was when they moved in to make an arrest. Prostitutes had to be on the lookout for men, women and couples now, and their attempts to avoid detection increasingly lost them business. Lillian knew prostitutes 'were among the hottest critics of the Government's decision to appoint policewomen'.

At other times, Lillian investigated alone. For three months in 1918 she kept an eye on eighteen-year-old Millie Sinclair. Millie rented a flat in Kings Cross which was far beyond what an average earner could afford. This drew Lillian's suspicions and she followed Millie to dance halls and seedy parts of the city. When questioned by Lillian, the young woman claimed she was married. Lillian was having none of it and asked her which man was her husband, seeing as Lillian had witnessed Millie with several different men. Millie claimed her husband was recovering from fighting at the Western Front and had told her to have a good time while he was away.

Lillian wasn't convinced and her investigation continued. She shared the story with Detective Sergeant Tom O'Brien. As their careers and cases crossed over, Lillian and O'Brien became close confidants and relied on each other in their related investigations. O'Brien went on to lead the Flying Gang, a group of plain-clothes officers sent out to break up the sly-grog rackets from the middle of the 1920s. In another case in 1925, Tom O'Brien was punched in the neck and body as he tried to arrest a man in Darlinghurst for using indecent language. The offender was already annoyed at O'Brien for having arrested an underage girl in his house. The magistrate sentenced him to over two months' hard labour in Long Bay if he couldn't pay the fines and reminded him that while O'Brien was 'a strict officer', he was fair and just. The same description could be applied to Lillian Armfield and this was one of the reasons they worked well together.

Back in 1918 and reviewing the Millie Sinclair case, Tom O'Brien informed Lillian that Millie used to work as a housemaid until a few months back and couldn't possibly have enough money to afford a flat in the Cross. O'Brien also pointed out that Millie had already been arrested for soliciting. His actual words, smacking of the culture of the time and police-speak, were: 'She's been vagged twice.' Women arrested on suspicion of soliciting were often charged with vagrancy – unable to demonstrate a lawful means of support – so this would have raised Lillian's suspicions. She investigated further.

Millie couldn't be honest with Lillian because she knew all too well the social stigma around prostitution. Prostitution was labelled the 'great social evil' and women who entered into it were seen as having 'fallen' from femininity. Evangelical religious movements argued that the female prostitute needed to be saved to prevent the further degradation of society. Young unmarried men and husbands were apparently being lured into immoral lifestyles by streetwalkers and brothel-keepers. Church leaders argued that prostitution led to marriage breakdowns and posed a significant threat to society through the spread of venereal diseases. One church minister told a Christian convention in 1898: 'There is perhaps not another city on the face of the earth in which vice has more completely established her dominion than the capital of New South Wales.'

World War I had also put pressure on the police to more closely supervise young girls on the streets and living in rental accommodation. Venereal diseases had long been associated with wartime conditions, dating back to the Crimean War of the mid-nineteenth century. Prostitutes were characterised as a health threat passing on sexually transmitted diseases to soldiers on leave or returned from active service. Following on from the Crimean War and an increase in venereal diseases among troops, the British government legislated to restrict the spread of these diseases in the armed forces. Port towns were the main targets. Here police could arrest any woman suspected of prostitution and subject her to a compulsory check for venereal disease. If she was found to be suffering from VD, she would be sent to a locked hospital until she was fully recovered. The sexual double standard was clear: women were targeted, not their male clients.

The Australian colonial governments also looked to introduce *Contagious Diseases Acts* to control the spread of venereal diseases in the late nineteenth century. Queensland and Tasmania passed *Contagious Diseases Act*s in 1868 and 1879, but New South Wales and Victoria failed to pass similar legislation. Although a *Contagious Diseases Act* was not introduced in New South Wales, containment areas were established.

Prostitution was blamed for a lowering of social standards and reformers – 'from the church, the state, the medical profession, philanthropists, feminists and others' – wanted to control and end prostitution. The social purity movement dreamed of a world where prostitution no longer existed and pleaded for the social, medical and legal regulation of the 'fallen' woman. The prostitute had fallen out of respectable society and, as social reformer Grace Ferguson wrote to the newspapers, carried the mark of shame:

> All women 'on the streets', as we call it, are not totally depraved and devoid of all shame, by a long way. Some poor girls, from folly and silliness or absolute ignorance have fallen, and failing to gain a footing in respectable society again, have gone under. Others have found the battle of life too hard for them – God help them – and have sold their bodies to sustain life or help their families, but they still retain their sense of shame.

Millie Sinclair didn't outwardly demonstrate a sense of shame about selling her body for sex but she still denied her involvement in prostitution to the police. Perhaps this was also because she was concerned about a criminal conviction if she revealed how she earned her money.

Social workers tried to offer prostitutes places to stay away from the brothels and off the streets. By the 1890s the Sydney Rescue Work Society had an establishment called the Open

All Night Refuge for Women. If they were left to wander the streets, prostitutes were increasingly at risk of being charged with 'idle and disorderly' or vagrancy, especially with the passing of the new *Police Offences Act*. It was far easier for police to control prostitution if the business could be contained in certain parts of the city and within brothels.

In 1918 Lillian visited the flat where Millie was staying and found her living with three young women. This could possibly have explained why she was able to pay the rent but Lillian wasn't convinced. She took the girls' names and details and quizzed Millie further about her means of support. She seemed to be the only one claiming to have work. Millie couldn't supply work details and had no paperwork to support her marriage. She would have had to have a very good paying job to provide the high rent – four guineas.

Millie and the three girls living with her were convicted as vagrants, with Millie singled out as having led the girls into prostitution. In court, Millie admitted she wasn't married but was enjoying a good time before her boyfriend came back from the war. Suddenly a young man appeared in the courtroom. He was dressed in a Royal Australian Navy uniform and took the stand to vouch for Millie's story. The magistrate let Millie go with one hour's detention and she left the court building in the arms of the young officer.

The three other girls were not as lucky. One was sent to a maternity home, another to the Salvation Army Home and the third was placed in the care of her sister.

Lillian came across Millie in the street a few years later. She had a baby in her arms and a toddler at her side and looked happy and healthy. Lillian was pleased the magistrate's decision hadn't backfired but 'couldn't help feeling that Millie Sinclair was a lot luckier than she deserved to be when I thought of the three young girls she helped to ruin'.

Sydney's prostitutes were depicted as both vulnerable and dangerous, and in need of rescuing. The police, courts and media – influenced by public opinion – promoted an image of prostitution as turning formerly good women into fallen, impoverished wrecks of womanhood. Pushed into brothels or allowed to solicit on the streets as long as no one saw, prostitutes were also portrayed as a threat to the health of the state. Some reformers were concerned for women who could not get out of prostitution and who felt trapped working on the streets or in the brothels. Sexual slavery likewise entered into public debates about the need to regulate prostitution. It was a serious situation where prostitutes could not get out of the work and might be subjected to violence and exploitation.

Despite the legal restrictions, threat of imprisonment and growing social stigma, women continued to solicit on the streets. For Lillian Armfield, streetwalkers were a normal part of life on the streets of inner Sydney. They conducted their business 'from dusk till dawn'. By the 1920s, popular religious figures such as Reverend R.B.S. Hammond claimed: 'Everybody knows that prostitution is prevalent in Sydney', and were able to single out prostitutes' main thoroughfares.

This didn't mean, however, that the streetwalkers weren't under pressure to avoid police attention.

Streetwalkers evaded attempts to regulate their behaviour by keeping close with locals. Prostitutes in the first decades of the twentieth century generally lived, worked and were a recognised part of their community. In the inner-city neighbourhoods of Sydney, prostitutes were resourceful in gaining local acceptance. Some helped their neighbours out and looked after young children while mothers went off to work. Former resident Mary Baker remembered the level of acceptance she grew up with in eastern Sydney:

> Oh there were girls in our street that we knew were on the game, more or less. But strangely enough, I don't remember that anyone ever looked down on any girls that were involved in prostitution, because they kept their business to themselves, and people didn't interfere into other people's business. You said good morning or good afternoon to anyone, irrespective of what people did, as long as they didn't interfere with you.

Lillian Armfield had to understand the individual circumstances of the women working in prostitution. Just as she had with runaway girls, she kept an eye on the different women about the streets and made sure they knew she was there to help them if they needed assistance. Lillian wanted to gain their trust. Around eastern Sydney streets where there was almost an inherited mistrust of the police, Lillian had to show the streetwalkers and brothel workers that she was there to police crime but her main goal was to ensure they were protected in their work. She knew she would never rid the city of prostitution; despite all the restrictions and the severity of laws, prostitution could not be suppressed. What she did was to ensure that she offered some level of social reform and looked after the girls and women living off prostitution, as best she could. Most police information on prostitution came directly from the women working on the streets and in the brothels. If she gained their trust, Lillian could better police prostitution. She knew many of the prostitutes by name and got to know them over many years, developing a personal relationship, as well as a professional one. She became godmother to some of the children born to prostitutes in Kings Cross and tried to 'keep an eye on them' as they grew up. Lillian's family remember this as representative of her genuine commitment to the women in the communities she policed.

Lillian could never have made any headway in her investigations without developing an understanding of the brothel business. If she was going to strike a blow to prostitution and keep young women away from the business, she needed to know where all the brothels were and who was running them. One of the first places she looked for runaway girls was near or in brothels and in notorious rental accommodation about the city. The brothel madams began making a fortune after 1910 when legislation was brought in allowing men to be arrested for living off the proceeds of prostitution. Women found their loophole and used it to full effect.

Police favoured underworld regulation, particularly through the containment of prostitution in brothels, but stepped in when business got out of hand or locals complained. The first call-girl establishments were set up by two Frenchwomen in Kings Cross in the early twentieth century, but they were not prosecuted if they carried on discreetly. The professionalisation of prostitution transformed the prostitute into a 'business identity' and led to greater publicity for the underworld managers, who were targeted for their inability to contain and regulate their businesses.

In a sensational case from 1929, Lillian Armfield worked in a taskforce investigating a French prostitution racket. For a number of weeks, police had been watching the same group of men greeting young women arriving in Sydney Harbour. When questioned, they claimed the women were their wives arriving from France. It might have been true were it not for the fact they seemed to greet many wives. The men said they were now greeting sisters-in-law. Detectives suspected the men were running a prostitution racket but they needed evidence beyond women arriving by boat from overseas.

While the detectives watched the harbour, Lillian began watching the city cafés to see if any of the men and women showed up. By chance, she was walking past French Jack's café on Cathedral Street when she caught sight of the group. Lillian reported the meeting back to Detective Syd Thompson (later the head of the Vice Squad). Thompson had joined the police in 1915, the same year as Lillian, and they developed a mutual respect for each other's work.

Thompson and Lillian's friend Detective Sergeant Tom Wickham – who would make a name for himself leading police operations targeting organised crime during the Razor Wars – began investigating the leader of the group, Salvatore Bua. Wickham was the best man for the job. He couldn't be bought, despite the efforts of crooks, drug peddlers and pimps. One cocaine trafficker tried to bribe Wickham in 1929: 'if I had you fellows with me I could corner the cocaine market, and we could make a packet out of it'. He made the proposal to the wrong man: Wickham had the trafficker's premises raided soon after.

Lillian knew the team needed more than suspicious activity to make an arrest. She made her way into Salvatore Bua's business by befriending two of his prostitutes. A key part of Lillian's early investigations into prostitution was her ability to talk to girls and young women and coax information out of them. Knowing the women were French, she endeared herself to them by asking if they needed any assistance as newcomers to the city. Lillian was likeable enough to win their trust but when one of them was seen with a black eye, Lillian knew she had to tread very carefully. Bua was keeping the women in his racket through intimidation and violence, and he wouldn't be shy in doing worse to a police officer sniffing around his establishments.

Over many weeks of investigations and surveillance work, the police team amassed enough evidence to question Bua. They met him in his flat in Kings Cross, requesting more information about his business. The meeting was waylaid when one of Bua's women lunged at Detective Thompson. Lillian came to his aid and subdued the woman by holding on to her arms until she calmed down. She thrashed about, screaming blue murder at the detectives, but eventually gave in. She was no match for the tall country officer who had years of experience restraining asylum patients. While Lillian was busy with the woman, Bua charged at Thompson with what looked like a walking stick. Thompson was quick on his feet and grabbed the stick, suddenly realising it was a razor-sharp sword stick. The game was up for Bua and his racket. They were deported and the police kept the stick as a souvenir.

Palmer Street featured in Lillian's investigations as one of the most notorious spots for brothels. It is ironic that the very street named for a social reformer, a man who had toured the streets in 1859 identifying the worst spots for prostitution, became so closely associated with the trade. By the 1920s the street was firmly under the control of a woman who loathed the Women's Police – especially their boss, Lillian Armfield.

•

Matilda 'Tilly' Devine (nee Twiss) made a name for herself on the streets of London well before she was a household name in Australia. Born in Camberwell, London, in 1900, she met a young Australian soldier, James Devine, while she was soliciting on the streets of London. Tilly was one month shy of her seventeenth birthday when she married Jim. He was an army misfit with one of the most disreputable service records in the Australian forces. Jim was born in Victoria but had been working as a shearer in Queensland before enlisting. He was repeatedly detained during his wartime service for being absent without leave and was declared an 'illegal absentee' by May 1918. He returned to Australia in 1919.

Tilly was reunited with Jim the following year when she arrived in Sydney on board a war-bride ship. They rented a flat in Paddington and worked together in prostitution, thieving and extortion around eastern Sydney. Jim took up work as a hire-car proprietor but the police knew the cars were never hired out. They were used to ferry Tilly and other prostitutes to and from jobs around the city streets. Jim was basically Tilly's pimp in a getaway car. By the middle of the 1920s, Tilly owned a number of brothels, and both she and Jim were peddling cocaine. In her first years in Sydney, Tilly was arrested nearly eighty times for prostitution.

Tilly was well-known to the police and regarded by them as 'a prostitute of the worst type and an associate of the worst type of Prostitute, Vagrants and Criminals'. She was also known to resort to extreme violence when someone crossed her. In May 1925 she was convicted at the Darlinghurst Sessions with maliciously wounding Sydney Corke two months beforehand. Tilly slashed him across the hand and watched as blood spurted from the wounds over his face. Corke was rushed to hospital but didn't regain full use of his hand. Police testified that Tilly had close to eighty previous convictions and was incorrigible. A month before her court appearance, Tilly had thrown her shoe at a constable at Central Police Station.

Appearing on the malicious wounding charges in May, Tilly fainted in the dock and then, when revived, sobbed as the magistrate handed down a two-year prison sentence.

By the end of the 1920s, Tilly no longer sold her body for sex. She had plenty of women selling theirs for her in the brothels she ran in Woolloomooloo, Darlinghurst and Surry Hills. By the 1930s, she had thirty brothels across eastern Sydney, and one of her most successful was at 191 Palmer Street. Her 'vice empires' made her one of the city's wealthiest women. She later boasted to reporters she had more diamond rings than the Queen: 'And better ones too.'

It didn't stop the law catching up with her. Lillian and other officers in the Women's Police launched an ongoing investigation into Tilly's businesses. They cornered her workers, kept a close eye on Tilly, and raided her brothels whenever there was a suspicion of drugs and violence alongside prostitution.

Tilly Devine loathed the Women's Police. She would hiss 'I hate you' at the special constables as they walked near her on the streets. One local story has Devine cornering Constable Peg Fisher in a lane off Palmer Street. After some harsh words, Devine started to violently attack Peg. As locals watched on, Kate Leigh ran up behind Devine and hit her. Tilly fell to the ground and Kate sat on top of her. You can imagine how furious Tilly was to be in such a humiliating position.

Lillian and other members of the Women's Police were told by their superiors never to attempt to arrest Tilly alone. Lillian noted that 'She was more than a handful, even for my male colleagues. She even attacked a huge Fijian sailor on one occasion. She was frightened of nobody . . .' In July 1929 Tilly appeared to support her husband Jim at Central Court. He was fined for carrying an unlicensed gun. During the proceedings a criminal rival caught Tilly's attention. After the hearing, she followed the woman outside into the court-yard, started a fight and bit the woman's finger. She refused to let go until a constable intervened.

The law had had enough of Tilly Devine by 1930. She was ordered out of the country that year by a magistrate and she decided to use it as an opportunity to visit her sick mother in London. Tilly claimed to be over Sydney and glad to be rid of the place: 'you people did not like me because I am English. If I had been an Aussie girl there would have been nothing said.' She returned to Sydney after nine months. Tilly and Jim appeared in court in January 1931 after a violent domestic incident between the pair at their house in Maroubra. They had moved out of eastern Sydney to the beachside suburb and turned this house into their centre of operations. It was a tactic employed to evade the police who were targeting crime in Darlinghurst and Surry Hills.

The Devine marriage was a violent, volatile one. There were numerous reports of domestic violence over the years at both their Darlinghurst and Maroubra addresses. 'Big Jim' Devine was charged in January 1931 with attempting to murder Tilly. The pair had argued and when Tilly fled the house, she told police, Jim fired a shot at her. Jim was remanded on a hefty bail but when the case was heard a few days later, Tilly refused to give evidence against Jim and the attempted murder charge was dropped.

The marriage was over by August 1943 when Tilly divorced Jim on the grounds of cruelty. Also in 1943 when Tilly's Palmer Street house was declared a 'disorderly house' – a brothel frequented by thieves – she lost her composure very quickly inside the courtroom. Already facing a charge for malicious wounding and committed for trial, she was sentenced to six months' imprisonment as the owner of the disorderly house. Tilly screamed back at the magistrate and challenged him to put her away for longer. She screamed all the way to the cells where she had to be subdued by a number of officers.

Tilly continued on in the sex business for many years and didn't sell her Palmer Street home and brothel until 1968. Though her criminal career slowed down by the 1950s, she had over 200 convictions to her name.

With increased police patrols and crackdowns on soliciting through the 1910s and 1920s, streetwalkers were forced to look for work in the brothels and this was what made a fortune for Tilly Devine. It wasn't an easy process for the streetwalkers. Firstly, a woman had to know someone in the brothel business who could provide an introduction to the owner. It was important for women to establish a connection with another worker so that they could operate together, pass information on by word of mouth, get commissions from taxi drivers and look out for each other in the brothel. Impressing brothel owners was harder, especially with more streetwalkers looking for work after being pushed off the streets by the police. Brothel madams like Tilly Devine could be more selective about whom they hired.

The two Frenchwomen, Madame Louise and Madame Marie, who had established Sydney's first call-girl establishment in Kings Cross were very particular about their workers. Lillian Armfield added their apartment to her patrols of the area. The young women inside had been 'carefully chosen'. They were 'very pretty, and were always fashionably dressed' so that they could mix throughout society which, according to Lillian, 'they often did'.

Brothel work was dependent on the status of the establishment women were working in. The higher-class brothels – such as the Frenchwomen's apartment – allowed women to build up a clientele, serve an apprenticeship and adhere to the owners' set standards and practices. A wider variety of sexual and emotional services were required as part of their daily work but they generally earned more money and were protected inside the business. High-class establishments were less likely to engage with low-level crooks, and they were intent on ensuring discretion for both their clients and workers. At the lower end, in brothels mainly operating on quick 'pent-up' business, the pay was less along with more limited protection and security.

We don't have a lot of descriptions of the inside of the brothels from those who were there, either as prostitutes or customers, but some recollections have survived. Bank robber Darcy Dugan recorded his impressions of one of Tilly Devine's brothels in his memoirs:

The premises had gaudy wallpaper and furnishings. The carpet in the reception lounge was red, punctuated with bright-green floral patterns. It smelled of stale cigarettes and human sweat. Three heavily made-up women in flimsy, frilly dresses lounged on an enormous settee, smoking.

Tilly worked hard to build up her business by the 1930s and when Dugan visited in the 1940s, she was the owner of medium-range brothels. They were not high-end establishments catering to an exclusive clientele but neither were they the worst of what eastern Sydney had to offer. Tilly and other wealthy brothel owners decked their houses out with good furniture, music and working spaces. In low-end brothels, described in the newspapers as 'terraces of the rabbit-warren type', business was conducted in 'squalid single rooms rented at blackmail rates'. Tilly Devine knew that if she created the pretence of a more respectable brothel, rather than a 'disorderly house', she would face fewer prosecutions for offending the public order.

Lillian Armfield came to know the women inside the brothels very well. One young woman caught her attention in the middle of the 1920s and quickly showed Lillian she was very different to the other prostitutes the Women's Police came into contact with, who were 'victims of men and poverty'. Lillian already knew that some women were 'quite brazen' about their work. According to Lillian they were:

in their sorry trade for what they regard as an easy living, and who have their own peculiar sense of honour – perhaps it would be better to say a sense of obligation – to those men they solicit. They have their price and they bargain their bodies and they are satisfied with that . . .

Nellie Cameron was one of these women. While Lillian would never agree with her lifestyle, she was impressed with Nellie's beauty, tough character and devil-may-care attitude about the world she lived in.

Known as the pretty girl of the underworld, Nellie was born in the inner-city suburb of Waterloo. Her father fought in World War I but deserted his family not long after his return. Nellie's mother remarried and they moved to the wealthy North Shore. Despite a private school education, Nellie ran away from home and began associating with known criminals around eastern Sydney. She was the lover of leading gangsters and worked as a prostitute for Tilly Devine. Nellie became a prostitute, according to Lillian Armfield, 'for no other reason than she wanted to be one'.

Nellie charmed the crooks and police alike because she carried herself with what Lillian called 'a charm that was all her own . . . and a natural dignity that she never lost in the hectic circumstances'. They all knew, however, that she was behind some of the violence erupting in eastern Sydney from the late 1920s. Many of her male admirers could have enjoyed her business in the brothels but so great was Nellie's beauty and charm, they wanted her all to themselves. Jealousy was the root cause of many fights between gangsters over Nellie and, for Lillian, it 'was responsible for more than one murder'.

The newspapers called Nellie a 'gangster's moll' but Lillian and other women in the police force recognised that Nellie was often the one in control of the gangsters.

Nellie's first lover was Ted Pulley. He was a standover man and thief originally from New Zealand. He was killed by Redfern crook Florrie Riley, who alleged Pulley tried to attack and rob her. She and her friend were so frightened, Florrie shot him in self-defence. The city coroner agreed and Ted Pulley's death was ruled as justifiable homicide.

Frank Green was next on the list of Nellie's lovers and the pair created a notorious reputation for themselves. Green had a razor scar down the side of his face and was a ruthless standover man for Tilly Devine. He was eight years older than Nellie and had a long criminal record. He was a hard drinker and cocaine addict, and could be volatile in just about any situation. Somehow he attracted the attention of many of eastern Sydney's most desired women, including Nellie Cameron. He once told her: 'I've got so many bullets in me I rattle when I walk, and I'm satisfied no bullet will ever kill me.'

At the same time as Nellie took Green's fancy, another young crook started paying her attention. Guido Calletti was a young Italian–Australian street thug who had spent some of his youth in reformatories in Gosford and Lillian's home town of Mittagong. By the 1920s, he posed as a labourer and fruit-barrow owner, and later bought a greengrocers in Paddington. The police knew him as the leader of the Darlinghurst Push. When he set his sights on something, he rarely backed down, and this was what happened with Nellie Cameron. She was

Frank Green's girl but Calletti wanted her for himself. Lillian recalled an incident where Green and Calletti fought 'bare-knuckle' over Nellie in the Domain: 'Green got the better of it, but afterwards he had five bullets fired into him and he survived by a miracle.'

Nellie chose Calletti over Green and gushed about the news in a conversation with Lillian, who reckoned she was one of the first to learn about their secret marriage. At one point they planned to give away crime and focus on the fruit and vegetable shop in Paddington. Lillian thought it would probably just become a front for a sly-grog shop and, while she knew Nellie could not be reformed, Lillian accepted it: 'Nellie Cameron was the one girl I knew was beyond any hope of redemption . . . Her record and Calletti's were too bad for me to believe that.'

By the 1950s Frank Green was living in a shabby place in Paddington and regularly argued with his lover, Beatrice Haggett. Green drank heavily and, on the night of 26 April 1956, he and Beatrice had an argument over his constant nagging and accusations she was having an affair. Beatrice drove a carving knife into Green's chest, just below the collar-bone. He died shortly after. Quizzed about whether she would attend Frank Green's funeral, Kate Leigh, demonstrating the rivalry of the underworld, laughed and told reporters she had no intention of going but would happily 'dance on the bludger's grave'.

The love affair between Nellie and Calletti didn't last. While Nellie was in Queensland in the late 1930s – no doubt avoiding the police – he took up with Mary Eugene Markham. Like Nellie Cameron, Mary Markham refused to be reformed and enjoyed the attention she got from working as a prostitute. She went by the nickname 'Pretty Dulcie'. Her police record was extensive and included convictions in New South Wales, Victoria and Western Australia. She started out in the prostitution underworlds of eastern Sydney in the late 1920s when she was only fifteen and was another of the young women Lillian came to know well on the streets of Sydney. According to Lillian, she 'used to say it was easy to get a hundred pounds a night at the brothels'. Dulcie refused Lillian's efforts to reform her and in Lillian's book this meant she 'was completely incorrigible'. She associated with well-known gangsters and flitted between them on a number of occasions, further adding to gang rivalry.

Dulcie was also known as the 'Angel of Death' around eastern Sydney. Police believed at least eight male associates and lovers were gunned down in front of her with scores more killed while keeping company with her. Dulcie's first boyfriend was stabbed to death in a shop doorway in 1931. Police believed his killer was in love with Dulcie and wanted her boyfriend out of the way.

Many other men were associated with Dulcie but the most famous of them was Guido Calletti. He should have been warier about her reputation. Calletti died in her arms after he was gunned down at a party in Darlinghurst in August 1939. Five thousand people turned out for his funeral, including his former lover Nellie Cameron. When the case was brought to court, Dulcie fled rather than give evidence. She took off to Lithgow and returned weeks later.

The 'Angel of Death' lost another lover the following year. This time her new husband, Frank Bowen, was gunned down in Kings Cross.

Another world war came and went and little changed in Dulcie's lifestyle. When Dulcie moved to Melbourne, Lillian kept up with her antics through her contacts in the police and in the sensational newspaper stories reporting Dulcie's run-ins with the law. She was shot in the thigh during a gun battle at her house in St Kilda in 1951. A young boxer was killed in the battle and his brother badly wounded. Two men were acquitted of the murder and Dulcie carried the scars of yet another violent confrontation in which a man died in front of her.

Her second husband, Melbourne underworld identity Leonard Lewis, was also shot but survived. Dulcie moved back to eastern Sydney shortly after the shooting and was known as the 'limping blonde' to locals around Darlinghurst and Surry Hills. She owed the police some gaol time and did six months in Long Bay Prison for a 1946 consorting charge.

Dulcie seemed to settle down in her fifties, at odds with the Swinging Sixties, and by the 1970s she was living in a house in Bondi, telling reporters she was a happy housewife and enjoying her third marriage. She died in 1975 in a house fire, caused by a cigarette she had been smoking in her bed. Death had finally caught up with eastern Sydney's infamous 'Angel of Death'.

•

Women like Nellie Cameron and Dulcie Markham were confident, tough and in control of their prostitution work. However, it wasn't always like this and the more the brothels became the meeting places of gangsters and other underworld identities, the harder Lillian had to work to ensure the women inside were safe. Lillian policed the brothels with a stern, unfailing toughness. Peg Fisher was recruited into the Women's Police in the 1940s and recalled Lillian taking her into the main brothels and telling the criminals inside: 'If you do anything to this policewoman, I'll shoot you.'

Toughness was essential to Lillian's work, especially when she crossed paths with some of Sydney's most violent gangsters. One of the worst was George 'The Midnight Raper' Wallace. Wallace had little respect for women and attacked women with no connections to Sydney's crime scene in their beds at night. Streetwalkers were even lower on his list. He had no sense of remorse for the violent standover tactics he used in Sydney's underworld, which included using rape as a threat against prostitutes. Wallace was well known about Sydney from the late 1920s and featured in newspapers with reporters repulsed by his reputation:

> His nickname leaves little doubt of his vile habits. It was pasted on him by his unsavoury attacks on women. It was his custom to sneak into women's rooms by the window, usually when they were in bed and wreak his filthy way upon their helplessness. He did not confine his depredations

to within bedrooms. He has been known to assault them on street corners and in quiet doorways and dark lanes. For many months he had women who were compelled to venture forth alone in his districts absolutely terrorised.

George Wallace was part of what the newspapers dubbed an 'Unholy Trio' of underworld crooks, including Frank 'Razor Jack' Hayes and Norman Bruhn. Bruhn was a thuggish Melbourne criminal with connections to underworld identity Squizzy Taylor. Bruhn staked out his claim in Sydney's crime scene through violence, extortion and mugging other drug traffickers. He led a gang that extorted money from rival gang members under the threat of the razor. In December 1926, welterweight boxer Billy Chambers confronted Bruhn, Hayes and Wallace while they were arguing with and threatening a woman in Darlinghurst. Chambers' Christmas Day present was a visit from the trio who pistol-whipped him. He was knocked to the ground, unconscious, and a large razor gash was cut down his leg. While Chambers bled and his boxing career was ruined, Bruhn, Hayes and Wallace emptied his room of anything of value.

Norman Bruhn's gang members were all known for exacting standover payments from prostitutes but George Wallace was the most violent. Lillian Armfield had first learned about Wallace in her earlier work tracking runaways rumoured to be working on the streets or in brothels. Wallace wasn't the kind of man you easily forgot and he taught Lillian that entering the murky world of prostitution put her in danger too. During some of her undercover work, Lillian witnessed firsthand how Wallace dealt with prostitutes. Wallace wouldn't take lightly to finding out a female officer was at the centre of investigations into his dealings with prostitutes and the drug peddlers he was trying to put out of business. In her efforts to protect and police prostitutes, Lillian put her own life on the line. In a later article looking back on the Razor Gangs, *Truth* newspaper singled out Lillian as a 'Gallant Woman' in the investigations and the threat posed to her life: 'If her identity had become known, her life would have counted for nothing and frequently she placed herself in situations of great personal danger.'

It wasn't hard, therefore, for police officers to feel particularly driven in trying to put George Wallace away for his crimes. The police might turn a blind eye to some illegal activities, so long as they were contained and away from the public, but violent crimes were swiftly investigated. Sometimes, however, the underworld did them a favour. Norman Bruhn was shot dead in Charlotte Lane, Darlinghurst, in June 1927. Razor Jack was shot the following year in Crown Street; he survived but took off to Germany. Wallace accrued over 130 convictions during the course of his criminal career, mainly for assaults and the use of outlawed weapons.

George Wallace also met a violent end. Pushed out of Sydney by gang violence, rivalries and police crackdowns, he continued his criminal spree in Brisbane and Melbourne before moving to Perth in the late 1940s. He was stabbed with a carving knife outside the European Club in Perth in the early hours of 23 November 1948. Wallace died two weeks later in Royal Perth

Hospital. His assailant, Leonard Levy, took off to Melbourne but was found by police a few weeks later and extradited back to Perth. Despite pleading self-defence, Levy was sentenced to death for the murder. Looking pale and unsteady on his feet, Levy made a statement from the dock in which he said his conscience was clear and he had a 'reasonably fair trial'. Now all he could do was 'abide by the jury's verdict'.

Few police officers across the country were saddened by the passing of George Wallace. Certainly not Lillian Armfield, who was repulsed by the 'Midnight Raper': 'Wallace was a coward and a sadist.'

•

Policing Sydney's prostitutes was seldom straightforward for Lillian Armfield and it deeply affected her through the years, trying to help as many women as she could. She told reporters, 'It's a dreadful, sordid life, when you see it from within the walls of police work as I do.' It was not simply a case of getting streetwalkers off the streets, either sent off to an institution, put back into the workforce in a different way or, if they would not give up sex work, trying to find them work in a brothel. Prostitution was only one part of the criminal economy driving the rise of organised crime in Sydney. The drug trade – first through opium and then cocaine – destroyed many lives and Lillian watched too many prostitutes combine soliciting with drug addiction. Cocaine knew no social boundaries and ruined the lives of men and women from across the city and different walks of life.

Lillian's policing work also led her into the dark worlds of drug addiction and trafficking. Her drug investigations placed her right at the centre of Sydney's opium and cocaine trade, and under the watchful glare of the city's other most feared underworld figure, Kate Leigh.

7

Showdown with Kate Leigh

IT WAS A REGULAR EVENING IN SURRY HILLS IN JULY 1930, WHICH meant the police were waiting to kick in a door. Detectives Tom Wickham and Syd Thompson of the CIB Drug Squad had the house surrounded but they needed to move carefully. Lillian Armfield and one of her female officers were also waiting nearby. There were cockatoos watching the street for any police presence and while the light of streetlights didn't penetrate darkened alleyways, the sudden approach of car headlights could give the game away. The detectives watched from across the street, waiting for the standover man to vacate his position outside the front door of one of the most notorious addresses in eastern Sydney.

In an instant, they were on the move. Forced-entry raids are adrenaline-fuelled, highly dangerous busts. They often turned violent in the underworlds of inter-war Sydney. As the detectives tried to remain calm while knowing what could be in store for them inside the Riley Street house, their minds and hearts would have been going at a hundred miles an hour.

Racing across to the house, the detectives snuck inside and found a group sitting at a dining table. The place smelled of nicotine, sweat and just a touch of fear. The people at the table were too calm. Someone had tipped them off. Wickham and Thompson searched the room and found what they were looking for. There was cocaine in a vase and more scattered on the floor. The owner of the house, Kate Leigh, could be volatile and violent, which meant the police had to remain calm and careful in their approach. She feigned innocence as two female officers followed her up the stairs to search her bedroom. Kate had amassed a fortune from cocaine, prostitution, and sly-grog sales and she knew the police would be keen to pin anything on her to put her away.

The detectives needed enough evidence for a conviction. Raids can only ever have a chance at success if the chief investigating officer has gathered enough intelligence to make a case for a warrant in the first place. Busting down doors doesn't alone turn up drugs or other illegal activities. Surveillance over days, weeks or months is essential to building up enough evidence of suspicious activities and providing the detectives on the ground with an idea of the best time to strike.

The Surry Hills raid was an example to other underworld crooks that their luck was running out. As organised crime continued its rise in the harbour city, the NSW police had to gain the upper hand in their war on drugs. Since 1927, cocaine had replaced opium as the main drug of choice and it was ruining the lives of a wide range of people – from low-level crooks and prostitutes to middle-class mothers who believed the doctors who told them the drug wasn't addictive and could be used for medicinal reasons.

It wasn't just cocaine. Sydney was in the grip of a surge in crime sponsored by gangs, prostitution, illicit booze and a local economy benefiting from the spoils of stolen goods. Sydney's inner-city neighbourhoods were the heartlands of crime. To outsiders, the residents were rowdy and immoral, and houses around Campbell, Riley and Bourke streets were said to harbour a hard, mean and violent community. Tomahawk and bottle fights were the area's 'daily medley', according to the newspapers.

The police had to step in and break down doors to find the drugs. The coordinated raid on Kate Leigh's house in July 1930 was central to these city-wide crackdowns. May Smith – Botany May – had been taken off the streets a couple of years beforehand but Kate had quickly stepped into the gap in her business and was making a fortune from dealing cocaine.

Kate Leigh was as tough as they came in the criminal underworlds of Sydney. Born Kathleen Mary Josephine Beahan in Dubbo in country New South Wales in 1881, she grew up in a large Irish–Australian Catholic family and learned to look after herself from a young age. Kate Beahan took on the school bully and won and from there earned herself a fearsome reputation. In her teens she started hanging out on the streets with her young brothers and some known criminals. Her parents were at a loss and supported the local authorities in making the decision to send Kate off to Parramatta Industrial School. After living in an institution that broke so many other young girls' spirits, Kate walked out of the front doors determined to take charge of her own life. She was tough, street-smart and ruthless in her pursuit of wealth through criminal businesses around eastern Sydney. By the 1920s, she was a well-known criminal identity and was building an empire funded by sly grog and cocaine.

Getting on Kate Leigh's bad side could prove fatal. When cocaine addict and rival crook Snowy Prendergast threatened Leigh inside her house only months before the Drug Squad raid, Kate shot him dead and claimed self-defence. That she convinced the judge of this was even more startling. The newspapers were scathing in their reporting of Kate's shooting of Prendergast. *Truth* produced a disparaging portrayal of Kate (going by the new name of Kate Barry after her second marriage) as 'Sydney's Vicious Harridan of the Underworld':

It is a strange world when that vicious old harridan, Kate Barry, wishes to pose in it as a woman with a generous heart. But unbelievable though it may seem, that was this notorious woman's dearest wish — to be understood as a free and easy Lady Bountiful of the underworld . . . Around her drifted the worst people of the city . . . battered derelicts whom she rescued from the gutter and starvation, but not from crime. If they would not pursue a life of crime they could, and did, stay starving in the gutter as far as Kate Barry was concerned.

Kate was unfazed by her appearance in court. She told reporters outside the courtroom she wasn't afraid of anyone. She played the police at their own game. She passed on information in return for a heads-up when raids were scheduled on her houses in Darlinghurst and Surry Hills.

Kate Leigh was also supported in her crime businesses by her only child, Eileen, who was a chip off the old block. Eileen was caught and charged with soliciting on a number of occasions before Kate took her more firmly under her wing and brought her into the sly-grog business. Police preferred dealing with Kate rather than her daughter, and in the July 1930 raid they were hoping it was only Kate in the house with her associates. Eileen was as tough as her mother but a less likeable character. She didn't feel the need to endear herself to anyone.

The bust on Kate Leigh's house wasn't Lillian Armfield's first. Her war on drugs had begun back in 1915 when looking for runaway girls led her into the dark underside of addiction and the opium dens. If Lillian was going to prevent girls and young women from getting involved in the underworlds of criminal Sydney, she also needed to ensure they didn't end up in the throes of addiction, which would grip them in a merciless cycle of drugs, crime and prostitution.

Opium first made its appearance in Australia with the arrival of Chinese immigrants during and after the gold rushes of the middle of the nineteenth century. It wasn't illegal to bring in opium or to supply and smoke it but there were restrictions on the scale of opium sales through colonial trade laws. While the Chinese introduced the habit of opium smoking, opium was used beyond the Chinese–Australian population. Doctors prescribed it to women for menstrual pain and depression, and both doctors and nurses smoked opium to alleviate the stress of their work.

Opium dens were usually in inner-city neighbourhoods associated with Chinese immigrant populations. The dens were typically crammed full of beds where patrons could lie back and smoke opium from long pipes held over oil lamps. Some of the dens were quite impressive with expensive furnishings and an emphasis on good customer service for patrons. However, most of the dens in the major cities, particularly in Sydney, were squalid rooms at the back of overcrowded houses, shops and markets. Concentrations of dens were set up around Chinese immigrants living in The Rocks and then further along the city to the Haymarket. Dens also featured in the poorest neighbourhoods of Woolloomooloo, Darlinghurst, Surry Hills and Paddington.

From the late nineteenth century onwards, opium addiction and anti-Chinese racism led to major crackdowns on the opium dens and Chinese–Australian people supplying and selling the drug. The Sydney Anti-Opium League, formed in 1902, put pressure on the state government to enact legislation to tackle the opium problem. They argued the dens were corrupting the white race and leading young women into drug addiction and prostitution. Opium smoking was banned in 1908 under the *Police Offences (Amendment) Act*.

The opium dens also became a target of newspaper sensationalism, with journalists going undercover and reporting back to the newspapers on their experiences with the dens. In October 1904, a small group, including a police sergeant, investigated Sydney's dens for the *Sunday Times*. In a house off Goulburn Street in the city, they were taken to a room with a bed, lounge and chair where other people were smoking opium. In an alley off this main street, the group also came across a house where sixty to seventy people were living, alongside vegetable gardens, highlighting the squalor of inner-city living for Chinese immigrants, which in turn added to opium addiction and selling. At another den in Wexford Street, the party came across a teenage girl who was living there. She spoke to the women in the group, telling them she didn't have money or clothes to leave the den and was afraid of being picked up for vagrancy. She had moved to Sydney from another part of the country but soon spent her savings and couldn't get work; a Chinese man had offered her a place to stay. Then, at another establishment, the group came across an Englishman who told them he had smoked opium since 1878 and did it to get through his work each day.

One of the great fears associated with the opium dens was that girls would be lured into them for sexual services. While being sold for sex, they might be offered opium and from there develop an addiction. Investigating girls and women in opium dens was part of the general duties of the Women's Police.

Lillian's investigations into the opium dens were conducted undercover and she was also used in wider police investigations as a decoy into the dens. Lillian knew that being a woman allowed her to infiltrate the dens because the owners were on the lookout for male officers. She helped, in her own words, 'smash the drug traffic by gaining entry for police into opium dens, as a decoy to trap criminals . . .' Because her work infiltrating the dens wasn't publicised, Lillian was able to work undercover largely undetected. The newspaper publicity she received in her first years on the job mainly centred on her work with runaways and fortune-tellers.

The cockatoos outside of the dens therefore didn't pay much attention to Lillian. She strolled confidently past dens, went back and asked questions and gained entry easily enough. She would amass her evidence from observations inside the dens, then she would head back to the station and send in the male police officers to make the arrests. Even when den owners began to grow suspicious of the activities of the Women's Police, they weren't concerned about a fair-looking, unassuming, nicely dressed woman like Lillian. This was her forte and served her well throughout her service. Lillian didn't look like a police officer and she also didn't look like she was experienced in subduing and restraining some of Sydney's hardest crooks. The girl from the country did well to fool people with her appearance.

Lillian's first major successful raid was on an opium den in Milk Street (the street is now gone) in the inner city in 1919. Posing as a young woman looking for someone, she got past the cockatoos and was welcomed at the doorway of a house by Chitti Ah Foo. He was a known crook, adept at remodelling stolen jewellery so that it couldn't be traced. There were sounds of running feet and the lookouts were yelling back to him that the police were on their way. Ah Foo tried to close the door but Lillian made sure her full bulk was in the way and the entrance was open for her male colleagues. She was happy for the assistance, believing the den owner 'was looking at me as though he could slit my throat'. Ah Foo told her colleagues they had no right to be in the house, without warrant or invitation. Lillian watched as Sergeant Tom O'Brien corrected him: 'You didn't ask me and the boys in, but you asked this lady in, and she's in the police, like us.'

His statement that Lillian was 'in the police, like us' shows the respect she was gaining from within the force. It was affirmed when, days after the Ah Foo investigation failed to turn up hard evidence, Lillian organised another raid, supported again by Sergeant O'Brien, who hid in a car nearby. When Lillian hurried past the car on her way to Oxford Street, O'Brien thought the game was up. Lillian reassured him she hadn't been recognised and told him the girls needed a password to get in. O'Brien organised an informant to supply them with a password. Armed with the password, and knowing O'Brien and another officer were on standby, Lillian gained entry into the house. Ah Foo was startled but this time he resorted to violence. He pushed Lillian out onto the street. While she was taller than him and able to fight against his pushes, other Chinese men came to help Ah Foo.

O'Brien and two other officers quickly arrived and pulled Ah Foo off Lillian.

Despite the threat to her welfare, Lillian was determined to find the young women living in the den and using opium. She ran to an upstairs bedroom and inspected a large wardrobe. Like a character from C.S. Lewis's *The Lion, the Witch and the Wardrobe*, Lillian found a doorway in the cupboard. She tapped on it three times and a young woman opened the door, delighted that they had evaded 'those rozzers'. She was shocked when she realised the very same police were standing right in front of her. The doorway led to another house with young women and opium smokers inside. The game was up and Ah Foo was eventually deported back to China.

During another case, Lillian went undercover with two male officers and one female officer to gain entry to an opium den. Walking along Harbour Street, parading as couples with babies, they saw a den door open and rushed inside. Lillian blew her police whistle and reinforcements came along. The den owner was surprised to find the 'babies' in the women's arms were in fact only cushions.

The opium den investigations allowed Lillian to perfect her undercover work and develop a street-wise understanding of Sydney's connection to national and international drug trafficking. She made maps of the streets known for their drug dens and houses, and kept a close eye on court proceedings to see who was regularly up before the magistrates on drug-related charges. Lillian was developing her own 'rogues gallery' of men and women quickly establishing reputations as Sydney's most notorious and evasive drug dealers.

Kate Leigh had dabbled in the world of opium before Lillian was appointed to the Women's Police. She was named as a witness in a number of cases relating to opium dealing and use in the early years of the twentieth century, which hinted at the crowd she was associating with. Kate's first husband, James Lee (anglicised to Leigh), a young man of Chinese and Australian heritage, was an opium addict, when he wasn't gambling away his money. He and Kate married in 1901, after the birth of their daughter, Eileen, in 1900, and in the years that followed, he made money selling opium around the inner-city dens. The pair ripped off their land-lord, Patrick Lynch, in 1905. James told the magistrate in the court case that followed that he'd found Patrick in bed with Kate at the Tradesman's Arms Hotel and was so infuriated James hit him. Lynch told a different story. He claimed Kate asked him to check wallpaper and while he was looking at it on a ladder, she knocked him down. When he regained consciousness, James and Kate Leigh were trying to steal money from him.

Kate supported her husband in court, testifying that his version of events was correct. The magistrate didn't agree and charged the Leighs with perjury. They were acquitted of the charge but it meant James and Kate Leigh were now firmly on the police radar in eastern Sydney.

The Leighs went their separate ways in 1910, after James was convicted for opium possession. Kate claimed he had abandoned his family and she was once again left with her daughter to make ends meets in the rough streets of Paddington, Darlinghurst and Surry Hills.

A while later Kate Leigh made another sensational court appearance when she gave her boyfriend, Samuel Freeman, a false alibi for the shooting of a postal worker in 1914. Freeman and his mate, Ernest 'Shiner' Ryan, were up on other charges relating to what was called the Eveleigh Heist. The pair were accused of stealing wages delivered to the Eveleigh railway workshops in Redfern. Freeman was sentenced to twenty years in prison, including time for the earlier postal worker shooting, and Kate Leigh was sent away for five years for perjury. When Kate came out of prison in 1919, she turned her attention to the illicit sale of alcohol – sly grog – but also moved further into the drug scene.

By the time Lillian was investigating Kate Leigh for possession of illicit drugs in the late 1920s, Kate had well and truly moved on from opium. Cocaine was the drug of choice in Sydney after World War I. Kate Leigh could always smell a criminal opportunity from a mile away and she set her sights on running Sydney's cocaine traffic.

Cocaine first appeared in Australia in the 1860s when it was imported and used as a legal medicinal cure. It was mass-produced and sold by chemists over the counter. For years, chemists and newspaper advertisements sold the public the story that opium-based medicines such as Bonnington's Irish Moss, Ayer's Sarsaparilla and Godfrey's Cordial could cure a variety of ailments. Middle-class women in particular were drawn into the advertising and began buying these remedies for use in their family. Cocaine was also called a wonder drug that, if mixed with snuff, could cure hay fever and asthma. Famed Austrian neurologist Sigmund Freud advocated the use of cocaine for heroin addiction, and was a cocaine user himself.

Cocaine was also used in patent medicines. 'Secret remedies' mentioned on the packaging of medicines failed to disclose the use of cocaine and left some users unaware they were becoming addicted to the drug. The 'cocaine habit' was recognised from the 1880s, and Sydney newspapers published reports coming out of America that cocaine was a 'dangerous stimulant'. While cocaine addiction was not common, medical professionals were worried about the impacts on mental and physical health.

By the early years of the twentieth century, the medical profession had taken over greater control of medicines and increasingly made decisions about access to drugs based on the need for treatment. Cocaine was used as a local anaesthetic. Doctors tried to convince the public that cocaine addiction was 'practically impossible', but it became clear from those who suffered post-treatment addiction that there were serious social side effects to furthering medical knowledge.

It was only a matter of time before cocaine found its way onto the streets. Crooks looking to make extra money recognised the demand for the drug when doctors and dentists were not available, or willing, to prescribe it. All that was needed were a few corrupt chemists and dentists who would pass on cocaine to buyers, knowing they could make more money on the black market than from prescriptions.

Charles Passmore was one of the first in Sydney to seize the opportunity to make money from drug dealing. Passmore's criminal record stretched back a number of years but he made a name for himself in the underworld and in police notebooks when he started selling cocaine to prostitutes in the early 1920s. He was quickly added to the police Rogues Gallery.

One of Passmore's first convictions came in 1923, when police were increasingly under fire for failing to keep cocaine off the streets. In April of that year the *Daily Telegraph* blamed the police for the rise in Sydney's cocaine traffic, citing their inability to deal with the problem and the free rein chemists had over supply, which underpinned the corruption leading to deals with crooks. The following year, Sergeant Tom O'Brien, one of the male officers working closely with Lillian Armfield, didn't hold back in court when describing Passmore as 'representative of all things evil' in making money off addicts around Darlinghurst. Passmore was a kingpin of Sydney's drug trade by 1928 but moved into armed robbery. His undoing finally came when he was involved in a violent robbery at the Commercial Banking Company in Woollahra in September 1929, in which the manager and another worker were shot. The three main players, including Passmore, were convicted. They tried to appeal the decision but it was upheld. Passmore was bundled off to prison for ten years.

Police launched their first major drug raids around eastern Sydney in 1925. Along with finding opium stashes, the officers were alerted to a dramatic increase in cocaine being distributed around known drug houses. Raids on houses in Surry Hills in August 1925 turned up hundreds of pounds' worth of opium along with two tins of cocaine found under the bed of a woman feigning illness. It wasn't only in the poor, crime-ridden streets of Surry Hills that police found cocaine. In one house in Kensington, owned by a wealthy couple who employed a number of servants, customs officers discovered fifty bottles containing cocaine.

As a female officer, Lillian had to do the body searches of women after cocaine raids: 'such searches were very unpleasant for me, but they had to be done, and they had to be done thoroughly'. It required more careful detection on the part of the Women's Police than the usual work of finding bottles of knock-off beer or spirits. Women were able to conceal drugs in their clothing. Lillian often found stashes of cocaine tucked into 'special slits in their corsets and in the top of their stockings'. There were women who secreted cocaine inside their bodies. In one case, Lillian found a cocaine packet taped under the breast of a female dealer who thought she had gotten the better of the police.

By the time Lillian faced off with Kate Leigh in July 1930, she was a special sergeant. Fifteen years of tireless investigations into runaways, prostitution and fraudulent fortune-tellers had paved the way for her promotion. But she still needed the big busts to continue to prove her worth in the force. Lillian knew she was up to it and she had her supporters, especially Wickham and Thompson, who included her in their major investigations, such as the one on Kate Leigh's place in Riley Street.

Lillian and the special constable assisting, Nellie Mitchell, scanned Leigh's bedroom at the Riley Street house. Kate didn't take her eyes off either of them. She was surprisingly small – given her fearsome underworld reputation – and at five feet one was a good six inches shorter than Lillian. But Lillian and Nellie were not fooled by appearances.

There are important parallels in Lillian Armfield and Kate Leigh's stories. Both were from the country and were comfortable living as independent women. Kate would go on to marry for the third time in 1950 but her marriages failed in part because of her independence. Though their work put them at polar opposites – the crook and the cop – they had fought their own battles against a male-oriented world and found their own unique places within it. They were pioneers in their work but the battlelines were clearly drawn: Lillian as the nation's first female detective and Kate as one of the first female crime bosses, along with rival Tilly Devine. Kate respected Lillian, knowing her work would have been hard in the man's world of Sydney policing.

Lillian was a little bemused by Kate's respect: 'to me she was invariably polite and she accorded me with respect that always puzzled me, because she certainly didn't extend it to any other policewoman, nor to any of my male colleagues'.

One story, recalled by Lillian's colleague and friend, Peg Fisher, illustrates the respect and familiarity Kate Leigh extended to Lillian as Chief of the Women's Police. Kate stormed into Central Police Station one day in the middle of the 1940s and gave Constable Fisher a mouthful after she'd charged Kate with sly-grog possession. Lillian heard Kate out but took her aside to remind her the constable was only doing her job. Kate replied, 'Oh, I know that, Lil, but I can't be seen being nice to her.' Lillian Armfield was 'Lil' to one of Sydney's most notorious crime bosses. It was respect earned by Lillian's professionalism and genuine commitment to the local community.

And Lillian Armfield knew if you crossed Kate Leigh, she rarely forgot it, so you had to make sure you caught her fair and square.

For Lillian, though, it went deeper than just taking on Kate as a notorious crook. She had no time for anyone involved in the supply and sale of cocaine. She thought the drug trade was 'cruel and vicious and utterly degraded' and far worse than most of her work: 'It made prostitution seem respectable.' Drug dealers would try anything to make money from addicts. Lillian and other police officers regularly came across adulterated packages of cocaine where the retailers had included particles of ground glass when cocaine supplies were low.

Cocaine destroyed so many young lives, and one young woman in particular caught Lillian's attention in the late 1920s. She was the daughter of a jurist and was given an allowance to live in Sydney. Enjoying some freedom in the city's cafés and hotel lounges, she caught the eyes of drug peddlers who got her onto cocaine. She had the money to support her addiction and the dealers were willing to exploit it. They warned her off keeping her own 'store of cocaine' and told her to meet with peddlers whenever she ran out of the drug. Lillian watched the young woman closely, as she had done with numerous prostitutes. As the addiction took hold, the woman spiralled into drug-taking cycles and quickly went through her allowance. When she was arrested for associating with known criminals, the local newspapers got hold of the story but they held off naming her out of respect for her family. This wasn't a common occurrence. Wealth and privilege bought privacy. The young woman's family took her back home from Sydney and placed her in an institution.

When cocaine supplies were low, young women turned to substitute drugs, so great was their addiction. Lillian Armfield was particularly touched by the case of Dell Hutton. Dell started running with the wrong crowd – drug dealers and general crooks – as a teenager. She died of an overdose of veronal, a barbiturate she used when low in cocaine.

It wasn't always teenage women who fell prey to the drug runners and they weren't always in the city centre. One young married woman died from cocaine poisoning in country New South Wales in 1929. The drug traffic was travelling further out from the city, and Lillian and other members of the police, particularly the Drug Squad, knew they had to stop the supply coming into Sydney. That meant taking out the cocaine bosses, among whom was Kate Leigh.

The raid on Kate's house came after major police crackdowns on the drug trade in Sydney. Police powers were increased with the passing of the *Police Offences Amendment*

(Drugs) Act in 1927. The act was created to 'regulate the manufacture, sale, possession, distribution and supply' of dangerous drugs. In their efforts to suppress the narcotics trade, the police could prosecute chemists selling cocaine without a licence. This restriction was in direct response to cocaine being sold onto the streets by pharmacists, some of whom were unlicensed. While there was some resistance to the new laws from registered pharmacists, who felt unfairly targeted, most Sydneysiders supported them because people were concerned about the trade in drugs and the impact of cocaine use on lives across the city.

Detectives from the Drug Squad now had the power to arrest anyone in possession of a dangerous drug. Police prosecutions for drug possession naturally increased. In August 1929, police secured convictions for ten traffickers who were then given lengthy gaol terms by the court. The following month, Ronald Lee was sent to prison after he was caught handing over cocaine to someone in the street. He pleaded for leniency as a first offender but the magistrate imposed six months' imprisonment. Narcotics arrests reached more than 150 a year as members of the Drug Squad spent weeks closely watching drug runners in eastern Sydney.

The police war on drugs was led by an indomitable character, William MacKay. He had served in the NSW Police Force for more than twenty years but still sounded like he was fresh from working as a detective on the streets of Glasgow. MacKay had joined the NSW Force in 1910 and quickly worked his way up the ranks. He became Detective-Inspector of the CIB at Central Police Station in 1927 and was given the task of cleaning up the streets of Darlinghurst and Surry Hills the following year. MacKay was tall, broad, ruggedly handsome and completely intimidating. He used his deep, rough Scottish accent to full effect on the crooks who were often overwhelmed by him shouting at them with words they didn't understand.

MacKay was also known to smash down doors if the crooks didn't answer quick enough. Raiding a party in Riley Street, Darlinghurst, in January 1928, MacKay earned his promotion to detective-inspector after he 'engaged in a hand-to-hand struggle' in the kitchen with some notorious thieves. Fifteen people were arrested in the house for a mixture of offences, including being in a house frequented by thieves and possessing an unlicensed pistol. MacKay had stormed in the front door, frustrated at yet again having to tell the owner of the house to stop associating with known criminals. He wasn't in any mood to issue more warnings. Several other officers followed him into the house and began making their arrests. It quickly got out of hand. Officers found themselves being pulled between people and hustled onto the ground. MacKay stepped in and exchanged punches with the men while he pulled women off the male officers. When they all made their appearance in court a few days later, both the crooks and police pleaded innocence, blaming each other for provoking the situation.

MacKay knew how to frustrate the crooks and block their regular businesses in sly grog, drugs and sex. Kate Leigh had many 'sharp-eyed cockatoos' who would stand in front of or near her houses and shops, looking out for police. MacKay instructed two constables to regularly patrol the street in front of Kate's biggest sly-grog shop, where she was also peddling drugs. They walked up and down the street, stopping in front of Kate's place and talking for a long time, before walking back up the street. This went on for hours. Kate complained to her friends in local politics and they contacted the commissioner. MacKay was crafty. He claimed Kate's life was in danger and argued, 'It is my obligation to see that the threat of murder is not carried out. I intend to keep her premises under continuous surveillance so long as she is in my district.' MacKay won and Kate moved her business into Surry Hills.

MacKay didn't just take on the underworld crooks. He set up surveillance of unemployed workers and kept a close eye on union workers, particularly around riots near the wharves and on the inner-city streets. He was called on to give evidence in court into a riot at Wentworth Park in August 1929 when 700 men armed themselves with stakes in a show of solidarity for out-of-work union labourers. MacKay followed on from this work with investigations into the Communist Party, which earned him a reputation as one of the toughest police enforcers.

Lillian Armfield came to know William MacKay well while he served as Detective-Inspector of the CIB at Central Police Station. He replaced Tom Mankey who had worked closely with Lillian from those first years of looking for runaway girls. MacKay appreciated the inside knowledge Lillian had built up over the years by talking to women about eastern Sydney and getting to know some of the leading female crime figures. MacKay included Lillian in more investigations and won her respect, something that would count for a great deal in the years ahead as they faced gang violence in eastern Sydney.

When MacKay was sent over to Darlinghurst Station in the late 1920s, Lillian and her colleagues around Sydney knew he was there to take down organised crime figures. MacKay was now in the heartland of their operations and was ready to strike a blow to the drug trade and gang violence. He was tough and perfectly matched to eastern Sydney but if he wanted to infiltrate the gangs run by Kate Leigh and Tilly Devine, he needed Lillian on board. He knew the women of the underworld would rather talk to Lillian than a big, burly Scotsman who had a reputation for being quick in using his fists to get information. Lillian now started working across the main inner-city police stations.

Firm action was needed from MacKay to deal with the increase in violence in inner and eastern Sydney. In a bid to control the importation, distribution and supply of cocaine, criminals were organising into rival gangs and maintaining their businesses through violent standover tactics. Gang-related violence also made locals think twice about talking to the police and giving up suspects in attacks. Fearing retribution, few witnesses came forward after violent brawls and shootings. Gun violence dominated some of the leading crime stories reported in the newspapers. In 1927, *Truth* used the shooting death of gangster Norman Bruhn in Charlotte Lane as further evidence the police needed more regulations to render them less 'impotent' against the crooks. The drug trade needed to be stamped out, along with the gun violence associated with it.

The NSW Police Force introduced a *Pistol Licensing Act* in 1927 that outlawed the use of guns on the streets of Sydney. The side effect of this new licensing was that the crooks opted for razors instead, preferably the 'Bengall' cut-throat sort available from most chemists and grocers. Razor slashings increased by the hundreds and, again, the press made the police look a laughing stock. The razor took urban warfare to new heights of violence. Local gang member Bill Lloyd's face was slashed in December 1927. The wound from his 'hair to his neck' required sixty stitches. Police pressed Lloyd for information, but he wasn't giving anyone up. By 1928, razor slashings were such a problem that James Mitchell, now commissioner, requested an extra 200 officers be appointed to deal with the violence. The newspapers supported the request, telling readers there were only 3000 police officers across New South Wales to a population of over 2.3 million. This was one officer to almost 800 people.

Worse was still to come. The following year, in 1929, the stock market crashed on Wall Street and sent world economies plummeting towards depression. Sydney entered into another frightening era. Gang violence escalated to the point where Sydney was earning a reputation as the 'Chicago of the South'. The year 1929 proved to be one of the city's most violent as it spiralled out of control during what would come to be known as the Razor Wars.

One of the worst incidents took place in May 1929. Locals called it the 'Battle of Blood Alley'. In Eaton Avenue, Kings Cross, over the course of about half an hour, a violent brawl broke out between Phil Jeffs' gang and rival gang members. Locals watched in horror as the punches flew and the blood spattered across the ground. Bodies were flung in all directions. Razors, guns, fists and feet collided in the bloody show-down. Jeffs had had it coming for a long time: he had been cutting cocaine with boracic acid and ripping off his many customers. Word got around and both the dealers and users were unhappy. They wanted Jeffs' blood. When the police arrived around 10.30 pm, everyone was wearing the wounds of one of the most violent brawls the city had ever seen.

Police thought 'Blood Alley' might have settled the score for a while, but violence erupted again in July. Some of Kate Leigh's men ambushed members of Tilly Devine's gang in the 'Loo. The violence continued out to Maroubra when Big Jim Devine shot at Leigh associates outside his house. Kate's close friend, bodyguard and lover, Walter 'Wally' Tomlinson, was injured and Gregory Gaffney was shot dead. Jim Devine was later found not guilty at his trial. It didn't help the police case that no one in the underworld was willing to give any information about exactly what had happened.

Another battle caught the police off guard yet again in August. The 'Battle of Kellett Street', once again in the Cross, saw Leigh's and Devine's gang members fight it out for control of cocaine and booze in eastern Sydney. Bottles and rocks flew about the place and the forty-strong brawling group took to one another with guns and razors. More than a dozen injured men lay about the street when police turned up. Not one soul would identify his assailants.

In its efforts to end the violence of the Razor Wars, the NSW Police Force recognised it needed all the help it could get. Lillian was needed across major investigations in eastern Sydney. The newspapers were taking note, too. In fact, Lillian developed something of a following in the papers as they reported developments in police efforts to deal with the city's 'incorrigible criminals'. Arguing for greater police powers to prevent criminals consorting with each other and to be able to prosecute 'those who aid and abet razor-slashers, bottle-thugs, and gunmen by refusing to testify against them', *Truth* singled Lillian out as central to police efforts to break up the gangs. The drug traffic and 'the wiles of the underworld's women' were suffering through Lillian's 'tact and resource'.

The *Truth* story was accompanied by a photograph of Lillian wearing a cloche hat pulled close to her eyes and with her favourite string of pearls around her neck. She looks serious, stern and focused – the picture of a tough, strong woman who had fought hard for respect and recognition in the man's world of the NSW Police. Ten years beforehand, such a photograph would have severely compromised Lillian's undercover work into runaways and fortune-telling. Now, however, she was well known about the streets of eastern

Sydney as the crooks regularly came into contact with her as part of the wider police crackdowns and raids.

As *Truth* declared, Lillian's work was winning her 'respect and admiration from police and public'. With her knowledge of underworld women and the main players in the Razor Wars, she was proving herself to be indispensable in the police force. The police needed to ensure she could defend herself with more than a handbag, fists and her wits. Female officers were not officially given guns until the 1970s, but during the early years of the gang wars, Lillian's superiors issued her with a gun.

In 1926, Lillian apprehended two rapists she was investigating after an attack on a young woman in the city. She confronted them in their office in Pitt Street and told them to stay and wait for her colleagues. This all seems meek and mild in the world of policing if not for the fact Lillian raised a revolver at the pair and warned them it was loaded. Both men were eventually sentenced to ten years in prison for intent to rape, attempted sodomy and indecent assault on a female.

Drugs were central to the rise of organised crime in Sydney and if the police were going to break the violent hold of the gangs in the eastern neighbourhoods, they needed more powers to prosecute known criminals involved in the business. The newspapers were right: more police powers were needed to prevent the crooks from meeting and prosecute those who were aiding the drug trade and rise in underworld crime.

Drug dealing relies on the 'deals' and group members meeting to carry on the trade across all levels of the criminal operation. The hierarchical structure of traditional organised crime, such as existed in Sydney in the 1920s, meant suppliers didn't know the traffickers who didn't know the mid-level dealers who in turn did not know the street-level dealers. The overall deal would rely on drug runners who met the provider at each level. It might be the same person meeting the trafficker, supplier and lower-level dealers but a smart outfit would use more than one person at each level so they could not inform on all the main players. In this structure, the person coordinating the trade – the syndicate boss – would remain isolated from the suppliers and dealers.

The CIB detectives knew they had to prevent the main players in Sydney's underworld from being able to meet to traffic and supply cocaine if the police were really going to strike a blow to the drug trade. New legislation introduced from 1929 allowed them to do exactly this. The *Vagrancy Act* was extended to include 'criminal consorting' clauses allowing police officers to arrest any Sydney crook consorting with 'bad characters' and known criminals. Underworld criminals faced guilt by association but were rarely innocent. The main people targeted by the police had long criminal records.

Facing up to six months in prison, eastern Sydney criminals became crafty about how they met, preferably behind closed doors and away from police surveillance. To maintain her isolation from the rest of the group, Kate Leigh used runners to communicate with the main players, supported by drug suppliers. The runners and main players were paid to keep their mouths shut and knew if they informed on their boss there would be violent retribution. Criminal associates of Kate Leigh and Tilly Devine would rather take the fall for their boss in court than inform on her. After the consorting legislation was introduced, crime bosses distanced themselves even further from operations and others involved in the drug deal might not even know who was coordinating it.

Sydney's organised crime bosses, though publicly isolated from the business, nevertheless still had to be involved and informed about drug deals. Underworld business was reliant on their leadership. The CIB detectives and Big Bill MacKay were intent on taking out the leaders but Tilly Devine and Kate Leigh were smart criminal operators who closely coordinated their businesses. The police persisted, all the same, hoping to prevent them from meeting any of their associates in public or in private. Facing a long stint in Long Bay Prison, neither Kate nor Tilly wanted to be done for consorting.

The NSW Police Force established a Consorting Squad to suppress organised crime through enforcement of the consorting legislation. The cocaine trade was their main brief but its links with wider organised crime meant they could break down the gangs across their wider operations too. This team of fifteen officers, which included Detective Sergeants Wickham and Thompson along with officers from the plain-clothes division, had been handpicked based on their previous police experience and intricate knowledge of the razor gangs. While Lillian Armfield was not an official member of the squad, she was involved in consorting investigations.

Criminals didn't have to be caught consorting in the streets. People could be arrested in homes, at work, and in cars or taxis. The first consorting case was brought before the courts in December 1929 when a group of men were charged and found guilty of consorting with 'reputed criminals'.

There is some debate about who the first woman was to be charged with consorting. The beautiful prostitute and lover of some of Sydney's most notorious gangsters, Nellie Cameron, has often been singled out as the first. Nellie's first consorting charge was in March 1932, when she was arrested and charged with consorting with 'reputed criminals', one of whom was her lover at the time, Frank Green. However, there was another sensational consorting case two years beforehand, in February 1930, when seven women were charged with consorting with 'women of ill-repute'. Nellie Cameron was not among the women charged. The distinction here might be that while other women were charged with consorting with known prostitutes, Nellie was the first one charged with 'consorting with criminals'.

Consorting prosecutions were effective in breaking up the gangs. The police happily told the newspapers that underworld crooks were taking off to the other states to avoid time in prison. By the start of 1930, police reckoned as many as a hundred gangsters had fled the state.

The consorting powers were even more effective if police also caught underworld leaders red-handed with drugs. This is why Lillian Armfield was not about to let Kate Leigh out of her sights in the Riley Street house in 1930. Lillian knew

Kate was smart and would do her best to hide any cocaine from being directly linked to her: 'We had to match our wits against hers, and she was so cunning and experienced in every police tactic that it seemed we would never catch her with the cocaine.' Lillian had already pre-warned Constable Nellie Mitchell to be ready to catch Kate out but, in that moment in the bedroom, it was Lillian and Kate who were really facing off.

Suddenly, Kate was on the move. She grabbed a tobacco tin from the dressing table and threw it in the fire. Lillian had to be quick; the evidence would be destroyed in the flames. She pushed Kate out of the way, lunged at the fire and snatched the tin back out. Hurling abuse at each other, Kate and Lillian wrestled with the tin while Nellie called out to Wickham and Thompson downstairs.

This was the great showdown of underworld Sydney. We've heard a lot about Kate Leigh and Tilly Devine and their long feud, but this moment, inside Kate's house, evokes more of what was at stake in eastern Sydney between those who ran the criminal empires and those who wanted to break them. It was a definitive moment for both women.

Kate Leigh and Lillian Armfield were fearsome figures around eastern Sydney. If Lillian managed to nab Kate with cocaine, it would be a career highlight. If Kate went down for cocaine possession, she knew her cocaine dealing days were numbered. And if Kate got away with it, she could delight in having taken on the toughest woman in the police force and beaten her. There was much at stake between the two women in 1930.

The game was up. Kate backed off from Lillian and the realisation hit that she had finally been nabbed for cocaine possession. She was even more furious that Detective Wickham was there to see her downfall. She knew he would take particular delight in the moment. Wickham had been intent on getting her for cocaine possession for at least the last couple of years.

By now a small crowd had gathered outside Kate's house, eagerly waiting to see if Kate or the coppers had come off best. Kate Leigh was placed under arrest and screamed blue murder as detectives carried her out the front door. She kicked, screamed and struggled her way into the waiting police car. It was a satisfying scene for Lillian Armfield.

Kate Leigh was convicted of cocaine possession and faced a lengthy prison stint. Detective Wickham, giving evidence against Kate, seized the opportunity to tell the courtroom what he really thought of the underworld leader:

I have known this woman for 15 or 20 years . . . She is a principal in the cocaine traffic in this city. Not only does she peddle it herself, but she is one of the biggest suppliers to other peddlers. She is titled the Uncrowned Queen of the Underworld and there is no doubt that she wields a powerful influence in the underworld of Sydney. She boasts her privilege of obtaining preferential treatment of prisoners in the gaols and of her influence with high political and legal people. I regard her as a menace to the community.

She is a low moral type – a most dangerous type – capable of committing any crime in the criminal calendar.

The detective also labelled Kate a bad mother who had led her daughter down the path of ruin. When Wickham called her 'the worst woman in Sydney', Kate was incensed.

Lillian listened to Wickham then watched as Kate Leigh's defence lawyer delivered his closing argument and waited for the sentence to be handed down. A storm was brewing; Lillian knew it from previous experiences with Kate. She looked on as Kate was sentenced to twelve months in prison and walked down from the defendant's box, ready to be taken to the cells. Then the storm broke. Kate turned and started shouting at Wickham. She was still furious at being called the 'worst woman' and yelled abuse at him all the way to the cells. Worse than this, he had called her out on being a bad mother. For most of their lives, Kate and Eileen were close. Certainly, Kate had shown her daughter the criminal ropes and lived a life where criminal activities were normalised for Eileen from a young age. However, Kate was furiously loyal to her daughter and considered herself to be a good mother. The Queen of the Underworld had a high moral opinion of herself.

The Riley Street raid shows Lillian Armfield could match her wits against one of the toughest crooks in the country. While the male detectives took the credit in court for the planning that had gone into the arrest, Kate Leigh was stung by Lillian and one of her loyal female officers. Kate would also have noticed that Lillian was training other women with her valuable skills and knowledge.

The NSW Police Force had also started to take notice. The cocaine raid of 1930 showed her superiors they were right in promoting her to sergeant. By 1935, Lillian was Chief of the Women's Police.

Kate Leigh and Tilly Devine's hold on eastern Sydney crime was loosened and would never recover to the heyday of the Razor Wars.

By the late 1930s, the NSW Police Force pulled off a remarkable victory against the traffic in cocaine. It is now commonplace for Australian police to investigate transnational drug routes, but back in the 1930s NSW police officers were entering new territory in their efforts to investigate overseas cocaine supplies. Their work paid off, and large imports of cocaine were prevented from entering Sydney and elsewhere in New South Wales.

Crime bosses such as Kate Leigh and Tilly Devine were losing money quickly and had to go back to their mainstays. For Kate it was sly grog, while Tilly relied again on prostitution. However, the consorting laws continued to affect their businesses. Tilly Devine was charged with consorting in April 1931 and sentenced to fourteen days' hard labour in prison for it. This was alongside convictions for assault and stealing, which would land her more time in prison if she couldn't pay the fines. The police maintained their pressure on the underworld leader and she was again charged with consorting in October 1931. Tilly could not properly run her brothels if she couldn't associate with her staff. There was also less likelihood of her being able to peddle cocaine to her prostitutes.

Devine and Leigh might have been an even more formidable force against the police if they had united in their criminal efforts but a deep animosity remained between the pair. Their rivalry, so violent during the Razor Wars, was pitched in a very different manner during the 1930s. They both enjoyed the limelight and the public relations campaign they could run through regular news stories detailing their notoriety and hatred of each other. The main aim was to convince the public one of them was better than the other. After several years of violence, standover tactics and ruthless control of Sydney's crime scene, it was not an easy task.

Truth newspaper – the nation's scandal sheet with offices in each major city – sensationalised the rivalry and had reporters and photographers follow Devine and Leigh. Sydneysiders read regular reports about the rivalry between the warring underworld queens. In one *Truth* article, photographs of the two women were positioned alongside the heading: 'Says Tilly to Kate: Underworld Hymn of Hate'. Tilly Devine wrote a letter to the newspaper from London, responding to recent comments against her by Kate Leigh, and stating: 'I am writing this letter asking a favor [sic] to keep my name out of the papers in any connection with Kate Lee's.' Tilly went on to call Kate a 'virago' and added that she believed she herself was a 'class above' a woman who objected to being called the worst woman in Sydney but settled for being known as notorious: 'The underworld all took their hats off to me and class me a lady beside her.'

The public mudslinging continued. Kate Leigh told *Truth* in 1930 that she was not the 'worst woman in Sydney' because that 'title was Tilly Devine's'. Tilly was said to have once responded to Kate's claims that she had never sold her body for sex by remarking, 'Sure Kate never worked as a prostitute. Who'd have an old bag like her on anyhow? She wouldn't get any takers if she offered it for free.' In 1943, a decade after the heyday of the Razor Wars, Kate Leigh stood up in the Licensing Court and expressed her disdain at being compared with her inner-city rival: 'I'm here to give evidence and not to be insulted ... I've never heard such a thing in my life. Fancy daring to mention me in the same breath as that woman. I refuse to listen to her name. Even the mention of it disgusts me.'

Truth continued to regularly report on the women's feuds, arrests and appearances in court. It also enjoyed wide access to them, knowing they would grant interviews if it meant the other could be outwitted in her efforts to win over the public. This blurred the lines between what was actually happening and what each woman wanted the public to think was taking place. The name of the game was muddying the other woman's reputation as much as possible.

Tilly and Kate had their favourite photographers and sometimes tipped off reporters when they were making an appearance in court. Kate Leigh's favourite press photographers at *Truth* knew she liked flattering images printed in the paper. In one staged photograph for *Truth*, she lay back 'in her big limousine, one heavily jewelled hand dangling idly in its flashing array of diamonds, while the other stroked the fluffy Pomeranian to which she was so attached'.

Their rivalry even went as far as their dogs. Tilly and Kate both owned Pomeranians they carted around like accessories. In one newspaper photograph, Tilly kneels down with her three Pomeranians. It is an attractive photograph of Tilly as she looks softer than usual with her wavy hair loose about the shoulders. In another *Truth* photograph, Kate poses in a large hat, smiling for the camera and cuddling her two Pomeranians. One local story handed down has Tilly rushing out to buy her third Pomeranian after she saw Kate posing with two. She had to go one better and have three dogs.

There were moments when Kate and Tilly tried to make amends. They performed a dramatic show of support for the newspapers in 1948. In one photograph, Kate leans down close to Tilly's face, smiling and looking for a response. Tilly, meanwhile, continues to puff on her cigarette. In another, the two women attempt to embrace but it is an awkward moment, reminiscent of when you go to hug someone, misread their body language, and pull away embarrassed. The vice queens have their heads tilted, looking at each other, but still keep each other at arms' length. The legacy of many years facing each other down in the street and attempting to do each other out of business is clear in the photographs. Police were always surprised they hadn't killed each other. *Truth* may have claimed that the pair were close friends by the late 1940s, but the staged photographic embraces are far removed from any genuine closeness. Nevertheless, for two women who were so adamantly opposed to each other, even a staged show of friendship was a break with the past.

By the late 1940s Kate Leigh was trying to cultivate an appealing matriarchal identity in Surry Hills. It was in part fostered through real actions and her public relations efforts in the newspapers. Both Kate and Tilly donated money to children's homes and helped out the needy in their neighbourhoods, but Kate went one step further and provided free entertainment for the poor kids of Surry Hills. She gave Henry 'Jack' Baker, her standover man and lover for many years, money to buy Shetland ponies that she used to give kids rides in a vacant block of land at Ward Park. But it was the Christmas parties that were the highlight of the year for the kids.

Each year from the early 1940s, she would block off Lansdowne Street and set up a street party. Tables would be surrounded by eager children waiting for food and enjoying the celebrations. In 1946, more than 300 local kids attended Kate Leigh's party. She told the press, 'Kiddies of Surry Hills have very little but I will not see them unhappy at Christmas.' It didn't matter too much that most of the gifts given to the kids were from Kate's haul of stolen goods. It was like taking from the rich and giving to the poor.

In one 1950 *People* article on life in Surry Hills, Kate is photographed waving to children below her terrace house, alongside Santa. The caption reads:

All hail Kate Leigh. All hail the Yuletide spirit embodied by a caparisoned friend of Kate's who volunteered to assist her distribute her bounty to the underprivileged neighborhood [sic] kids from the balcony of her Surry Hills residence. The children also crowd her smallgoods shop.

In another photograph, Kate reaches out to a small child crying in the arms of Santa. Taken in 1948, the photo captures Kate in an apron looking every bit the elderly matriarch. Many children trying to get close to Santa shroud her. There is a look of genuine affection on Kate's face as she tries to soothe the upset child. If you knew nothing else about Kate Leigh, you would look at this photograph and think it was a kindly old woman trying to help a sad child. Yet Kate's notoriety should not detract from the fact that she really did want to help children in her community.

The locals knew most of Kate's gifts for the kids had been knocked off, and they made sure their kids didn't ask too many questions. One newspaper reporter, writing a story about Kate's popular Christmas parties, witnessed one child ask his mum, 'Where does Old Kate get all the dough for this sort of thing?' The mother grabbed him by the ear, hurried him around the corner and out of earshot of Kate.

Kate Leigh's criminal celebrity resonated more with the eastern Sydney locals than did Tilly Devine's. One of the fundamental differences between the women was that Kate was a local girl – raised in the country before coming to the city – and Tilly was English.

Henry 'Jack' Baker's loyalty to Kate was unfailing. In court he once testified: 'There's never a better woman lived. I've lived with her as man and wife for fifteen years. You always talk about her bad points. What about her good ones? She has a heart of gold.' Henry Baker's grandson, Hal Baker, often visited Kate in Surry Hills when he was a kid. For Hal, it was obvious why more people liked Kate than Tilly. Being English put Devine 'behind the eight ball' where there was 'almost a hatred of English in these parts', where old diggers were still reeling from the actions of English officers in World War I. Tilly Devine also lost favour when she moved out to Maroubra, whereas Kate Leigh remained in Surry Hills for the rest of her life, telling a journalist in 1950: 'I've been in the Lansdowne Street place for 17 years. And I've never once missed giving a Christmas party for the kids round here. I love them and they love me.'

While Kate was tough and violent, and could never be trusted, her reputation among the police was better than Tilly's. Tilly was reviled by the police, and few in the force changed their opinion of her, even years after the heyday of her criminal career in the 1920s and 1930s. Kate had a low opinion of the police, particularly the policewomen she regularly dealt with, but she developed respect for Lillian as the boss of the Women's Police.

Even Kate Leigh, the 'worst woman in Sydney', could acknowledge the professionalism, hard work and persever-ance of Sergeant Lillian Armfield. Tough country women who created a unique place for themselves in the eastern Sydney crime scene in the first decades of the twentieth century – albeit on opposing sides – Kate Leigh and Lillian Armfield respected each other for sticking it out in a man's world. They both wanted more respect for women in their chosen professions, though on opposite sides of the law.

8

'Darkest Sydney'

LILLIAN ARMFIELD'S WORK IN THE WOMEN'S POLICE CONTINUED to draw her further into Sydney's dark underside in ways she could never have imagined in her first days on the job. Though she was mainly responsible for offences against the person and offences relating to public order, Lillian's policing work included knowledge of all crimes included in the *NSW Crimes Act* of 1900, the legislation guiding police work even today, with a staggering 582 sections defining and listing punishable offences. Lillian's work was based around the main duties of the Women's Police – relating to girls and women specifically – but the actual scale of the work she was involved in is remarkable. In policing work today, different major crimes are dealt with by specific policing teams, such as the Organised Crime (Targeting) Squad or the Sex Crimes Squad. Lillian and her colleagues worked all manner of crimes and investigated, among many other offences: murder and manslaughter, child murder, infanticide, child abandonment, suicide, sexual assault and rape, sexual servitude, abortion, procuring prostitution, consorting, riots, public drunkenness, and peeping or prying. It was an extensive policing brief and the nature of some crimes was particularly harrowing.

Though it wasn't the Razor Wars, the work was still dangerous and draining. As a senior officer in the NSW Police Force, Lillian was required as a key investigator on some of the hardest and most emotionally taxing cases Sydney would witness in the 1930s and 1940s. This coincided with her own heartache over her sister Muriel's marriage breakup.

By the late 1930s, Lillian had moved to a small one-bedroom place in Darlinghurst. Now the violence of the Razor Wars was over she felt she could live back there. Lillian's relationship with her sister Muriel became even closer in these years. Muriel had moved to Sydney around the time Lillian started in the police force and the pair were in regular contact. In 1938, Muriel's husband, John, left her as a single mother of eight children. Four of her kids were old enough to have jobs but the younger ones helped their mother by looking out for each other. John was an alcoholic and his drinking had deeply affected the family. Though only two when his father left, Muriel's son, Norm, remembers running away from the house at one point, with an older brother, to escape their father's drinking. According to Norm, this seems to have been the moment that broke the relationship for his mother.

Lillian felt even more connected to her sister in their close relationship supporting each other and her brother-in-law's departure may have further deepened Lillian's mistrust of men. The sisters remained close and as a marker of respect for Muriel being there for Lillian in her first years in the police, Lillian frequently visited her nieces and nephews and made sure Muriel was able to support her family as a single mother.

Back out on the streets and investigating serious cases with the CIB detectives, Lillian was further exposed to the depravity of people who would deprive a person of their liberty and, in the case of murder, take their life. Following on from the Razor Wars, which had largely subsided by the early 1930s, Lillian was reminded in the most brutal way possible of just how important her work was in protecting women on the streets and in their homes. Lillian's work brought her into close contact with what the newspapers had referred to as 'darkest Sydney'. She worked on two of the most sensational homicide cases involving Sydney police in this period: the 'Pyjama Girl' case of 1934 and the murder of Connie McGuire in 1949.

Homicide detectives investigate some of the worst crime scenes imaginable. As former detective Charlie Bezzina has revealed in recent years, after his retirement from the Homicide division in Victoria: 'A homicide investigator needs to be prepared – mentally, emotionally and even physically – to see the most repugnant sights imaginable.' It starts with the discovery of a dead body. Police might take a call at the station or a member of the public comes in to report it.

Detectives are sent out immediately, along with constables – uniform officers – who will secure the scene and keep the public and media away. The scene has to be preserved and due caution given to the identity of a person or persons not being revealed before family have been notified. Today, in the social media age, this is becoming increasingly hard to police. A medical professional is then called in to consider cause and time of death. If the death is allegedly suspicious, which the attending officers will usually have a pretty good idea of, a full homicide investigation will be launched.

Homicide investigations can take days, weeks or months. Sometimes they take years, as in the recent case of the Claremont serial killings in Western Australia where a suspect was arrested in December 2016 after a twenty-year investigation. At the very start, in those raw first moments, the initial forty-eight hours are crucial. The trail is hot and the evidence is fresh. Witnesses' memories have not been subjected to the questioning mind that, over time, combines other sources of information on top of what was seen or experienced. A person's recollection of an event naturally becomes more unreliable with the passing of time. For police officers, the first hours of an investigation are fuelled by the need to catch a killer at large in the community.

When a woman's body was discovered near Albury, New South Wales, on 1 September 1934, Sydney detectives were sent for. This wasn't usual practice, given the local police would normally run a homicide investigation, but assistance was immediately needed from an 'experienced detective' at the Sydney police headquarters. Local police knew from their first moments at the gruesome scene that it was one of the worst murders in the state's history.

Leading the investigation from Sydney, Detective Sergeant Alf Wilks – later deputy director of ASIO – sent two of his best men for the job. Detective Sergeants Allmond and MacRae travelled down to Albury to lead the investigation there. Tom MacRae was renowned within the force and would go on to become the Chief of Sydney Homicide. In 1933, assisted by members of his team, which included DS Allmond, MacRae led an investigation into five brutal attacks and murders of girls and young women in Sydney parks. Within days of being assigned to the job, MacRae had located a suspect, who was later sentenced to life imprisonment.

In Albury, local man Thomas Griffith had found the young woman when he stopped by the road and caught sight of what he thought was a body half-concealed at the end of a stormwater drain. As he moved in closer, his suspicions were proved correct and he was horrified to discover the body was charred and the legs were drawn up into a foetal position. The woman's clothes were mostly burned and her head was covered with a jute bag.

The crime scene is the most important part of any homicide investigation. It holds the clues to what happened and is essential to building evidence to find and convict the murderer or murderers. Today there is greater understanding that a crime scene should not be contaminated. Overalls, overshoes and masks are now a requirement at all crime scenes and only the most essential people involved in the investigation are allowed access, mainly the chief investigating officers, a police photographer, a video operator, and forensic specialists. Back in 1934, however, officers would walk through a crime scene and touch items, including the body. They would walk around the scene, looking for clues and contaminating it at the same time. This wasn't incompetency: it was before the widespread professionalisation of forensic science and DNA testing.

Some police methods have not changed, however, and officers turning up to the scene where the young woman's body was found in 1934 reacted in a similar manner to today's officers. They knew they would have to work as quickly and best they could while the scene was cordoned off. The first officers on the scene would have stood and taken in the position and condition of the victim, the location and environment, and looked for the entry and exit points for whoever dumped the body. They would then have recorded this information in their notepads while the police photographer stepped in to record a visual account.

The scene awaiting MacRae and Allmond at Albury was ghastly and they knew immediately the victim had suffered. A few days later, the crime scene was described in newspapers across the country. Readers were confronted with the gruesome details at the start of most reports, including this one from Queensland:

> The body of a girl aged about 20 years, clothed in white and yellow silk pyjamas, was found to-day in a culvert on

the Howlong-Road, four miles from Albury. The forehead had been cruelly battered, and the legs and lower part of the abdomen charred to a black mass. Part of the body was in a charred cornsack.

With this news report and so many others in the days that followed, the woman came to be known as the 'Pyjama Girl'. Not all newspapers used the title to describe the victim but it would come to be a key part of how the case was remembered.

Once the body was photographed and studied at the crime scene, it was taken by ambulance to Albury Hospital where the woman was examined by the government medical officer, Dr Leslie Woods. He confirmed that the woman had been burned with kerosene, which the police had found on grass at the crime scene. The doctor also investigated in more detail the wounds sustained to the woman's head. Eight wounds were found on the left side of the head and the bone around these areas was smashed. There was a deep gash to the forehead that exposed the brain.

Under X-ray, Dr Woods found a bullet lodged in the woman's neck. It had entered just below her left eye. This information was not published in the newspapers as police wanted to keep it under wraps, as is common in homicide cases where a suspect has not been found. Suspects can often give away information that only the killer and police would know.

Detectives MacRae and Allmond had to work backwards from the woman's body to establish what had happened and to identify any potential suspects. It was clear from the autopsy that the victim had been dumped at the site in Albury, but from where they were not sure and police could not be certain she was a local until they interviewed residents.

Family and friends are usually the first to be investigated. A common thread in homicide cases is the victim, more times than not, knows their attacker. For the officers working on the Pyjama Girl case, the task was harder: they didn't know who their victim was. As Detective Sergeant MacRae would later say, 'Identification is half the battle in a murder investigation.'

Detectives decided to transfer the woman's body for public display. Her body was kept on ice at the Albury morgue and hundreds of people came to look at her. However, her face was not on display, rather it was a mask made for public identification. Some thought they might have known the woman, others were already worried about a missing friend or relative, and still others had a morbid interest in viewing the body. No one recognised the dead woman.

The newspapers became an essential part of the police operation to identify the victim and find who had killed her. Unsolved homicides impact deeply on the victim's loved ones and can make the wider community fearful and anxious.

In the meantime, one police officer was frantically working her way through photographs of missing girls and women to compare them with the police photograph of the Albury murder victim. The newspapers stated that despite no local girls being reported as missing, the young woman could be 'one of those on record as missing, and for whom the chief of the women police (Sergeant Lillian Armfield) is looking'. It was no easy task looking frequently at the face of the victim and comparing it to those of other young missing women, but Lillian was dedicated, like others on the case, to finding the person responsible for such a horrific crime.

While Lillian and her team compared photographs and conducted their own investigations into reports of missing women from Sydney and the wider New South Wales region, their male colleagues sent detailed descriptions of the victim to all police stations in New South Wales and Victoria. The woman's fingerprints were sent to all police headquarters across the country. The police were hopeful people would start coming forward with information once they saw an artist's depiction of the victim that was published in the leading newspapers nation-wide.

By 12 September 1934, the police had no breakthrough in the case and decided to send the body to Sydney, where it was thought the woman was from. The hope was it might be viewed by a friend or family member. The body was preserved in formalin and publicly displayed at the University of Sydney. This was an important decision by officers of the Homicide Squad: if the body was buried, it would not be preserved, and their chances of identifying the victim and finding the perpetrator would be severely reduced.

The NSW Police faced early criticism in the case, as is common with homicide cases that are not quickly solved. Nearly two months after the discovery of the body, *Truth* newspaper in Sydney declared police were 'baffled' and 'at a dead end'. Meanwhile, Lillian and her team in the Women's Police continued to compile their list of potential victims from the hundreds of young women who had been reported missing in recent years. In total they would search 2000 files on missing women from across New South Wales.

Professor Burkitt at the University of Sydney had also become involved in the case, providing an anatomical examination of the body. The professor considered the woman to be between twenty-two or twenty-three and twenty-eight. The police had little else to go on.

A possible victim surfaced from the middle of the 1930s. Linda Pratt, an Englishwoman, had married an Italian immigrant, Antonio Agostini, in Sydney in 1930. The pair moved to Melbourne to remove Linda from 'undesirable influences' in her Sydney friendship group. Some friends of Linda had thought the body on display might have been her but other friends were unsure. Antonio was interviewed by police in Melbourne in 1935 but he claimed his wife frequently left him. He did not think the fact she was still missing was out of character, given the volatile nature of the relationship. At the time of the discovery of the Albury murder victim, Linda Agostini was twenty-eight, matching the upper end of the age estimates.

Measuring the success of a homicide investigation is complex. Traditionally, a 'good' homicide investigation is measured against the identification, prosecution and conviction of a guilty offender or offenders. With or without a conviction, an investigation might also be termed successful if all procedures were followed professionally and detectives were able to reduce the social impact on the community. If the public can be reassured that the police have done all they can and there is no direct threat to the wider community, with or without a conviction, then public confidence can be restored.

In the decade following on from the discovery of the Pyjama Girl, police measured their success in this complex manner. There was no conviction – mainly due to lack of knowledge about the victim – but investigators argued they had followed all procedures and believed there was no ongoing threat to the community. Detectives were always keen to remind the public that most homicides involve someone close to the victim and this was likely the case with the unidentified female corpse.

Three years after the murder, *Truth* was persistent in its criticism of the police investigation. It argued for an inquest into the death because, the newspaper alleged, the police were keeping things 'Hush Hush'. While the paper recognised the importance of confidential police information, it also argued for a 'thorough probe by an experienced coroner'. The role of the media in a murder case is important but the press can also hamper a case if too many details are revealed, particularly if the perpetrator of the crime reads the newspapers and learns more about the police investigation.

It was a frustrating few years for Detective Sergeant Tom MacRae. He told reporters in 1938 of his hopes that the victim would be identified and her killer brought to justice:

If only we could get this girl's identity, we would have a chance of success. The police are still hoping that some day one of the tens of thousands of people who inspect the victim in her formalin bath in Sydney may recognise or remember having seen her somewhere.

An inquest was held into the death in January 1938 but lasted only a day. The main witnesses were police officers and Thomas Griffith, the young man who had found the body. Griffith was faced with persistent rumours that he had in fact killed the young woman and then reported it to the police as a discovery. Other rumours were spread that Thomas and his family were all implicated after a party at their home nearby. The police did not investigate the rumours, firmly believing them to be unfounded community gossip.

The inquest failed to establish the identity of the Albury victim, despite many of Linda Agostini's family and friends coming forward to identify her as the victim. Police rested more of their case on the dental records which were declared not to be a match for Linda.

A few months later, in May 1938, an Italian shopkeeper went to police claiming the dead woman was Linda Agostini. He had known Antonio and Linda and believed an image he had seen of the victim was very similar to Linda. Police were suspicious as no photograph had yet been published, only the artist's depiction, and so they thought he must have been referring to that. The shopkeeper had decided to come forward after the recent inquest sparked his interest and led him to question what he knew of the Agostinis. However, with the police still misled by the dental records, the shop-keeper's evidence was put to the side.

In the meantime, the Albury victim's body was transferred from the University of Sydney to police headquarters. The case was seemingly becoming very cold.

In April 1943, close to a decade after the murder and with no suspect or suspects brought forward, *Truth* again claimed police incompetency. Under the headline of 'Pyjama Girl Muddle', *Truth* protested that the police wanted to forget the case and allow it to become another unsolved murder.

Truth also entered into growing speculation that the victim was a young woman by the name of Anna Philomena Morgan. Philomena, as she was more generally known, had been reported missing to police two weeks after the discovery of the body in Albury. Her family situation was fraught with accusations of incest and abuse, and police investigated the possibility that her mother had killed her and disposed of the body. Philomena's grandmother was said to have viewed the body on display at the university and believed it to have been her granddaughter. There was, however, no firm evidence at the time to definitively link the body to that of Philomena Morgan.

The investigation continued. By the early 1940s, Lillian's work in the Women's Police had become a team effort, with over a dozen women working for her. They had amassed a list of 125 women who could be the Albury victim. One of Lillian's officers, Grace Hopkins, would become an important part of the investigation. Hopkins was nicknamed the 'glamour girl of the NSW Police Force' and served for twelve years before she married in 1955.

A small group of investigators was set the task of bringing the case to a close. Police Commissioner William MacKay handpicked the officers, including Grace Hopkins, and wanted a result.

Police ordered new dental charts for the victim and when they were shown to match Linda's records, police again interviewed Antonio, who had spent four years in an internment camp during World War II. In the course of this interview, he pleaded guilty to the accidental killing of his wife.

In a lengthy statement that took a constable three hours to type up, Antonio Agostini told Commissioner MacKay he had struggled with his wife's heavy drinking for years and they often lived apart. She ran away frequently and sometimes threatened his life. He awoke one night with Linda holding a gun to his head. They struggled violently across the bed and when he tried to get the gun out of her hand it went off, killing her instantly with a shot to the left side of her eye. Antonio claimed he did not report the death to police because he did not want to bring shame on the Italian community. Instead, he drove to Albury and disposed of the body.

The coroner's hearing in April 1944 established the corpse was Linda Agostini. Antonio was convicted of manslaughter – police believing his statement of accidental death – and he was sentenced to six years in prison. He served out four years and was then deported to Italy where he died in 1969.

Despite Agostini's conviction, the Pyjama Girl case, one of the most sensational in Australian crime history, to some extent remains a mystery with debate about whether or not Antonio Agostini was responsible for the death of the young woman found in Albury. There seems to be general agreement that he killed his wife but whether it was her body in Albury is still questioned. Historian Richard Evans has pointed out that the Albury woman's eyes were brown while Linda Agostini's were blue. The nose shape was also different and when Antonio told police about the murder weapon, he referred to a revolver, when in fact police forensics had traced the bullet to an automatic weapon.

The case is, however, important in demonstrating the manner in which Lillian Armfield's team at the Women's Police had made themselves indispensable in such investigations. When a female homicide victim needed to be identified, their list of missing women was consulted and Lillian was brought in to check photographs of the victim against missing girls and young women. Grace Hopkins was also singled out in the press as a leading detective in the case. Women were slowly getting the wider recognition they deserved – and which Lillian Armfield had fought so long for – in the police force, while working more often alongside the male detectives.

•

As Chief of the Women's Police and now with over two decades of experience on the job, Lillian Armfield knew prevention was a key part in her work protecting women, but there were painful reminders that, despite her best efforts, some women could not be reformed or protected from the dangers around them. Constance 'Connie' McGuire was one of these women and her refusal to listen to Lillian and get the help she needed proved fatal in 1949.

Lillian Armfield first met Connie McGuire in the late 1930s when she faced a charge of offensive behaviour. It wasn't her first. To Vice Squad detectives she was a 'well-known street woman' – prostitute. Connie was more harmful to herself than the rest of the community and the police appreciated that she tried to keep her streetwalking contained to known soliciting areas and away from the general public. She 'always acted in a good-mannered way'. Yet the police were still intent on turning her away from sex work. Special Sergeant Lillian Armfield took on Connie's case and tried to convince her to give up prostitution. Connie's biggest problem, however, was allowing herself to be easily led by her lovers. 'She was,' Lillian later recalled, 'a good girl gone wrong. She never touched liquor, and never used bad language, and she kept herself scrupulously clean.'

Though her character was flawless, Connie's lifestyle led her into associations with less salubrious Sydney characters. In the 1940s, after separating from her husband, she met and fell in love with a notorious gunman, Rex Llewellyn Flanagan. He lived off the earnings of women who prostituted themselves and he pushed Connie back out onto the streets to earn more money for him. He listed his occupation as a cook but preferred to loaf about on what Lillian Armfield saw as immoral earnings. Flanagan was married – since 1939 – and continued to live on and off with his wife and Connie. He was nothing more than a 'hoodlum' in Lillian's eyes and she knew Connie could do much better. Connie, unfortunately, didn't have as high an opinion of herself and looked to Flanagan for protection and security.

Lillian had seen it all too many times before. Flanagan cared little for Connie, other than what she could make for him on the streets. When she didn't earn enough, Flanagan would resort to taunts and threats. The pair moved in together but their relationship deteriorated. Registering as man and wife, they argued over Connie's earnings and Flanagan threatened her with a loaded revolver. By 1949 their relationship seemed beyond repair. During a visit to Connie's brother in Rozelle, the pair argued and Flanagan pulled out his gun. He held it point-blank at Connie and fired. Rooted to the spot with fear, Connie fortunately wasn't hit but the bullet lodged in the woodwork behind her.

There were regular arguments between the pair wherever they lived. Connie tried to leave Flanagan several times and moved into an apartment in Quinton Road, Manly. It didn't take long for Flanagan to find her, particularly after she registered under the name Connie Flanagan. Lillian tried to convince Connie to leave Flanagan for good. Lillian was hopeful her regular chats with Connie – on the street or visiting her at home – would allow her to see sense and start a new life. Lillian pleaded with her, 'You're still young,

Connie, and you've got a chance in life.' Lillian shared stories of other women who had worked the streets and turned their lives around. With the assistance of the Women's Police, they could get new work and accommodation. But Connie had to want this herself, and Lillian was disappointed when she realised Connie wasn't sure she wanted to leave Flanagan, which also meant giving up prostitution.

Though she had booted him out several times, Connie allowed Flanagan back into her life and by September 1949 he was living on and off with her at the Manly apartment. Their arguments escalated and Connie expressed grave concerns to Lillian. She worried about how angry and violent Flanagan was during arguments. Lillian knew about the shooting incident at Connie's brother's house, thanks to local gossip and talking to Connie's friends on the streets, but Connie refused to make a formal complaint about it. Lillian again tried to convince her to leave Flanagan, telling her she and the other policewomen would give her all the help she needed to start afresh. As Lillian said to Connie: 'Everyone's entitled to start a clean sheet, and we'll give you all the help we can.'

Late on the evening of 12 September 1949, an argument broke out in Connie's Manly apartment. It was a heated, angry and violent confrontation that would prove to be her last. Witnesses would later tell the police they heard two people shouting and Connie pleading not to be hurt. Connie's last moments were terrifying. Mrs Emily Lilley, a neighbour, heard Connie call out, 'Oh, Rex, don't, don't.' She yelled the words loudly before her voice dropped and two shots were fired. The silence following the shots was broken by the sound of footsteps hurrying down the stairwell outside the apartment.

When police arrived they found Connie slumped in a chair with a bullet wound above her right breast. On the table next to her was a teapot and two cups, confirming for officers that she had entertained someone before being fatally shot. Connie had known her attacker, and the detectives knew exactly where to look. Based on what Lillian Armfield told them of her conversations with Connie, and now with statements from neighbours, a warrant was put out for the arrest of Rex Flanagan.

Detective Sergeant Gordon Jack and Sergeants Armstrong, Blackwell and Gilmore ran the investigation and cordoned off the crime scene. Fingerprint and photograph experts from the CIB Scientific Investigation Bureau were sent in. Connie was killed not by the first bullet but the second. She had run out of luck after the incident at her brother's place. Police found the first bullet lodged in the plaster behind her.

Homicide investigations depend a great deal on the immediate actions of the murderer and police need to establish the route a person has taken after leaving the scene. At first light, officers traced a route they thought Rex Flanagan might have taken back to his wife's house and on the way scoured the beach near Connie's apartment. In his haste leaving the murder scene, Flanagan had panicked. Police found a Smith and Wesson .38 revolver buried in sand near rocks at the beach, not far from the apartment complex. Grease and vaseline found on the teapot in Connie's apartment matched that found on the revolver. The police had their murder weapon and now needed to find the murderer.

Lillian joined the investigation and door-knocked around the apartment building and houses nearby. It was heartbreaking for Lillian knowing how much she had tried to help Connie out, but for the time being she was more focused on finding the killer than grieving. Lillian and the other officers also had to show that the earlier shooting at Connie's brother's house was linked to the murder scene. Lillian interviewed women in Rozelle who gave evidence about the incident and when officers examined the house on Nelson Street, they found a bullet in the wall of the bedroom where Connie and Flanagan had stayed. It matched the bullets found at the murder scene and had been shot from the same gun found in the sand at Manly. When police arrested Rex Flanagan, he denied any part in the murder.

While the police continued collecting evidence and building their case against Flanagan, Connie's family needed support. The families of victims are another key part of homicide investigations. Former Homicide Detective Charlie Bezzina worked for seventeen years on murder investigations. For Charlie, murder cases were always grounded in finding 'justice for the victim and their loved ones'. Lillian Armfield knew Connie McGuire well and had listened to her talking about her mother, brother and ex-husband. They were naturally devastated by her death, and at her funeral Connie's mother inserted a card in flowers on her daughter's casket with the words: 'To my dear Connie, with all my love, Mum.' Connie's ex-husband, Charlie McGuire, paid for most of the funeral and included on his funeral card: 'In remembrance of our happy days together.' The pair had been separated for eight years but, as Charlie told *Truth*, paying for the funeral was his way of showing his final respects: 'If she was good enough to bear my name, she was certainly good enough for me to bury.'

Lillian had to be very careful in her dealings with the family because, despite evidence to the contrary from the police and reports in the newspapers, Connie's mother and brother denied her soliciting history. Even under normal circumstances, few families would have talked about prostitution outside of their private conversations about a family member. The shock of Connie's death also made her mother and ex-husband hold on to precious memories of her. They told newspaper reporters – always keen for an exclusive inside story from a victim's family – that she was a beautiful 'bookish' woman who 'always had her nose in a book'.

The case came before the courts late in 1949 and reached its climax in April of the following year. Rex Flanagan tried his best to win over the jury. He wore an immaculate blue suit and red tie to court with a handkerchief placed in his top pocket to give off the air of a man who didn't look like he could commit such a cold-blooded murder. He pleaded innocent to the murder charge and provided an alibi. On the evening of the murder, according to his police statement, he had been at home with his wife, Mrs Nellie Flanagan, and had not left the flat until 11.45 pm, after Connie was killed in Manly.

Dressed in black and wearing a pearl necklace and earrings, a bespectacled Nellie Flanagan changed her tune in court. Detectives revealed a long list of convictions for prostitution going back many years. She was also known to run houses of ill fame and went by a number of aliases. With her reputation crumbling, and hesitant to provide her ex-husband with an alibi for murder, Nellie Flanagan testified that he had in fact left her flat at 10.45 pm. This was now well before Connie was murdered at 11.20 pm.

It took the jury twelve minutes to return a guilty verdict. Rex Flanagan was sentenced to death for the murder of Connie McGuire. It was commuted to life imprisonment but for Lillian Armfield and the other officers involved in the case, there was justice for the victim. It was still, however, a senseless killing.

Connie was laid to rest with a cross of violets in her folded hands covering the fatal wound in her chest. The kind heart Lillian had appreciated had been fatally broken. Connie's ex-husband worked extra shifts for months after her death to pay for a headstone over her grave at Botany Cemetery. In the end, Lillian was left to mourn for a woman she couldn't save from the darker depths of Sydney life. Her murderer was behind bars but, for Lillian, it 'wouldn't do much for poor Connie McGuire'.

9

'A Gallant Woman':
Chief of the Women's Police

IN A DARKENED CITY STREET ON A FRIDAY EVENING IN DECEMBER 1931, a whistle and a cry goes out into the night. Feet scurry along the road, doors slam and the lights go out. Lillian Armfield smiles and tells the reporter from the *Arrow* that the noise is a signal. She's been spotted. The reporter, Jean Hull, is walking the inner-city streets with Lillian, writing a feature article on 'Sydney's Smart Police Woman Sergeant'. The city's streetwalkers and crooks know Lillian well and while some hide away in houses on Campbell Street, Jean has already seen another side to Lillian's work back at the police station. There, a streetwalker by the name of Rene had been charged yet again with an offence against good order but she had been pleased to see Lillian and asked if her cold was any better. When Lillian and the reporter left Rene, they headed upstairs to Lillian's 'spick and span' office and could hear drunken women singing in the cells below. Lillian had smiled and told Jean: 'We hear some beautiful voices at times.'

On their walk around the city streets, Lillian is reflective. She wants the readers to understand her work but also to know she is a regular person too:

Some people imagine that I am a hard-hearted callous woman, always prying into others' affairs. But I assure you I am just a normal person, who, when work is over, likes to get out on to a tennis court or into a bright bathing suit among the waves at Bondi.

But it took 'a strong nerve and plenty of energy' to get the job done. As a sergeant, Lillian had to adapt to the job and separate her work life from her private life, 'otherwise you would find the sordidness of the everyday happenings stunting your viewpoint of life as a whole'.

By the time of the newspaper interview, Lillian Armfield had worked tirelessly for years to ensure women had a place in the police force and she was successfully running her own team of female constables. This achievement is captured in a photograph from 1938. Eight women are busy going about their work in a small room with concrete flooring and tall, open filing cabinets. Six of the women are seated at what look to be three tables pushed together to make up a larger working space. Two of the six are working on typewriters as the other four jot down information in their notepads. One woman stands at the back of the room, showing her notebook to a woman seated at the centre of the tables. With her thumb and forefinger pressed around her jawline, the seated woman is considering the other woman's work.

There is much to draw us into this photograph. The ink wells of a bygone era; the large typewriters which we now appreciate take a lot longer than computers to compile work on but conditioned the typists to work carefully. The mass of paperwork that in our digital age is another hallmark of the past. The women either have short, wavy, crimped hair or their hair is tied up to the neckline. They are dressed in skirt suits with blouses and sensible low-heeled shoes, the 'uniform' first worn by their boss back in 1915.

All eight women are working at the back of the CIB in Sydney. Their boss, Lillian Armfield, is the one seated at the back-centre of the group and thoughtfully looking at paper-work presented to her by one of her officers. These female officers – Eva Rosser, Geraldine Croke, Katie Ledger, Margaret Jeffrey, Nellie Mooney, Nellie Mitchell and Ethel Burton – were handpicked by Lillian, allowed into the Women's Police to carry on the work she had started back in 1915. It was no good being the head of the Women's Police with no succession plan. Here, in 1938, Lillian could sit back with a sense of achievement that there were now seven other women in the NSW Police Force along with another few volunteers. While she wanted more women and would continue to petition her superiors and the state government, the Women's Police 'experiment' had paid off.

By 1938 the other Australian states had their own Women's Police. A few months after Lillian Armfield and Maude Rhodes were appointed as the first female constables in Australia back in 1915, South Australia introduced its own female officers. Women had conducted park and street patrols for a number of years around Adelaide for the State Children's Department but their duties were unclear and they didn't have to report to local police. A more formal appointment of women to contribute to the protection and welfare of young girls and women, in the form of the Women's Police, made even more sense after the state government closely watched developments in Sydney. South Australia's first two female constables reported for duty on 1 December 1915.

Victoria followed suit in July 1917 and the ripple effect continued on to Tasmania in October of the same year. Like their South Australian counterparts, the Victorian Police watched progress in New South Wales and wanted to build on what was already working there or needed improvement. Wonderful interstate rivalry meant the Victorians would be looking to beat the New South Welshmen at their own game. The rivalry was given more fire when Victoria's chief commissioner reportedly received no reply to his correspondence to NSW Inspector-Chief James Mitchell asking for more information about the Sydney experience. Despite the snub, the Victorians continued on in their plans for the introduction of female officers. Madge Connor and Elizabeth Beers were the first female officers appointed to the Victorian Women's Police. Madge was not unlike Lillian Armfield in some respects with her cloche hat and pearl necklace. By 1921, bettering their NSW rivals, the Victorian Police Force allowed for women to be sworn in with the same powers as their male colleagues.

The nation's largest state, Western Australia, introduced the Women's Police in September 1917. Like their equivalents in the eastern states, the West Australian special constables were expected to control the sexuality of young girls and women and protect them from abuse on the streets. One Women's Christian Temperance Union spokeswoman summed up the moralistic arguments for introducing female officers:

There is a great probability that women police patrols would greatly help in the protection of the weak, and the punishment of those who deliberately plan their destruction. In Great Britain, woman police are said to be a 'walking conscience'.

West Australian parliamentarian Edith Cowan believed policewomen would save young women from 'social degradation and from disease'.

The emphasis on protection was clear, as was the need to serve women in Western Australia.

Helen Dugdale and Laura Chipper were selected as Western Australia's first female constables. Like their Sydney counterparts, they carried the full weight of the aspirations of the women's organisations. Dugdale and Chipper worked under the Inspector of Police at the Metropolitan Branch in Perth, but they were listed as a 'minor' branch. The inspector instructed them to wear plain clothes to gain the trust of women on the streets. The work prerequisites in Western Australia were the same as in the other states. The police hierarchy preferred women who had worked as nurses or with welfare organisations. Helen Dugdale was a former nurse and Laura Chipper had worked for fifteen years with the Salvation Army at their Perth Rescue Home. In her time at the rescue home, Laura had firsthand experience with the young women she would be required to police out on the streets: from runaway girls to streetwalkers and women caught in a cycle of offending and incarceration. Salvation Army volunteers and staff worked tirelessly to try to prevent repeat offenders from coming before the courts and being imprisoned again.

Esther Warden was one of the women the Salvation Army tried to save and she met Laura Chipper on a number of occasions, both at the rescue home and later when Laura was serving as a police officer. Esther was known as the 'terror' of the West End of Fremantle and had a lengthy record around Perth too. The Salvation Army tried numerous times to take Esther in and break her cycle of reoffending. Esther was having none of it and, as with the women Lillian Armfield resigned herself to being unable to help in Sydney, the Salvation Army couldn't do anything more for Esther. By the time of her death in November 1942, aged sixty-nine, Esther Warden had over 200 convictions.

From 1917 to 1939, the West Australian Women's Police consisted of, on average, around five female constables and never exceeded ten across the state. In the early years, Dugdale and Chipper kept detailed records of their work with women and children on the streets of Perth and Fremantle. In one annual report in June 1921, Constable Dugdale recorded her work in following up inquiries into female misconduct, neglected or destitute children, and cautioning women for drunkenness, immorality and vagrancy. Dugdale interviewed close to 400 women in her office and cautioned a further 171 girls and women. One of her main duties listed was helping women who had been found drunk in public.

Progress was slow in coming to the remaining federal, state and territory police jurisdictions. Women had to wait until 1931 for an opportunity to join the force in Queensland and even longer, 1961, in the Northern Territory. Women were introduced into the federal police force in 1947.

As women were steadily introduced into the various policing forces across the country, Lillian Armfield continued to focus on her job leading the Women's Police in New South Wales. She could now delegate work and train other women to be involved in major cases, as evidenced with the Pyjama Girl case. The work of the Women's Police, under Lillian's command, had come a long way since 1915 but Lillian wasn't about to let the 'experiment' falter with her tenure. She was a tough boss with high expectations of her staff. Earning her respect was no easy task, as Peg Fisher found out in the 1940s.

Peg Fisher worked for Army Investigations during World War II and at the close of the war decided to apply for the NSW Women's Police. Peg endured the parade in front of the senior male officers, and when she made it to Lillian Armfield it was just as hard. Lillian wanted only the toughest, most intelligent women working for her. Lillian's officers had to be mentally and physically strong, ready to handle all types on the job and wear criticism and mockery.

Peg was nervous meeting Lillian, having read about her in the newspapers and having followed her career for some time: 'I felt like a wet sponge. She was a very tall woman . . .' It wasn't just Lillian's height that caught Peg off guard; the meeting was a test in which Peg would be subjected to a tough grilling. Lillian shouted at Peg to 'Stand over there!' and gave her the once-over. She stared long and hard at Peg and then spoke slowly and clearly: 'If you're no good, I'll give you hell.' Peg was rooted to the spot, trying not to show nerves and fear. Lillian continued: 'The first time you bloody well do something to upset me, the first time you let me down, I'll kill you.' Peg held firm, knowing it was a test and would determine whether or not she got the job.

Lillian had investigated pimps, prostitutes, drug traffickers and sex offenders. She'd faced down the most notorious eastern Sydney gangsters and underworld leaders and had had to cope with seeing some of the worst of what life could offer on the streets. She couldn't work with other women who could not handle the realities of the job. She had to be hard on Peg on that first day and ensure she was up to everything a policing life could throw at her. If Lillian didn't test Peg's resolve, it could crumble on the streets, and the crooks would see it all unfold.

Chief Armfield was tough and expected the same from her constables. 'She swore like a trooper,' Peg recalled years later, and could hold her own in any of the criminal haunts about eastern Sydney. She was strong and intimidating when she needed to be and would pull rank to put someone in their place. Peg's experiences might well explain why Maude Rhodes clashed with Lillian in those early years. On one occasion, Lillian questioned Peg about why she never second-guessed or defied her orders. Peg dutifully answered that Lillian was the boss. She respected this and knew it was what drove Lillian through her many years in the job.

Peg Fisher passed the test and developed a close rapport with her boss. They worked on various cases together and Peg found Lillian 'terrific' to work with, once you had proven yourself worthy in the role. The pair were, according to Peg, 'married to their job' and it made them even better friends. Of all the women she worked with, it was Peg who Lillian relied on the most: 'if she needed the least little thing she'd send for me . . . it was always her and me together'.

Being 'married to the job' is a common description given about and by police officers. It was a crucial part of the personal sacrifice Lillian made when she joined in 1915. Going into the job, female police officers accepted that they had to remain unmarried, leave the job when they became married or apply for police work once they were widows. It could be a lonely life with a restricted personal identity outside of it.

When Peg Fisher joined the NSW Police Force in the 1940s, Lillian Armfield was living in a tiny room in Darlinghurst.

Though she had family in Sydney and in the Southern Highlands, she lived alone around days working shifts and amassing criminal investigations. Her friendship with Peg was important because, in Peg, Lillian found someone else who devoted just as much of herself to policing.

Lillian chose a number of police widows to work with her from the 1920s. Their experiences were different – they had married and some had children – but they knew the demands of police work from having supported family members in the role. Six of the eight women featured in the CIB photograph of 1938 were widows from police families. Officers Burton, Jeffrey, Ledger, Mooney, Mitchell and Rosser had either been raised by a father in the police force or married a police officer.

By the 1940s, the NSW Police Force extended the Women's Police to other districts across the state, beyond the city. Constables Jeffrey and Weaver were sent to Dubbo in 1941. By the end of the decade, over thirty women were stationed at different districts across the state.

As Chief of the Women's Police, Lillian attracted a considerable following in the press from reporters who had closely followed her career and wanted to share the unique aspects of her work. In a 1938 story titled 'Now We Know What Policewomen Do', the *Sun* gushed at meeting the police sergeant, but the reporter was a little surprised that she was not an 'Amazon', mythical women who were bigger and stronger than normal – as this was the expectation for a woman taking on an unconventional gender role. The reporter captured some of the essence of Lillian in a few short minutes: 'Behind those penetrating brown eyes, beyond that kindly smile, you find the realist.' For a woman who had avoided creating a prominent media profile for herself – staying true to the wishes of her first boss, Mitchell, in keeping a low profile – talking to the media from the 1930s was another way in which Lillian gained more recognition for the work of the Women's Police. Lillian was also mindful of how she would be remembered. By the 1940s, when she sat down to talk to Elisabeth Lambert from the *World's News*, Lillian was 'a tall, greying and elegant' woman but she had quite a story to tell about her interesting career.

It certainly was an interesting life policing Sydney's crime streets. Besides the runaway girls, fraudulent fortune-tellers and organised crime – enough in itself to keep anyone busy – Lillian policed a number of cases through the years that show the eclectic nature of policing work, including investigating vandalism of graves, jewel thefts, kidnappings and house-breakings.

One of the most fascinating housebreaking cases involved an unlikely young mother, Nettie Burnham. Nettie was described as one of the best housebreakers by well-seasoned detectives and was known to break in to second-storey places and take off quickly with the loot. The curious thing for Lillian was that Nettie was always caught for housebreaking while she was pregnant. The first time she was let off with a warning from the magistrate but two years later she was sent to prison when again pregnant. Nettie seemed to have an irrational urge to commit a burglary when pregnant. It might well have been, as Lillian initially suspected, that Nettie was trying to get more money to set up her family life. However, after the birth of each child, Nettie stayed home, looked after her children and did not commit any crimes. Lillian recognised that, during each pregnancy, something obviously changed in Nettie's mental health that induced her to commit burglaries.

Where once Lillian had feared the mob of locals who wanted to step in and take a runaway from her in Surry Hills, by the late 1940s policewomen were respected in the neighbourhoods they policed. Constable Peg Fisher didn't feel scared anymore in eastern Sydney: 'Even the prostitutes and no-hopers in Darlo would take my side if they saw me in trouble.' It's hard to imagine that happening without Lillian Armfield's tough and fair stance in the eastern Sydney crime lands through two world wars, the Razor Wars and the rise of organised crime.

From brothels and fortune-telling rooms to sly-grog shops and railway stations, Lillian investigated and raided addresses few would go into alone. In March 1947, however, she was invited to one of the finest addresses in the state. It was work-related but Lillian wasn't on the job that day. The NSW Governor, Lieutenant General John Northcott, requested Lillian's presence at a ceremony to recognise her service in the police force. Standing at Government House, supported by some of her male colleagues, Lillian was awarded the King's Police and Fire Service Medal for distinguished conduct.

This was the first time the award was presented to a woman anywhere in the Commonwealth. It was yet another first for Lillian Armfield.

News of Lillian's award made it back to Mittagong where, in the local newspapers, she was named as the 'sister of Jim Armfield of Mittagong and Miss Ruby Armfield of Bowral'. Lillian's star was great in Sydney but back where she came from, she was known by association with her family. In her unassuming manner, Lillian liked it this way. She had left Mittagong as a young woman pursuing a career in the city but her humble, hard-working and resilient life in the Southern Highlands of her younger years had guided her through one of the toughest careers.

Two years later, Lillian was sixty-five and had arthritis in her hands, which racked her with pain every day. Lillian's nephew Norm saw how painful and debilitating the condition was for her: 'It ran in the family. Her hands were like claws. All gnarly and bent.' She was frustrated by the arthritis and spent years covering it up as best she could, but the hands that had written down so many of Sydney's great crime notes and handled the toughest of underworld crooks had had enough. Lillian found it hard to give up the work that had defined her life for over three decades but she was unable to continue.

On 2 December 1949, Lillian Armfield retired from the police force after nearly thirty-five years of service. She had reached retirement age, which in itself was something of an achievement, having survived the Razor Wars and years of risky undercover work in 'darkest Sydney'. As she told a reporter a few years before her retirement, 'one of the under-world threatened to run me down. But so far no car has bumped me – much less killed me.'

Lillian's career and retirement were celebrated across the nation's leading newspapers. Referred to as a 'Gallant Woman' in one *Truth* piece, featuring a large photo of Lillian, she was the officer who had 'played a brave part in the police campaign against the razor-gangs'. In Adelaide the *Mail* reflected on a career in 'every branch of police work, from drab routine to murder investigations'. Lillian would be remembered, the newspapers said, for 'her work among women and girls, diverting and rescuing them from lives of crime and vice'.

As the tributes flowed and NSW police officers congrat-ulated one of their own, Lillian faced a financially unstable future. She left the Women's Police with no superannuation and was not eligible for a police pension. The NSW Police Force explained this was because Lillian had joined the police six months older than the cut-off age, making her ineligible for membership in the Police Force Pensions Fund. The Lord Mayor of Sydney, Alderman E.C. O'Dea, was appalled by this and formed a committee to raise funds for Lillian, hoping to give her enough money to live on beyond the old-age pension given to all pensioners. The fund had some support but not as much as the mayor had expected.

Lillian was not alone in being overlooked in her retirement. In November 1952, almost three years after Lillian's retire-ment, Adelaide's *Mail* newspaper included a short piece from Sydney highlighting a number of other women who had left public service jobs with little financial security. Matron Shaw of the Crown Street Women's Hospital retired after thirty years of working sixty-hour weeks. She had helped deliver more than 100,000 babies and was known as a 'protector of unmarried mothers'. She retired with only the money from a public fund which raised £1000.

For Lillian's family, her retirement reminded them of how she could be both celebrated and overlooked at the same time. She didn't have the same privileges as male officers and bore most of the uniform or ancillary costs. For her nephew Norm it was all 'through ridiculous male club pettiness' but 'Lillian earned her place' despite this.

In 1965, when Lillian was eighty, the NSW Government granted her a 'special pension in recognition of her services'. She received an extra pension from the state government but it was kept at a level that avoided her losing any of her Commonwealth pension. It was an important gesture but it came fifteen years after she had retired.

It was also in her elderly years that Lillian Armfield agreed to sit down and talk to journalist Vince Kelly for his forthcoming book on her policing career, *Rugged Angel*. She had been out of the force for over a decade and, with the passing of years and the value of hindsight, was able to look back on her career and consider what she would tell Kelly. Lillian knew his book would influence how people remembered her, and as an investigative journalist, Vince Kelly did his own research and included wider details around cases and experiences. He talked to former officers and looked through old newspaper reports and government records. For Kelly, Lillian was a 'rugged angel' and he shaped his story mainly around her policing career.

Because of Vince Kelly's interest in Lillian Armfield's career, we have a record of her recollections of her work and what it meant to her. Kelly brings the job to life through her eyes. Lillian is portrayed as the first policewoman and credited with so much of the early work of the Women's Police. We know Maude Rhodes joined at the same time and left late in 1919, four years after their appointment, but Maude mainly appears in the background in Kelly's Women's Police story. This isn't surprising, however. Lillian was asked to recall what the job had been like for her and so placed herself in the middle of the cases the Women's Police worked.

Vince Kelly's biography of Lillian, published in 1961, concludes with Lillian as a retired officer looking back on her career. Little attention is given to her private life. This is a reflection, too, of the manner in which Lillian separated her work from her family life. Earlier on in her career it was a matter of protection. During the violent years of the Razor Wars, she did not want to put her family in harm's way by revealing too much of her private life. Underworld crooks maintained their criminal empires through fear and retribution, and the police were not beyond this.

Though her policing career dominated so much of her life for close to forty years, Lillian was also a devoted daughter, sister and aunt. Her family provided her with the encouragement to achieve her policing career goals. At a time when there was a lack of opportunity for women to be able to get a career – particularly when it meant sacrificing getting married and having children and upholding traditional female roles within society – Lillian's family supported her unconventional pathway in life. It would not have been easy for her parents to watch their daughter leave their country home to work in an asylum and then take on even riskier work as a police officer. But throughout her career, the support from Lillian's family was unwavering. She was very close to her sisters, Muriel and Ruby, and lived with family for a short while later in her life.

Lillian's family supported her into retirement. Muriel's son Norm recalls visiting his aunt Lillian at a Norton Street house in Leichhardt before Lillian moved in with his family: 'I remember we built a room off the back of the house for her.' This was at Norm's parents' house at 16 Hampton Street, Hurstville Grove. There's a family photograph of the three sisters, taken after Lillian's retirement, in which they are posing for the shot. Their arms are locked and all have happy, warm smiles in each other's company. Their closeness is obvious.

Lillian's contributions to the wider community also didn't stop with her departure from the force. For Lillian's family, her work in the Women's Police was a reflection of the community-minded person she was in both her personal and professional lives. She helped out at fundraising stalls and local events around Sydney and in the country at Bowral, Berrima and Mittagong in her retirement years. Norm remembers his aunt as a person devoted to making life better for others and reaching out to the wider community:

> Her kindness to people, especially the downtrodden. Her toughness and resilience. She had such a hard time in a man's domain. Yet she stuck it out. Shows her commitment to improving the lives of so many.

Though she led a quiet life away from the public eye in her retirement years, Lillian kept in touch with her old workmates and liked to be updated about the careers of new women in the force. The first reunion of the Women's Police was held in July 1965 at the Police Club in Sydney. Over sixty ex-policewomen gathered to celebrate the fiftieth anniversary of the creation of the Women's Police. Eighty-year-old Lillian Armfield was there to look back on her long career and how far the police force had come since the introduction of two female constables in 1915.

Every year after her retirement, Lillian's old colleagues treated her to a cruise along Sydney Harbour for her birthday. Seated amid women who, like her, had experienced just how tough and rewarding the job could be, Lillian enjoyed the companionship. The day trips got harder as the pain from her arthritis became more debilitating over the years but she still appreciated the sentiment. Lillian was a tough but fair boss and, for this, the women who had worked for her respected her well after they needed to in the job.

Riddled with arthritis and trying to make ends meet without a full police pension or superannuation, Lillian

Armfield nevertheless proved to be the last woman standing from the women who'd dominated Sydney's organised crime wars of the 1920s and 1930s. She outlived Sydney's most famous female underworld figures, including Nellie Cameron, Kate Leigh and Tilly Devine.

Lillian had been quite taken with Nellie. Although Lillian thought Dulcie Markham was prettier, she didn't think Dulcie had 'the rare and curious indestructibility' of Nellie's beauty: 'she maintained her air of rather disdainful nonchalance, and she continued to queen it over men'. Nellie Cameron's life was short. She survived the most violent years of the Razor Wars, and carried the bullet wounds as evidence of just how hard it had been, but became depressed and reclusive from the late 1940s. In November 1953, she placed her head inside the oven of her Taylor Square apartment, and turned on the gas. She was just forty-one. With all the 'pomp and ceremony of a national celebrity', Nellie was taken into the chapel in Darlinghurst in a rose-covered coffin. She was farewelled by a thousand mourners including brothel madam Tilly Devine, who was overcome with grief for a woman she loved like a sister. Lillian Armfield was also there to farewell Nellie but thought the service was too dignified: 'Nellie would have been happy if there had been a brawl at her funeral, a real ding-dong affair in which a few would have been wiped out. That's the sort of funeral Nellie would have liked for herself. She was only forty-one, but she had lived up every day of it.'

Kate Leigh lived past the youthful Nellie Cameron and was still as tough as nails in the 1950s. In 1954, at the age of seventy-three, she was charged with assaulting a taxi driver and threatening another man. But, just as had happened throughout Kate's criminal career, there was always someone willing to take the blame. Electrical fitter Roy Fowler-Glover told the magistrate it was his fault Kate was enraged. Apparently he'd bought two bottles of beer from Kate's Devonshire Street house, only to find they contained water. Roy had headed back to Kate's place in a taxi and confronted 'Mum' – Leigh's affectionate sly-grog nickname – at the front door. Roy told the courtroom he thought it was one of Kate's 'coots' that had robbed him of his beer. He made the mistake of threatening to throw bottles through the front window of Kate's house. Kate ran inside, grabbed a rifle and came back out the front, pointing it at Roy and the taxi driver, and yelling, 'Get going, you mug, or I'll blow your brains out.' The two men bolted and the taxi driver made a complaint to police. When a detective questioned Kate, she replied, 'Wouldn't you take a gun to them? The mug was going to throw a bottle through my window.' On closer inspection, the detective found the gun was unloaded. Kate avoided a conviction for assault but was fined for sly-grog selling.

The tax department also came knocking. Kate Leigh pleaded poverty in the Bankruptcy Court in August 1954, saying: 'You could turn the place from Sydney to England and you would not find a penny piece belonging to me. I am stony broke.' The State Receiver wanted to take over her house at 212 Devonshire Street to pay her debts, which amounted to seven times her assets. Kate claimed she sold alcohol on the 'sly' but had 'gained nothing by it' in years. She reckoned police were the real money makers, raking in fines. When asked how she had paid back a large sum of money to the tax office, Leigh claimed it came from old friends. A few months later she was back in court and was told to pay back some of the money owed to the tax department. If she wasn't broke before, she was now.

Kate Leigh's time as the country's biggest sly-grog seller was well and truly over. In February 1955, the New South Wales government introduced a 10 pm closing time, effectively doing away with the 'six o'clock swill'. While the papers lamented that the liquor referendum had not been an 'earth-shaking clash between the beer-barons and wowsers', late closing was the final nail in the coffin for Kate's time as the wealthy sly-grogger of Surry Hills. The locals to whom Kate had supplied backdoor booze for many years could now purchase beer and other drinks in pubs later into the evening. 'Mum' had served them well but her business was no longer needed.

Kate Leigh aspired to be a community identity later in her life and liked to tell reporters that she had high morals, having never drunk alcohol, smoked or sold her body for sex. While magistrates would attest to Kate having never drunk alcohol or smoked, there's a question mark around whether she sold her body for sex. It is possible she prostituted herself in her younger years, especially when she was a single mother looking for work and trying to pay the rent. However, there is no conviction in Kate's criminal record relating to prostitution, making her claim more plausible.

Leigh retreated from public life in her last years, but remained close to her nephew William Beahan and other family around eastern Sydney. She rented out rooms in her Devonshire Street house to pay the bills as her health rapidly declined. A massive stroke ended one of the most successful criminal careers in Australian history. Kate took her last breath at the hospital that had been the scene of so many bloodied arrivals during the worst years of the Razor Wars. Huddled in a bed in St Vincent's, Darlinghurst, she died on 4 February 1964, one month shy of her eighty-third birthday.

As they had done a decade before for Nellie Cameron, a motley crew of ex-cons and young crooks turned out to bid farewell to one of Sydney's most famous underworld identities. They gathered with family members and neighbours to farewell Kate Leigh at St Peters Church on Devonshire Street, Surry Hills. Her coffin was taken into the church only metres from her home and former sly-grog shop. Some joked that Tilly Devine turned up just to check her old rival was really dead. Frail and thin – a shadow of her former self – Tilly sat down next to journalist Bill Jenkings and told him she was only there to sticky-beak. Police were in a forgiving and sentimental mood that day. Detectives and senior police overlooked the violent, cunning woman Kate had been in her youth to eulogise her as having 'another side to her life'. Former Deputy Commissioner of Police W.R. Lawrence told reporters: 'Certainly she had a criminal record, but she did all she could to help the needy and young offenders. She warned many of the youngsters about the futility of crime.' Kate Leigh had over a hundred convictions to her name but had redeemed herself in the eyes of the police through her 'matriarchal' identity in Surry Hills.

Lillian Armfield was also there to farewell Kate. Although the former underworld leader had mellowed in her later years, her morals could never have matched those of her former adversary. Lillian Armfield could never be bought.

The woman Lillian regarded as 'even more violent' than Kate Leigh, Tilly Devine, passed away in November 1970. She had suffered from chronic bronchitis for some twenty years but died of cancer. She was given full Catholic rites and buried under her married name of Matilda Mary Parsons. One patron at the Tradesman's Arms in Surry Hills proposed a toast, remembering it as one of Tilly's favourite drinking spots. No one else lifted a glass. In direct contrast to police descriptions of Kate Leigh on her death, Police Commissioner Norman Allan described Tilly as a 'villain'. Ron Saw, writing for the *Daily Telegraph*, labelled Tilly a 'vicious, grasping, high-priestess of savagery, venery, obscenity and whoredom'.

Like Kate Leigh's, Lillian Armfield's last years were the quietest of her life. The arthritis was unbearable and her tall, strong body was racked with pain. Her movements slowed and her body, frail and pained, became thin and brittle. Lillian needed professional care and moved into the Harold Hawkins Court Hostel for Senior Citizens in Leichhardt. Her days mainly revolved around visits from family and reading her favourite detective novels.

Family and former colleagues knew by the middle of 1971 that Lillian didn't have long to live. Word got around to Police Commissioner Norm Allan and he visited her with an offer to help out with her funeral. As frail as she appeared, her mind was as clear as ever and still conveyed the tough spirit that defined so much of her career. She told Commissioner Allan she didn't want a police funeral. She wanted a quiet family service and cremation.

Lillian Armfield died at Lewisham District Hospital on 26 August 1971. Later that evening, Commissioner Allan told the press: 'Her death has closed an era. She was a pioneer, a pathfinder for the present-day policewoman.' Allan also captured the essence of Lillian when he said: 'She was a gallant and very lovely woman.'

Australia's pioneering policewoman was farewelled by her closest family and friends at the Northern Suburbs Crematorium. Commissioner Allan honoured Lillian's request and didn't organise a police funeral. He did, however, send a police guard of honour as a mark of respect for her work.

Even in death, Lillian could not be separated from her beloved sister Muriel. Their ashes are next to each other at Bowral Cemetery. In the end, the woman who had created such an incredible career in the city, and was known across the country as the founding Chief of the Women's Police, travelled back in spirit to the Southern Highlands where it all started for her.

In a life spanning eighty-six years, Lillian Armfield still got one over eastern Sydney's warring underworld queens. She was three years older than Kate Leigh and sixteen years older than Tilly Devine when she died. With Lillian's death, as her friend Peg Fisher said of the death of Kate Leigh, 'a bit of good old Australian history' had also passed.

Lillian Armfield's policing career is a reflection of the person she was and the contributions she wanted to make to the wider community. Policing success is often measured in terms of results that equate to the volume of cases investigated and cleared, and the positive effects on the wider community. Lillian found hundreds of runaway girls by developing a daily routine that included a dawn patrol of the streets and close surveillance of arriving trains and rental accommodation. Given the task of investigating men and women believed to be fraudulent fortune-tellers, Lillian prosecuted dozens and earned herself a reputation as one of the toughest police officers in the state. She successfully investigated brothel madams and drug dealers, denting their businesses and putting some of the state's leading underworld leaders behind bars. She played an instrumental part in police crackdowns during the infamous Razor Wars and ensured eastern Sydney was a less violent place by the late 1940s than it had been two decades before. Newspaper reporters praised her police service, declaring it 'a good day for N.S.W.' when Lillian was appointed.

In over thirty years in the job, Lillian saw the worst of what people could do to themselves and each other but she was committed to making a difference in her community.

This was especially true of her dedication to the young women she policed and protected. In her own words:

> Some were vicious and dangerous. Some were just weak and easily led astray. The varying degrees of their wickedness made life for me always interesting, and often more than exciting, but I always felt that most of them had a chance at redemption and I tried to see that they got that chance.

A true measure of Lillian Armfield, however, is how she gauged her success as a police officer. For Lillian, trailblazing her way through the force, making a place within it for other women was important: 'I do honestly believe that the women police who carry on the work I pioneered are a wonderfully potent influence for good. I was very proud of them and am grateful for their help and loyalty. They are doing a grand job.' There was much for Lillian to be proud of in the early 1960s. There were now fifty women in the NSW Police Force and in 1961 the department made the decision to allow female officers to remain employed after marrying. The restrictive walls were starting to come down for women in the force.

Lillian Armfield battled against the unequal standards to create more opportunities for women like her who wanted to make a difference in the community through police work. Lillian holds a unique place in Australian policing history and, mainly through her own efforts, ensured a pathway was created for the women who followed her into the force.

A year after Lillian's death, women gained greater equality across the country. Gough Whitlam was elected prime minster and introduced a raft of social changes seeking equal pay for women, federal funding for women's health, refuge and crisis centres, and parental leave for Commonwealth employees. Prime Minister Whitlam also established a single mother's benefit and appointed a Woman's Adviser to the Prime Minister, the first of its kind in the world. Lillian's unequal working conditions and her fight for better social services and support for women were now part of a wider national campaign for social justice for Australian women.

Lillian Armfield's story reminds us, and hopefully inspires our children to see, that one person can really make a difference to the world around them. Be fierce, push the boundaries, aim high, and know that change often comes from someone having the commitment and tenacity to lead by example. Lillian led an extraordinary life. She may not have always seen it that way herself, believing she was merely doing her job, but her example – her legacy – has left a lasting impression on Australian policing history and allowed so many other women to follow in her shoes.

Epilogue: In Her Shoes

ON A CRISP, SUNNY DAY ON 3 SEPTEMBER 2015, SEVEN HUNDRED women took to the streets of Sydney. They marched from the Hyde Park Barracks through the inner-city streets, past State Parliament and along Macquarie Street to the Opera House. They stopped there at Circular Quay, stood to attention, and smiled for the cameras. Joined by the highest-ranking female officer, Deputy Commissioner Catherine Burn, they were gathered in their uniforms to celebrate the centenary of women in the NSW Police Force. The state's longest-serving female officer, Superintendent Doreen Cruickshank, was impressed with the celebrations and offered her own reflections on what female officers had achieved: 'The women came through the gates at Bourke Street with a notebook and the guys came out with their firearms.' One of Doreen's colleagues, Senior Constable Pam Amloh, also reflected on the achievements of women in the force: 'We're just the same as the boys.'

One hundred years beforehand, all Lillian Armfield could do was hope to set an example and pave the way for other women. The policing stories of the women who followed her reflect the changes that came through in the police service after Lillian's pioneering efforts, but also convey just how hard it has been for women to be accepted into what was, for many decades, a male world. It took perseverance, resilience and complete dedication to the job to ensure female officers would be counted alongside their male counterparts. These are some of their stories.

•

Amy Millgate was the first Australian woman appointed to the Traffic Police in 1947. Policing was a family affair for Amy. She was the daughter of a detective sergeant and the sister of two police officers, and went on to marry one herself – a man who would go on to become assistant police commissioner. At the age of sixteen, Amy joined the Women's Australian National Service and when war broke out she served two years in New Guinea before being discharged. When she arrived home she applied for a position in the NSW Police Force. Her detective sergeant father made the first introductions, setting up a meeting with Commissioner William MacKay, and asking him to consider her life experience despite the fact she was younger than the required twenty-five years for entry into the Women's Police. MacKay was a hard man to win over but he offered Amy the chance to prove herself. It started with making tea and toast for

MacKay and other senior officers. When Amy went home to complain to her father, he told her that she was the junior member and everyone started at the bottom.

Amy Millgate persisted and started working for Lillian Armfield in the dawn patrol that Lillian had introduced back in 1915. In her first years on the job in the late 1940s, Amy came to know Lillian well and found the Chief of the Women's Police was happy to share the knowledge she had acquired from decades of 5 am patrols and time spent getting to know women around eastern Sydney. Amy enjoyed the work, investigating 'with the boys from the Vice Squad, taking statements', but she had to learn the ropes very quickly about Sydney's streets: 'You had to learn the rules – you had to have tact, common sense, and not overdo it by speaking up too much and putting your foot in it.'

Amy met underworld leaders Tilly Devine and Kate Leigh outside a courtroom one day and was initially overcome, knowing exactly who they were: 'I nearly died.' Kate Leigh turned to Amy and said, 'Well, love . . . if you're half as good a copper as your old man is, you'll make a good one.'

An important part of Amy's work involved investigating young women living with American sailors stationed in Sydney during World War II. After the bombing of Pearl Harbor in December 1941 and Australian Prime Minister John Curtin's public acknowledgement that Australia would look to the United States for support in the region, naval and air bases were established to station US troops in Australia. Over 4000 US troops arrived in Brisbane from 22 December 1941 and continued to arrive in their thousands in Melbourne, Sydney and Fremantle in the following weeks and months. Some 2100 US servicemen arrived in Sydney in December 1941 alone. By the end of the war a staggering one million American servicemen had passed through Australia.

With a higher income than their Australian counter-parts, American servicemen spent more money in the cities but this also led to more alcohol being consumed in the pubs. A number of street brawls erupted in the major cities, including the notorious Battle of Brisbane where, over two nights, US and Australian troops rioted and fought in the pubs and streets.

The young women Lillian Armfield talked to during her patrols told her they found the Americans more glamorous and courteous than the Australian and British servicemen. Many of Sydney's teenagers and young women had only ever seen an American man in a Hollywood film, so when the US servicemen arrived with extra money to spend on dates and their 'exotic' appeal, the women quickly fell in love with them.

There was a darker side to the war romances. Lillian and her staff in the Women's Police were confronted with what Lillian called the 'ugly side of the war years on the home-front'. The involvement of young teenagers, sometimes aged thirteen or fourteen, was particularly worrying. Lillian and her officers, including Amy Millgate, often found American servicemen in bed with two teenagers at the same time. It was the job of the Women's Police to ensure teenage girls were not at risk of 'wrecking their own lives'.

One of the greatest risks was the spread of venereal diseases. Fears about this were raised in the press and in community and government health discussions. All of this had a direct impact on the work of the Women's Police. Amy Millgate later recalled:

> We'd find a girl in bed with a fella or trying to hide out on the tiny balcony. If she didn't meet the description of a missing person, or wasn't under age, we might let her go with a warning, a second chance. But she might be charged with having insufficient lawful means of support. Or with prostitution. VD wasn't rife then, but we had to stem it at the source. Our job was to protect women and children.

Despite the increased efforts of the Women's Police and detectives from the Vice Squad, business was also booming for streetwalkers and brothel madams during the war years. One special brothel was created above the Tradesman's Arms Hotel on Palmer Street, Darlinghurst, exclusively for African-American servicemen. At the time the White Australia Policy prevented non-white people from even entering the country so the Australian government had had to create a military order just to allow the servicemen in. Though they were allowed in to Australia, African-American servicemen were denied entry into some pubs and brothels. But Tilly Devine welcomed all the Americans into her establishments, arguing that she was adhering to government policy in supporting our new ally. She also profited from the boom in business.

When life settled back down after the war, Commissioner MacKay turned part of his attention to considering a police uniform for women. He had been consulting with police in London about their recent move to have female officers wearing a uniform to direct traffic. MacKay brought in the fourteen Women's Police constables and ran the idea past them, having already discussed this with their chief, Lillian Armfield. Amy Millgate and another officer were given the task of creating this new uniform and wearing it to direct traffic and give talks at schools. Amy thought creatively about how to create the uniform:

> I still had my Army tunic and skirt so I took it to the commonwealth clothing place for the tailor to have a look. I asked him to do the same in a navy blue with a shirt, collar and tie and stockings. They sent us to David Jones to buy two pairs of lace-up shoes as well. That's how it was that Gladys Johnson and I were chosen to trial the uniform for 12 months.

Amy Millgate and Gladys Johnson became the state's first uniformed policewomen.

Amy had to resign from the Women's Police when she married Bruce Taylor in 1951. Years later Amy was thanked for her service in the NSW Police Force and she has featured in a recent Justice and Police Museum exhibition. In her own humble manner, similar to that of her chief in the police, Amy has said that while we now talk about female officers as making history, 'I was just happy I was able to do something for my country and something for the job that I was in.'

Irene Rae, a police widow with years of service behind her, took over when Lillian Armfield retired as Chief of the Women's Police in 1949. Irene had worked closely with Lillian and had kept a relatively low profile, though she was regularly thanked by the police commissioner for her work as a detective sergeant and for leading the Women's Police.

Chief Rae was followed into the role by Margaret Jeffrey early in 1954 until her retirement in December 1956. While the transition from Armfield to Rae went largely unreported, Margaret Jeffrey captured considerable interest early on. The newspaper articles announcing her appointment are interesting. In one *Sun-Herald* article she is referred to as 'A good-looking, fair-haired grandmother', police widow and mother of a policeman. Even before we know anything of Margaret's suitability for the working role, she is identified in a matriarchal and motherly manner. Halfway down the article, the journalist finally reveals that the new Chief of the Women's Police has served for over twenty years in the force. In another shorter article in the *Sun*, Margaret is also identified as a police widow, mother and grandmother. She is publicly portrayed as the kind of motherly and firm character to look after young girls and women in need of protection and policing.

By the 1960s, conditions started to improve for women in the police. From 1964, women were entitled to superannuation and the Women's Police team had grown to over forty members. However, an important restriction remained. Promotion for female officers occurred under a separate system to that for men, leaving many women waiting much longer for a promotion compared with their male colleagues.

Irene Juergens joined the NSW Police Force in 1966, during the Swinging Sixties. She had long hair – a stark difference to the shorter, closely cropped styles of female officers in previous years – and wore a miniskirt outside of work. Expecting to have to leave if she married and had children, Irene made the best of the opportunities open to her. She spent six years mainly talking to schoolkids about road safety and walking the dawn patrol to protect young women. In 1971, Irene was crowned Miss Military Police and an accompanying newspaper story celebrated her win by referring to her as 'Constable 32-23-34'. The description wasn't welcome within the force and Irene was pleased to see some of the barriers were starting to come down. She was one of the first female officers to be formally licensed with a gun in 1979. Irene Juergens left the NSW Police Force in December 2012 as the longest-serving female officer at the time, with forty-three years behind her.

One of Australia's most well-known female police officers got her start in the NSW Police Force in 1972. Born in Manly in 1953, Christine Nixon was nineteen when she started the job and has said that she was a beneficiary of activism in the 1970s. She had grown up with some understanding of police work with her father, Ross Nixon, serving as an assistant police commissioner. Though her father objected to her joining the force, Christine became Women Police Constable number 173. She witnessed some important changes in policing after her initial appointment. Women were given handcuffs in 1975 but only twenty were selected to carry handguns. Sixty years after Lillian Armfield was appointed to the police, four women were included as part of a trial in 1975 that saw them appointed to general duties alongside male officers. For the first time in NSW policing history, female officers had been appointed to the broader force, beyond the Women's Police.

Christine reckons there were probably seventy men in the force for every woman back in 1972 when she started out. There were around 130 female officers and it still felt like they were 'something of a novelty'. The NSW Police Force was a 'proud, unapologetic, testosterone-fuelled culture', according to Christine, which she had to negotiate with 'dignity, femininity and strength'.

Like the women who had come before her, Christine Nixon was expected to direct traffic and give talks to schools, along with policing girls and women. Though women had been in the force for sixty years, there was still great resistance to their promotion. Six years after joining, in 1978, Christine applied to become a detective. She was turned down and given the option to pick up a rural policing spot or work with a colleague, John Avery, on a review of police education.

Women comprised 1.5 per cent of the police force in 1972. Ten years later this had risen to over five per cent and by 1991 doubled to over ten per cent. Despite this, however, less than five per cent of senior constables were women and a mere two per cent of officers promoted to superintendent were women. It was even more of an uphill battle when Christine was elected president of the women's branch of the NSW Police Association in 1974 and had to take on 'the resistant, blokey association hierarchy'. When Christine was sent to work at Darlinghurst Police Station with two other female officers in October 1976, the newspapers used the headline: 'The darlings of Darlo'. Suddenly it felt like not much had changed since Lillian Armfield joined in 1915.

There were other women like Christine Nixon who were also pushing for change. In 1981, Eileen Thompsett took a discrimination claim to the Anti-Discrimination Board after she was denied entry into the police force because she was married. Eileen was successful and the ban was finally lifted. Women were also included in the male seniority system from 1982.

After completing a Masters in Public Education at Harvard University, Christine Nixon returned to Sydney and began working on police reform with John Avery, who was now the NSW Police Commissioner. She worked tirelessly for better standards for women in the force, which often meant tackling the discrimination that continued within the culture of policing. As Christine has said:

> The occupational culture held that to carry out the tasks of policing you had to possess strength, bearing and self-confidence. These requirements and the culture fundamentally

excluded anyone less than five feet nine inches tall and lacking the required features. Those women who were allowed entry suffered as they still do from gender stereotyping.

Christine Nixon continued to work her way up the ranks and moved to policing in Victoria, becoming assistant commissioner. She was a career police officer so went where the opportunities presented. In 2001 she was appointed Australia's first female chief commissioner. Her greatest challenge came on 7 February 2009 when hundreds of bushfires raged across Victoria. Over 170 people were killed and over 400 injured as a result of the fires. Named Black Saturday, the bushfires put Christine Nixon directly into the public eye across the nation. She was criticised for her leadership style during the bushfires, with the media portraying her as taking a back seat while others worked to deal with the fires. Christine maintained she was leading by allowing her staff to do their jobs and lead the police and emergency efforts to contain the fires. It was a different leadership style and one in which Christine showed you don't have to lead in the same ways as others. However, it was not a popular approach during the devastating events of Black Saturday.

Before the bushfires Christine had announced that she would step down from the commissioner's job and she retired from the police service at the end of February 2009 to head the Victoria Bushfire Reconstruction and Recovery Authority. Since then she has become the Deputy Chancellor of Monash University and gives workshops on leadership and management.

One of Sydney's current top cops is a tough, tenacious and decorated officer from the western suburbs who barracks for the Parramatta Eels. Detective Superintendent Deborah Wallace has over thirty years of experience in the NSW Police Force. When she started out as a probationary constable at Blacktown in 1983, female officers had to initial all their reports with an 'F'. The meaning was obvious: there was a clear distinction between the work of male and female officers with less regard given to women investigating major crimes. Almost seventy years after the first policewomen were appointed, Deborah and the other female officers around her were still trying to convince their male counterparts that they could hold their own in 'the job'. On one of her first days at work, another, more experienced female officer told Deborah Wallace: 'Never lose your integrity or your femininity.'

Deborah learned the ropes quickly and knew if she got the job done, she would eventually be accepted and respected. She made her mark, becoming detective superintendent in the South East Asian Crime Squad, the Middle Eastern Organised Crime Squad (MEOCS) and the Gangs Squad. During her time with the MEOCS, Deborah and her team were responsible for disrupting the Brothers for Life gang who had been involved in a number of shootings in 2013. She has now set her sights on dismantling outlaw motorcycle gangs across Sydney.

Superintendent Wallace is straightforward in her approach to police work. Her job is to protect the wider community and bring criminals to justice. The arduous task of dismantling the bikie gangs doesn't faze her, though: 'They are just criminals and don't warrant any sort of special status.' While the 'darkness of human nature' continues to amaze Deborah, her tough, tenacious personality has allowed her to distance herself enough from her work to realise, 'you can't judge the rest of humanity by those who commit crimes'.

Deborah Wallace has earned her place as one of the state's finest police officers. She is the recipient of numerous awards and received the Police Medal in 2007 after twenty years' service. Wallace, however, maintains she has not done anything 'extraordinary'. She is simply doing her job.

Hundreds of other female police officers, like Deborah Wallace, have simply done their job and in doing so have achieved greater recognition for women as essential and equal within the police service. In the century since Lillian Armfield joined the NSW Police Force, they have all fought their own personal and professional battles to ensure women are pervasive in Australian policing.

In June 2016, Detective Superintendent Wallace travelled to the Southern Highlands of New South Wales to talk about her 'Life in Crime' at a luncheon organised by the Southern Highlands Business Women's Network. Deborah Wallace reflected on her journey from probationary constable to high-ranking officer in charge of investigating serious and organised crime. It is fitting, then, in light of Lillian Armfield's story, that Deborah Wallace's event was hosted at the Mittagong RSL.

The story of women in Australian policing is celebrated as starting in 1915. We might also like to think of it as beginning in 1884 with the birth of Lillian Armfield in Mittagong. It's hard to imagine now, all these years later, women being able to make a career for themselves in policing without the kind, elegant, tall and tough woman from Mittagong who read a job advertisement in a newspaper and thought she could make a difference in her community. Former Police Commissioner Christine Nixon, looking back on her policing career and life in her book, *Fair Cop,* has reflected on how the choices we make as individuals can have a profound effect on the society we live in. Christine joined the force half a century after Lillian Armfield and her words transfer well to Lillian's experiences and legacy. Lillian greatly affected the society in which she lived and allowed other women to follow on in her shoes as police officers.

Afterword

HISTORIANS LEARN EARLY ON IN THEIR PROFESSIONAL TRAINING
that the historical imagination is a powerful way in which
to connect with the stories being researched and told to a
wider audience. Two women have dominated my historical
imagination in the past few years. It started with Kate Leigh
and her notorious Sydney crime life and from retelling her
story I was drawn into Lillian Armfield's. Twentieth-century
Sydney, eastern Sydney in particular, has been brought to life
for me in ways that have allowed me to imagine what it would
have been like for Kate Leigh to run her criminal empire and
Lillian Armfield to police it, combined with the many other
aspects of her work in the Women's Police.

Having researched and closely considered Lillian's life and
work for the past few years, I thought I had a fair idea of who
she was and what she went through. However, during the
writing of this book a story surfaced that I had not expected.
It might provide further insight into Lillian's earlier life and

the depths of her empathy with the young women she policed. It could convey her emotional understanding of exactly what young women could go through at the hands of violent men. I share it here with permission from Lillian's nephew Norm.

Family photographs can reveal some interesting stories when we look beyond the familiar faces featured in them. There are a number of private family photographs from the early twentieth century that feature Lillian Armfield with her parents and siblings. Everyone in the photographs is accounted for, except for a girl who looks considerably younger than Lillian and her siblings. I have seen two of these photographs, taken around 1910 when Lillian was back visiting family in Mittagong. Lillian, by then in her mid-twenties, is seated in the centre of the image, flanked by her mother and father. Her siblings all stand behind – two brothers in the centre and a sister each on the left and right. The girl, younger than ten years old, is seated in front of Lillian, slightly to the left of her, and is dressed in her Sunday best with a ribbon in her hair. It almost looks as if Lillian has placed a hand on the girl's back, as if to get her ready for the photograph, keeping her still as you would do with a small child eager to run off.

The girl in this photograph, and others, is Pearl. One family story handed down from Lillian's sisters is that Pearl was Lillian's daughter. Lillian's nephew is unsure whether Pearl was the result of a failed romance or a sexual assault. Either way, there is suddenly another facet to Lillian's life. It is a deeply private story only known within the family.

In all the public records and in the retelling of her career, from newspaper reports and her interviews with the media, to Vince Kelly's *Rugged Angel*, Lillian is described as a single woman who devoted her life to her work. Her work in the asylum and then in the police precluded her from marrying and having children. This wasn't a problem for Lillian because she lived alone and didn't want to marry, and – in her moralistic work about Sydney – would not have wanted to have a child either. Marriage was one thing but a child born out of wedlock would have lost Lillian respect within the police force.

What if Pearl was kept secret to avoid Lillian being judged as a single mother and being sent off to a reformatory? What if Lillian was so intent on pursuing a professional career that she made the difficult decision to leave her daughter in the care of her parents? What if her work in Sydney, which brought her into contact with the worst of what society could offer, made her even more protective of her daughter so she kept her with family in country New South Wales?

Family stories are not always correct, as I have found in another recent book I've written relating to my husband's Straw family history. Events can be invented to suit a particular version of a person's life that sits best within the family memory. Pearl might have been confused with someone else. She could have been a cousin or a neighbourhood child who lived with the family at one point.

I couldn't find any record of Pearl having been born to Lillian Armfield. There is no birth certificate recorded for a child born as Pearl in Mittagong to Lillian. This doesn't mean she wasn't. Children born out of wedlock, particularly in the late nineteenth century, were tarnished with being illegitimate and could be adopted or brought up by married family members. Young single girls were sent off to reformatories or girls' homes to have their children in an institution, away from the prying eyes of the rest of society and the great shame this would bring to their families. While there was some acceptance of illegitimacy in very poor working-class communities, such as in the eastern Sydney neighbourhoods Lillian policed, single mothers were stigmatised right up until the 1970s and later. Having a child out of marriage almost always led to young women being labelled as sexually promiscuous. Little was said about the boys and men who had also contributed to the pregnancies.

It's not surprising, then, that in the small country town of Mittagong, regardless of the circumstances, Lillian's family might have covered up her pregnancy and not publicly and officially identified Pearl as Lillian's daughter.

Lillian might well have wanted to bring up her daughter but she may have had to work to support Pearl and her choice of career left no room for being a mother. Her long hours working in the asylum were in no way conducive to bringing up a child and one of the requirements of the Women's Police was that applicants were single. An unmarried mother applying for the job would have raised too many eyebrows, particularly when one of the main duties of female officers was to protect the morality of girls and young women in the inner-city streets. As the years passed by and she devoted more time to her work in the Women's Police, Lillian distanced herself more from Pearl. However, family members also state that Lillian sent money to Adelaide for many years, which they assumed was going to Pearl.

Does it matter if Lillian had a child?

Had the pregnancy been the result of a sexual assault, then Lillian would have understood how this felt when she talked to women on the streets of Sydney who had been assaulted. If so, Lillian's commitment to protecting women and ensuring she did her bit in keeping the city streets safe for them would take on a deeper, more personal meaning. Her concern for runaway girls being in harm's way would also be more intimate. Lillian worried about the young mothers at Kings Cross and became godmother to some of their children. Did she do this because of her own experience and with Pearl in mind?

If Lillian had been in a relationship and it failed, leaving her pregnant and then with a small child, it could better explain why some family members think she had a deep dislike of men. Or it could reveal a different side to Lillian's story as a young woman so intent on taking up a professional career that she left her child behind.

I could dismiss Pearl's parentage based on there being no written evidence to support a birth but an understanding of the society Lillian grew up and worked in tells us records were not always kept for illegitimate births. Dismissing Pearl as Lillian's daughter is also disregarding a family story. It is a family story that started with Lillian's sisters who were very close to her.

A question mark remains around whether or not the little girl in the Armfield family photographs was Lillian's daughter. Perhaps someone knows this same story or knew the Pearl featured in the photographs?

In exploring this publicly unknown and deeply personal part of Lillian's life, for me, the sacrifices she made to ensure women could work in the Australian police forces now take on even greater significance. One thing is certain: the gains Lillian made for herself and other women in police work came at a high personal cost.

Notes

Prologue

Botany May case

'Underworld Upheaval', *Truth* (Sydney), 26 November 1922, p. 5; 'A Drug
    Trafficker', *Lithgow Mercury*, 10 May 1928, p. 1; 'Impromptu Woman
    Searched for Cocaine', *Truth* (Sydney), 30 December 1928, p. 13; Vince
    Kelly, *Rugged Angel: The Amazing Career of Policewoman Lillian
    Armfield*, Angus & Robertson, Sydney, 1961, pp. 85–87; 'Apprehen-
    sions', *New South Wales Police Gazette*, 20 June 1928, p. 405, Archive
    CD Books Australia, digitised volume.

Chapter 1

Early Sydney and The Rocks

Grace Karskens, *The Rocks: Life in Early Sydney*, Melbourne University Press,
    Carlton South, 1997 (1998 paperback edition), pp. 1–17; Robert Hughes,
    The Fatal Shore, New York, Vintage Books, 1987; L.L. Robson, *The
    Convict Settlers of Australia*, Melbourne University Press, Carlton, 1994.

James and Elizabeth Ruse family history

'James Ruse', *Catholic Weekly*, 21 August 1952, p. 1; Penny Edwell, 'Lady
    Juliana', Dictionary of Sydney, accessed online 10 January 2016, <http://
    dictionaryofsydney.org/entry/lady_juliana#page=all&ref=note4>; B. H.
    Fletcher, 'Ruse, James (1759–1837), *Australian Dictionary of Biography*,
    National Centre of Biography, Australian National University, accessed
    online 25 January 2017, <http://adb.anu.edu.au/biography/ruse-
    james-2616>; Siân Rees, *The Floating Brothel: The Extraordinary Story
    of the* Lady Julian *and Its Cargo of Female Convicts Bound for Botany
    Bay*, Hodder Headline Australia, Sydney, 2001; Jan Kociumbas, *The
    Oxford History of Australia: Possessions 1770–1860*, Oxford University
    Press, South Melbourne, 1992 (reprinted 2004), pp. 32, 37–38.

Convicts and the NSW penal colony

Kay Daniels, *Convict Women*, Allen & Unwin, Crows Nest, 1998; Kociumbas,
    The Oxford History of Australia: Possessions 1770–1860, chapters 1
    and 2; Stuart Macintyre, *A Concise History of Australia*, Cambridge

University Press, 2004, chapters 2 and 3; Michael Sturma, *Vice in a Vicious Society: Crime and Convicts in Mid-Nineteenth Century New South Wales*, University of Queensland Press, St Lucia, 1983.

Samuel Marsden

A. T. Yarwood, 'Marsden, Samuel (1765–1838)', *Australian Dictionary of Biography*, National Centre of Biography, Australian National University, accessed online 11 January 2017, <http://adb.anu.edu.au/biography/marsden-samuel-2433>

Hawkesbury and thirty acres

Kociumbas, *The Oxford History of Australia: Possessions 1770–1860*, chapter 2; Macintyre, *A Concise History of Australia*, p. 40.

Dharug and frontier war

Sydney Gazette and New South Wales Advertiser, 17 June 1804, pp. 2–3; Grace Karskens, *The Colony: A History of Early Sydney*, Allen & Unwin, Crows Nest, 2009, pp. 482–3; Henry Reynolds, *The Other Side of the Frontier: Aboriginal resistance to the European invasion of Australia*, University of New South Wales Press, Sydney, 1982 (2006 edition); Henry Reynolds, *Forgotten War*, NewSouth Publishing, Sydney, 2013.

Ruse and Armfield genealogy

Armfield relatives have supplied family genealogical details that have been used in conjunction with family trees of Ancestry.com.au and the family history site, Geni, available online at <http://www.wgeni.com>. See, for example, the family trail from James Ruse, accessed online at <https://www.geni.com/people/James-Ruse/6000000002704496124>; NSW Government, 'History of the NSW Police Force – Significant Dates', NSW Police Force, accessed online 1 February 2017, <http://www.police.nsw.gov.au/about_us/history>

Convict birthstain

Babette Smith, *Australia's Birthstain: The Startling Legacy of the Convict Era*, Allen & Unwin, Crows Nest, 2008 (2009 edition).

Mittagong and Callan Park

NSW Government, Registry of Births, Deaths and Marriages (hereafter NSWBDM), 'Armfield, Lillian May', 16195/1885, reproduced birth certificate in possession of the author; NSWBDM, 'Armfield, George/Wright, Elizabeth', 3915/1882, reproduced marriage certificate in possession of the author; Personal communication with Norm and Eva O'Brien,

13 December 2016; 'Callan Park Asylum', *Sydney Mail*, 31 October 1891; Ben Pyke, 'Sydney's Shameful Asylums: The Silent Houses of Pain Where Inmates were Chained and Sadists Reigned', *Daily Telegraph,* 2 May 2015, accessed online 20 January 2017, <http://www.dailytelegraph.com. au/news/sydneys-shameful-asylums-the-silent-houses-of-pain-where-in-mates-were-chained-and-sadists-reigned/news-story/b4205dc9a17e8ee07 63711d93d720d04>; State Records Office New South Wales (hereafter SRNSW), 'Registers of Police 1913–1924', NRS 10945, 8/3259; 'Gossip from Sydney', *Goulburn Evening Penny*, 3 September 1915, p. 1.

Chapter 2

Rum Corps and early policing in New South Wales

James Morton and Susanna Lobez, *Bent: Australia's Crooked Cops*, Melbourne University Press, Carlton, 2014, chapter 2.

Police prerequisites

'Gossip from Sydney', *Goulburn Evening Penny*, 3 September 1915, p. 1; 'Women Apply to Join Police Force', *Barrier Miner* (Broken Hill), 12 June 1915, p. 5.

Constable Henry Chadban

National Archives Australia: First Australian Imperial Force Personnel Dossiers 1914–1920 (hereafter NAA AIF Personnel Dossiers), 'Chadban Henry: Service Number 2129', Statement of Service record, Series B2455, Item 3223612, accessed online 11 December 2016, <http://recordsearch.naa. gov.au/SearchNRetrieve/Interface/ViewImage.aspx?B=3223612>

Inspector-General James Mitchell

'Police Commissioner Mr Mitchell to Retire', *Narandera Argus and Riverina Advertiser*, 9 April 1929, p. 2; 'James Mitchell', *Australian Police*, accessed online 9 October 2016, <http://www.australianpolice.com.au/ nsw-police-history-index/police-commissioners-of-nsw/james-mitchell/>

Women's campaigns and first female appointments to the police

SRNSW, 'Registers of Police 1913–1924', NRS 10945, 8/3259; SRNSW, 'Registers of Police', NRS 10945, Reel 1974, 7/6213; SRNSW, 'Darlinghurst Gaol Photographic Description Book 1913–1914', NRS 2138, 3/6083; 'Women's Police', *Freeman's Journal*, 10 June 1915, p. 22; 'Policewomen Appointed. Two Pioneers in Sydney', *Sun* (Sydney), 24 June 1915, p. 7; 'The Feminine Touch. Sydney's Women's Police',

Daily Herald (Adelaide), 28 June 1915, p. 3; 'The Duties of Police-women', *Albury Banner and Wodonga Express*, 2 July 1915, p. 32; 'Women Police', *Armidale Chronicle* (NSW), 7 July 1915, p. 8; Kelly, *Rugged Angel*, pp. 8–11; Hazel King, 'Armfield, Lillian May (1884–1971)', *Australian Dictionary of Biography,* Australian National University, <http://adb.anu.edu.au/biography/armfield-lillian-may-5050>, accessed online 22 September 2016; 'Let's talk of Interesting People', *Australian Women's Weekly*, 17 November 1934, p. 3.

Peg Fisher on recruitment

Larry Writer interviewed Peg Fisher for his *Razor* book in the late 1990s, before Peg's death. During the course of the interviews, Peg revealed a great deal about her work in the Women's Police and her close friendship with Lillian Armfield. She asked to go by the pseudonym of Maggie Baker in the final publication. The quotations used here are taken directly from Larry's book, with his permission, and correspond exactly to the taped interview transcripts. See: Larry Writer, *Razor: Tilly Devine, Kate Leigh and the Razor Gangs*, Macmillan, Sydney, 2001 (2009 edition), pp. 242–246.

Risks to police lives

'The NSW Police Force. Annual Report', *Barrier Miner*, 20 June 1925, p. 6.

Women's Police assaulted

'Offences not otherwise described', *New South Wales Police Gazette*, 15 August 1917, p. 354, Archive CD Books Australia, digitised volume.

Police methods

'Helping the Helpless Forget: Life as Seen by Sydney's Smart Police Sergeant', *Arrow* (Sydney), 11 December 1931, p. 7.

Dawn patrol

'They're Proud of Lillian Down at Police H.Q.', *World's News* (Sydney), 2 March 1946, p. 3; Kelly, *Rugged Angel*, pp. 178–180; Kelly, *Rugged Angel*, p. 211.

Chapter 3

'They were looking for a runaway girl from Orange'

Kelly, *Rugged Angel*, pp. 28–33.

Eastern Sydney and crime

Christopher Keating, *Surry Hills: The City's Backyard*, Halstead Press, Ultimo, 2008, pp. 35, 53, 65, 74, 97; Anne O'Brien, *Poverty's Prison: The Poor in New South Wales 1880–1918*, Melbourne University Press, Carlton, 1988, p. 22; Phillip Knightley, *Australia: Biography of a Nation*, Jonathan Cape, London, 2000, p. 44; Ruth Park, *The Harp in the South*, Penguin Books, 1948 (reprinted 2009), p. 1; 'The Housing Problem', *Sydney Morning Herald*, 17 September 1912, p. 8; 'Housing Problem', *Daily Advertiser* (Wagga Wagga), 21 November 1918, p. 4; Writer, *Razor*, p. 7; *Townsville Daily Bulletin*, 5 February 1940, p. 10; *Sydney Morning Herald*, 12 September 1923, p. 14; Darcy Dugan with Michael Tatlow, *Bloodhouse*, HarperCollins, Sydney, 2012.

Albion Street Boys' Shelter

George Tarlington, *Street Kid: A Tale of Trouble and Survival Between the Wars*, Australian Military History Publications, Loftus, 2001, pp. 1–4.

Runaway girls

Robert van Krieken, 'State intervention, welfare and the social construction of girlhood in Australian history', TASA Sociology Conference, Flinders University, Adelaide, 10–13 December 1992, <ses.library.usyd.edu.au/bitstream/2123/902/1/Girlhood.pdf>; 'Danger to Girls', *Catholic Press*, 30 September 1915, p. 10.

White slavery

Raelene Frances, '"White Slaves" and White Australia: Prostitution and Australian Society', *Australian Feminist Studies*, vol. 19, no. 44 (July 2004), pp. 189–190; Raelene Frances, *Selling Sex: A Hidden History of Prostitution*, UNSW Press, Sydney, 2007, p. 140; Alana Piper, '"A growing vice": the *Truth* about Brisbane girls and drunkenness in the early twentieth century', *Journal of Australian Studies*, vol. 34, no. 4, 2010, p. 490; 'Boyd's Bagnio', *Truth*, 6 March 1921, p. 12.

Press stories, fears for young girls

'White Slavery. Ha! Ha!', *Truth* (Sydney), 21 December 1913, p. 7; 'Women Police', *Armidale Chronicle*, 7 July 1915, p. 8; 'Young Girl Missing', *Sunday Times* (Sydney), 24 January 1915, p. 2; 'Now We Know What Policewomen Do', *Sun* (Sydney), 18 August 1938, p. 30; Kelly, *Rugged Angel*, p. 176; 'Coroner Cannot Sheet Home Guilt', *The Gundagai Independent*, 23 May 1929, p. 3; 'Robert Mote's Family Tree', Ausigen.com, accessed online 15 January 2017, <http://www.ausigen.com/getperson. php?personID=I43298&tree=Ozigen>

Police Gazettes

'Missing Friends', *New South Wales Police Gazette,* 28 August 1918, p. 385, Archive CD Books Australia, digitised volume.

Sensational 1924 case

'Has Hunter-st, A White Slave Incubator?', *Truth* (Sydney), 20 July 1924, p. 13; 'White Slave Charge Fails', *Truth* (Sydney), 28 September 1924, p. 12; Kelly, *Rugged Angel,* pp. 118–120. Lillian told Vince Kelly the Lillian Howell case took place in 1919 but the records indicate it was 1924. In such a long policing career, Lillian may have mixed up dates in her recollections.

Metropolitan Girls' Shelter, Glebe

Christina Green, *The Life of Riley*, Parramatta Female Factory Precinct Memory Project, North Parramatta, 2014.

Stolen Generations

There are many personal stories, collections and histories of the Stolen Generations, some of which are available online, but the following two works provide a very good overview: Doreen Mellor and Anna Haebich (eds), *Many Voices: Reflections on Experiences of Indigenous Child Separation,* National Library of Australia, Canberra, 2002; Anna Haebich, *Broken Circles: Fragmenting Indigenous Families, 1800–2000,* Fremantle Arts Centre Press, Fremantle, 2000.

Esther Estler

'Apprehensions', *New South Wales Police Gazette,* 6 September 1916, p. 450.

Women's organisations and backlash

Ethel Turner letter to the editor, *Sydney Morning Herald,* 14 November 1917, p. 7; Kelly, *Rugged Angel,* pp. 11, 13–18, 27.

Mitchell's appeal to parents

'No White Slave Traffic', *Sydney Morning Herald,* 20 November 1920, p. 13.

Abortionists and Lillian on the work of the Women's Police

Peter N. Grabosky, *Sydney in Ferment: Crime, Dissent and Official Reaction 1788–1973,* Australian National University Press, Canberra, 1977, pp. 103–106; Kelly, *Rugged Angel,* pp. 210–212.

Chapter 4

Frank Fahy

Vince Kelly, *The Shadow: The Amazing Exploits of Frank Fahy*, Angus & Robertson, London, 1955, pp. 1–3, 5, 86; Norris Smith, 'The Shadow: An Undercover Pioneer', *Police Monthly*, April 2013, p. 23.

Fortune-telling history

Alana Piper, 'Women's Work: The Professionalisation and Policing of Fortune-Telling in Australia', *Labour History*, no. 108 (May 2015): 37–52; Circular from the Prime Minister's Office, 30 March 1917, Item 318941, Series 16855, Queensland State Archives.

Susie Simmons case

'Police and Prophets. Fortune-Tellers Convicted', *Sydney Morning Herald*, 25 August 1908, p. 7.

Young girl's suicide

Catholic Press (Sydney), 23 August 1902, p. 19.

Fortune-telling and war families

'Fortune-Tellers. Police to Take Action', *Sun* (Sydney), 7 May 1917, p. 2.

World War I

David Noonan, *Those We Forget: Recounting Australian Casualties of the First World War*, Melbourne University Publishing, Carlton, 2014, pp. 14–15; Alan Kramer, *Dynamic of Destruction: Culture and Mass Killing in the First World War*, Oxford University Press, Oxford, 2007, p. 251; 'The Australians' Landing', *Western Mail*, 18 June 1915, p. 20; Bill Gammage, *The Broken Years: Australian Soldiers in the Great War*, Australian National University Press, Canberra, 1974, pp. 156, 159, 235, 237; Les Carlyon, *The Great War*, Pan Macmillan, Sydney, 2006, p. 76; Joan Beaumont, *Broken Nation*, pp. 303–304, 389–392.

Corporal James Armfield

NAA AIF Personnel Dossiers, 'Armfield James: Service Number 2026', Statement of Service record, Series B2455, Item 3035188, accessed online 21 December 2016, <http://recordsearch.naa.gov.au/SearchNRetrieve/Interface/ViewImage.aspx?B=3035188>

Investigations

'Didn't Know a Detective', *Bathurst Times*, 28 May 1918, p. 4; 'Ferguson and Fortunes', *Truth* (Sydney), 14 August 1921, p. 12; 'A Clairvoyant Sent to Gaol', *Advertiser* (Adelaide), 13 August 1921, p. 10; 'P.C Sixtyfive', *Sun* (Sydney), 12 February 1918, p. 6; 'They're Proud of Lillian Down at Police H.Q.', *World's News* (Sydney), 2 March 1946, p. 3; Lillian's discussions about her policing work and use of notebooks have been compared with a June 2016 NSW Police Force Handbook available online at: <http://www.police.nsw.gov.au/__data/assets/pdf_file/0009/197469/NSW_Police_Handbook.pdf>, pp. 303–306; Kelly, *Rugged Angel*, pp. 196–200.

Undercover hats

'P.C Sixtyfive', *Sun* (Sydney), 12 February 1918, p. 6.

Young woman's suicide

'Fortune Told. Suicide Followed', *Sun* (Sydney), 2 March 1927, p. 16; 'Poisoned in Park', *Sydney Morning Herald*, 24 February 1927, p. 10.

Lillian reflecting on fortune-tellers

'Beware of Fortune-Tellers', *News* (Adelaide), 22 March 1950, p. 22; 'Helping the Helpless Forget: Life as Seen by Sydney's Smart Woman Police Sergeant', *Arrow* (Sydney), 11 December 1931, p. 7.

Sun *poem and article*

'P.C Sixtyfive', *Sun* (Sydney), 12 February 1918, p. 6.

Chapter 5

Park concerns

'Women Park Rangers', *Sydney Morning Herald*, 2 July 1915, p. 10.

Park violence

'Assaults on Women, Frequent in Sydney', *Riverina Herald* (Echuca), 15 May 1912, p. 4; 'Assaults on Women', *Daily Examiner* (Grafton), 11 June 1920, p. 2; 'Man Attacked in Moore Park', *Sydney Morning Herald*, 29 November 1920, p. 11.

Gangs

'Lust & Larrikinism', *Truth* (Sydney), 12 October 1913, p. 2; Melissa Bellanta, *Larrikins: A History*, University of Queensland Press, St Lucia, 2012, chapter 3; Kelly, *The Shadow*, chapter 12; 'Sydney bludgers', *Farmer and Settler*, 1 June 1915, p. 4; Alan Wright, *Organised Crime*, Routledge, London and New York, 2011 (first published 2006), pp. 29, 31, 41–42; Jacob Riis, *The Battle with the Slum*, Montclair, New Jersey, 1902; 'The Outrage Upon a Young Girl at Moore Park', *Sydney Morning Herald*, 13 September 1886, p. 4; Morton and Lobez, *Gangland Australia*, p. 15; Kelly, *Rugged Angel*, pp. 137–141.

Death of Constable Wolgast

'Constable Wolgast Dead', *Evening News* (Sydney), 21 January 1921, p. 8; 'Constable Wolgast Dead', *Newcastle Morning Herald and Miner's Advocate*, 22 January 1921, p. 6; 'Constable Wolgast. Public Funeral', *Sydney Morning Herald*, 24 January 1921, p. 10; 'His Last Post', *Sun* (Sydney), 21 January 1921, p. 8; 'Constable Wolgast's Death', *Barrier Miner*, 28 January 1921, p. 2; 'Rewards for the Detection of Crime', *Sunday Times* (Sydney), 30 January 1921, p. 1; 'Wolgast Murder. Centennial Park Practices', *Sun*, 10 February 1921, p. 7; 'Park Crime. Constable Wolgast's Death', *Sydney Morning Herald*, 11 February 1921, p. 10; Kelly, *Rugged Angel*, pp. 137–141. For a photograph of Charles Speechley see: Kelly, *Rugged Angel*, p. 85.

Lillian gaining respect of detectives

'They're Proud of Lillian Down at Police H.Q.', *World's News* (Sydney), p. 3.

Rogues Gallery

Between around 1910 and the 1960s the NSW police photographers took thousands of photographs of crime scenes, accidents, fires, police evidence and documents. Some 15,000 police and prison six-by-four–inch glass plate and acetate negatives were handed over to the Justice and Police Museum in Sydney in 1989. Working at the museum in the early 2000s, Peter Doyle began cataloguing thousands of negatives and over the course of a four-year research project discovered a window into Sydney's policing past that had been locked away for decades. Doyle's work, featured at the museum and in the photographic books *City of Shadows: Inner City Crime and Mayhem, 1912–1948* and *Crooks Like Us*, brings to life the mug shots that were a crucial part of NSW policing work at Lillian's time in the job. See: Peter Doyle, 'Public eye, private eye: Sydney police mug shots, 1912–193', *Scan Journal*, vol. 2, no. 3, December 2005, accessed online 2 January 2017, <http://scan.net.au/scan/journal/display.php?journal_id=67>; Peter Doyle, *City of Shadows: Sydney Police*

Photographs, 1912–1948, NSW Historic Houses Trust, Sydney, 2005; Peter Doyle, *Crooks Like Us*, Historic Houses Trust, Sydney, 2009; Kelly, *The Shadow*, pp. 1–5.

Chapter 6

Millie Sinclair

Kelly, *Rugged Angel*, pp. 170–174; 'Punched the Sergeant', *Sun* (Sydney), 30 July 1925, p. 12.

Prostitution background and history

Roberta Perkins, 'Control, regulation and legislation', chapter 2 in Roberta Perkins, *Working Girls: Prostitutes, Their Life and Social Control*, Australian Institute of Criminology, Canberra, 1991, <www.aic.gov.au/publications/previous series/lcj/1-20/working/chapter 2 control regulation and legislation.html>; Frances, *Selling Sex*, pp. 26, 31, 162; Emsley, *Crime and Society in England, 1750–1900*, p. 79; Nina Auerbach, 'The rise of the fallen woman', *Nineteenth-Century Fiction*, vol. 35, no. 1, 1980, p. 34; Emsley, *Crime and Society in England, 1750–1900*, p. 97; Jill Julius Matthews, *Good & Mad Women: The Historical Construction of Femininity in Twentieth-Century Australia*, Allen & Unwin, North Sydney, 1984 (1992 edition), pp. 125, 127; Lucy Bland, '"Purifying" the public world: feminist vigilantes in late Victorian England', *Women's History Review*, vol. 1, no. 3, 1992, p. 407; Daniels, *Convict Women*, p. 209; NSW Legislative Assembly, 'Select committee into the condition of the working classes of the metropolis', *Votes and Proceedings*, vol. 4, 1854–60, p. 68; Judith Walkowitz, *Prostitution and Victorian Society: Women, Class and the State*, Cambridge University Press, Cambridge, 2001 (first published 1980), p. 13; Havelock Ellis, *The Criminal*, Walter Scott, London, 1890, p. 218; 'Sydney's Worst Slum Area is Owned by City Council', *Sunday Times* (Sydney), 15 May 1927, p. 1; Paula Bartley, *Prostitution: Prevention and Reform in England, 1860–1914*, Routledge, London, 2000, p. 1; G.O. Ferguson, letter to *The West Australian*, 16 February 1918, p. 8; *The West Australian*, Monday 4 September 1899, p. 6; Kathleen Barry, *Female Sexual Slavery*, Prentice Hall, New Jersey, 1979, p. 283; Roger Matthews, *Prostitution, Politics & Policy*, p. 39; Chris McConville, 'The location of Melbourne's prostitutes', *Historical Studies*, vol. 19, no. 74 (1980), p. 90; Sharyn L. Anleu, *Deviance, Conformity & Control*, Pearson, Frenchs Forest, 2006, p. 198; 'Darkest Sydney', *Manilla Express*, 20 September 1902, p. 2;

'Immorality in Sydney', *The Braidwood Dispatch and Mining Journal*,
29 March 1905, p. 4.

Regulating prostitution, call girls and brothels

Frances, *Selling Sex*, pp. 134–135, 155, 244–47; Grabosky, *Sydney in
Ferment*, p. 126; Alfred W. McCoy, *Drug Traffic: Narcotics and Organ-
ised Crime in Australia*, Harper & Row, Sydney, 1980, p. 138; Judith A.
Allen, *Sex and Secrets: Crimes Involving Australian Women Since 1880*,
Oxford University Press, Oxford, 1990, pp. 73, 93–94, 174, 177; Kelly,
Rugged Angel, pp. 65, 67; 'Plea for Chastity', *Sunday Times* (Sydney),
6 November 1927, p. 5; Jeannine Baker, interview with her grandmother,
Mary Baker, 18 April 1998, transcript given to the author; George H.
Johnston, 'Vice Drives Girls into Depravity, Poverty', *Sun* (Sydney),
16 June 1949, p. 3; Personal communication with Norm and Eva
O'Brien, 13 December 2016.

Bua investigation

'"All Wrong." Man Denies Allegations', *Sun* (Sydney), 31 January 1930, p. 11;
James Morton and Susanna Lobez, *Gangland Australia: Colonial Criminals to the Carlton Crew*, Melbourne University Press, Carlton, p. 60;
'Has Hunter-st, A White Slave Incubator?', *Truth* (Sydney), 20 July 1924,
p. 13; 'White Slave Charge Fails', *Truth* (Sydney), 28 September 1924,
p. 12; Kelly, *Rugged Angel*, pp. 103–106, 118–121.

Tilly Devine

SRNSW, State Penitentiary for Women, Long Bay, 'Photograph Descrip-
tion Book 1910–1930', 'Matilda Devine', NRS 2496, No. 659, 3/6007;
SRNSW, State Penitentiary for Women, Long Bay, 'Photograph Descrip-
tion Book 1930–1970', 'Kate Leigh', NRS 2497, No. 155/92; Catie
Gilchrist, 'Tilly Devine', Dictionary of Sydney, accessed online 27 January
2017, <http://dictionaryofsydney.org/entry/tilly_devine>; Kay Saunders,
Notorious Australian Women, HarperCollins, Sydney, 2011, chapter 14;
Judith Allen and Baiba Irving, 'Devine, Matilda Mary (Tilly)', *Australian
Dictionary of Biography*, National Centre of Biography, Australian
National University, accessed online 29 January 2017, <http://adb.
anu.edu.au/biography/devine-matilda-mary-tilly-5970>; 'Tilly Devine'
National Advocate, 27 May 1925, p. 2; 'Tilly Devine's Shoe Hits
Constable', *Evening News* (Sydney), 22 April 1925, p. 7; 'Says Tilly to
Kate. Underworld Hymn of Hate', *Truth* (Sydney), 29 June 1930, p. 15;

'Husband Charged', *Sydney Morning Herald*, 10 January 1931, p. 8; *Daily Mirror* (Sydney), 24 November 1970, p. 9; Kelly, *Rugged Angel*, pp. 191–192; Writer, *Razor*, chapters 3, 12 and 18; Original police and court records are included in the following newspaper article online: Lucy Mae Beer, 'Chilling mugshots of the razor gang queens who ruled Sydney in the 1920s as they battled to control the criminal underworld – and their dirty deeds revealed in detail for the first time', *Daily Mail Australia* published online for Daily Mail UK, accessed 27 January 2017, <http://www.dailymail.co.uk/news/article-3607042/Photos-emerge-Tilly-Devine-Kate-Leigh-controlled-1920s-Razor-gangs-Sydney.html>

Kate Leigh sitting on Tilly Devine

This story was told to me by a local one day as I sat outside a Palmer Street house in Darlinghurst. I have heard different versions of this story, and while some of the details vary, the part about Kate Leigh sitting on top of Tilly Devine features in them all. Peg Fisher was the constable Devine attacked. See: Writer, *Razor*, p. 244.

Inside the brothels

Frances, *Selling Sex*, p. 219; Dugan and Tatlow, *Bloodhouse*, p. 26.

Prostitutes and the community

Kelly, *Rugged Angel*, p. 65; 'Plea for Chastity', *Sunday Times* (Sydney), 6 November 1927, p. 5.

Nellie Cameron

'Nellie's Emotions', *Arrow* (Sydney), 4 December 1931, p. 1; 'Death of Notorious Underworld Blonde', *Examiner* (Launceston), 10 November 1953, p. 4; 'Underworld Mourns Sydney "Queen"', *Advertiser* (Adelaide), 11 November 1953, p. 1; George Blaikie, *Wild Women of Sydney*, Rigby, Adelaide, 1980, pp. 181–82; 'Gangster's Girl of the City's "Lead Age"', *Sun-Herald* (Sydney), 15 November 1953, p. 88; Kelly, *Rugged Angel*, pp. 40, 42–43, 168–169, 191–192, 211; Writer, *Razor*, pp. 102–108.

Dulcie Markham

'"Curse" Strikes Again', *Sunday Mail* (Brisbane), 30 September 1951, p. 2; 'A Limping Blonde Who Lied for Her License', *Truth* (Sydney), 7 February 1954, p. 13; Blaikie, *Wild Women of Sydney*, pp. 183–199; Kelly, *Rugged Angel*, pp. 167–168.

'His nickname leaves little doubt . . .'

'"Midnight Raper" Stalks Sydney Again', *Arrow* (Sydney), 11 December
1931, p. 6; 'Man Charged with Murder of "Midnight Raider"', *Canberra
Times*, 29 December 1948, p. 2; 'Found Guilty of Murder', *Courier-
Mail* (Brisbane), 9 February 1949, p. 3; 'The Razor Gangs', *Truth*,
13 November 1949, p. 32; Kelly, *Rugged Angel*, p. 166; Writer, *Razor*,
pp. 61–63.

'sordid life'

'Helping the Helpless Forget: Life as Seen by Sydney's Smart Woman Police
Sergeant', *Arrow* (Sydney), 11 December 1931, p. 7.

Chapter 7

Kate Leigh cocaine raid

'Cocaine Raid', *Sydney Morning Herald*, 2 July 1930, p. 14; Kelly, *Rugged
Angel,* p. 191.

Kate Leigh back history

SRNSW, State Penitentiary for Women, Long Bay, 'Photograph Description
Book 1930–1970', 'Kate Leigh', NRS 2497, No. 839, 14/3137; Leigh
Straw, *The Worst Woman in Sydney: The Life and Crimes of Kate Leigh*,
NewSouth Books, Sydney, 2016; 'Says She Shot in Defence of Crown
Witness', *Truth* (Sydney), 30 March 1930, p. 13.

Opium dens

'Sydney Opium Dens', *Sunday Times*, 9 October 1904, p. 1; Kelly, *Rugged
Angel*, pp. 11, 46–54.

Kate Leigh and opium

'Whose Opium', *Sydney Morning Herald*, 12 January 1910.

First police raids and Charles Passmore

'Customs Raid. Opium and Cocaine Seized', *Sydney Morning Herald*,
28 August 1925, p. 9; 'Opium Raid', *Tweed Daily*, 7 August 1925, p. 3;
Kelly, *Rugged Angel*, p. 191; Writer, *Razor*, p. 36; 'Court Story of Daring
Daylight Raid', *Truth* (Sydney), 29 September 1929, p. 16; 'Court of
Criminal Appeal', *Sydney Morning Herald*, 8 March 1930, p. 14.

Cocaine ruining young lives

Kelly, *Rugged Angel*, pp. 129–130.

NOTES

Dell Hutton and other women

Kelly, *Rugged Angel*, pp. 130–131; 'A Cocaine Victim', *Dubbo Liberal and Macquarie Advocate*, 18 June 1929, p. 1.

Police crackdowns

'Drug Victims. The Curse of Cocaine', *Sydney Morning Herald*, 17 December 1921, p. 7; 'Cocaine Menace', *Sydney Morning Herald*, 10 April 1928, p. 101; 'Cocaine Runner', *Sydney Morning Herald*, 21 September 1929, p. 14; McCoy, *Drug Traffic*, pp. 121–122; 'The Blame', *Truth*, 26 June 1927, p. 1.

Increased police powers

NSW Government, *Police Offences Amendment (Drugs) Act*, reproduced online, accessed 12 February 2017, <http://www.legislation.nsw.gov.au/acts/1927-7.pdf>

William Mackay

Frank Cain, 'MacKay, William John (1885–1948)', *Australian Dictionary of Biography*, National Centre of Biography, Australian National University, <http://adb.anu.edu.au/biography/mackay-william-john-7381/text12829>, accessed online 30 August 2015; Kelly, *The Shadow*, pp. 202–203; 'House of Thieves?', *Truth* (Sydney), 29 January 1928, p. 8; 'Crowd of 700 Armed with Stakes Like Javelins, Says C.I.B Chief', *Evening News* (Sydney), 20 August 1929, p. 7.

Razor and gang violence

'60 Stitches', *Truth* (Sydney), 18 December 1927, p. 16; 'Mr Mitchell Asks for 200 More Police', *Sunday Times* (Sydney), 11 March 1928, p. 6; 'Gang War', *Sydney Morning Herald*, 19 July 1929, p. 13; 'Gang Feud', *Argus* (Melbourne), 10 August 1929, p. 25; 'Gang War. Women Involved', *Sydney Morning Herald*, 12 November 1929, p. 11; 'Man Shot Dead in City Last Night', *Truth* (Sydney), 10 November 1929, p. 20; 'Man Shot Dead', *Sydney Morning Herald*, 11 November 1929, p. 11; Writer, *Razor*, pp. 92–94, 113–114; Kelly, *Rugged Angel*, pp. 150–155.

Consorting

'Sydney's Policewoman. The Sterling Work of Lillian Armfield', *Truth* (Sydney), 25 March 1928, p. 12; 'New Crimes Act', *Evening News* (Sydney), 23 December 1929, p. 9; SRNSW, State Penitentiary for Women, Long Bay, 'Photograph Description Book 1930–1970', 'Nellie Cameron', NRS 2497, No. 792, 14/3137.

Devine and Leigh rivalry

'Says Tilly to Kate. Underworld Hymn of Hate', *Truth* (Sydney), 29 June 1930,
p. 15; 'Into Cells Again. Kate Leigh Shrieked at Judge', *Truth* (Sydney),
12 October 1930, p. 1; Blaikie, *Wild Women of Sydney*, p. 131; 'Kate
Didn't Like Being Classed with Tilly', *Mirror* (Perth), 27 March 1943,
p. 12; 'Notes from the City', *Scone Advocate*, 9 January 1948, p. 3;
Hal Baker, interview with the author, 16 August 2013; 'Kate Leigh Gets
6 Months' Gaol Term on Sly-grog Charge', *Truth* (Sydney), 21 March
1943, p. 11; '"Not British Justice," Says Counsel to S.M. in Sly Grog
Case', *Truth* (Sydney), 7 February 1943, p. 19; 'Study in Scarlet: An
Uncrowned Queen of Slumland Drips with Diamonds and Charity',
People (Sydney), 15 March 1950, p. 14.

Awkward 'truce' photographs

Fairfax Syndication Photos, 'Sydney crime figures and former rivals, Kate Leigh
and Tilly Devine, photographed on 20 August 1948', accessed online
30 March 2017, <http://consumer.fairfaxsyndication.com/C.aspx?VP3=Sear-
chResult&VBID=2ITP1GQBFSELM&SMLS=1&RW=1440&RH=776>

Kate Leigh's Christmas parties

'Xmas Party for Children', *Truth* (Sydney), 15 December 1946, p. 59; 'Study
in Scarlet', *People*, 15 March 1950, p. 13; 'Sydney underworld figure
Kate Leigh, at left, with Father Christmas, 5 January 1948', *Sydney
Morning Herald*, 5 January 1948, Fairfax Syndication, <professional.
fairfaxsyndication.com/archive/Sydney-underworld-figure-Kate-Leigh,-
2F3XC5NR2M6D.html>; 'Notes from the city', *Scone Advocate*,
9 January 1948, p. 3.

Detective Wickham on Kate Leigh

'Kate Storms in Court', *Truth*, 3 August 1930, p. 15.

Chapter 8

Lillian's sister Muriel

Information from Lillian's nephew Norm.

Homicide investigations

Charlie Bezzina, *The Job: Fighting Crime from the Frontline*, Slattery Media
Group, Docklands, 2010, chapter 12; Allan B. Smythe, *Homicide
Investigations: Criminal Justice, Law Enforcement and Corrections*, Nova
Science Publishers, 2009; Nick Petersen, 'Neighbourhood context and

unsolved murders: the social ecology of homicide investigations', *Policing and Society: An International Journal of Research and Policy*, 2015, DOI: 10.1080/10439463.2015.1063629; Fiona Brookman and Martin Innes, 'The problem of success: What is a "good" homicide investigation?', *Policing and Society*, 2013, DOI: 10.1080/10439463.2013.771538.

The Pyjama Girl case

'Brutal Crime. Girl Battered to Death', *Queensland Times*, 3 September 1934, p. 7; 'Baffled! Pyjama Girl Deadlock', *Truth* (Sydney), 21 October 1934, p. 20; 'Hold a Coroner's Inquiry!', *Truth* (Sydney), 26 September 1937, p. 16; 'Pyjama Girl Muddle', *Truth* (Sydney), 11 April 1943, p. 14; 'Sydney Detective Says Case of Pyjama Girl May Yet Be Solved', *News* (Adelaide), 10 December 1938, p. 2; Sue Doyle, 'The pyjama girl', *Journal of Australian Studies* (vol. 24, no. 64), 2000, pp. 34–42; Richard Evans, *The Pyjama Girl Mystery: A True Story of Murder, Obsession and Lies*, Scribe Publications, Melbourne, 2004. Richard Evans' book is based on his PhD research and uses a wide variety of police, court and newspaper records. His sources have been cross-checked and I am indebted to his work for creating an exemplary overview of the case up to the recent popular representations and continuing myths associated with the murder.

Connie McGuire murder

Lillian Armfield recalls this case in Kelly, *Rugged Angel*, chapter 28. See also: 'Dead Brunette was "Bookworm"', *Truth* (Sydney), 18 September 1949, p. 51; 'Tale of Three Spent Bullets and Death', *Truth* (Sydney), 23 October 1949, p. 10; 'Said Thanks to Judge for Death Sentence', *Truth* (Sydney), 16 April 1950, p. 6.

Chapter 9

Arrow *feature article*

'Helping the Helpless Forget: Life as Seen by Sydney's Smart Woman Police Sergeant', *Arrow* (Sydney), 11 December 1931, p. 7.

NSW *Women's Police photograph*

Historic Houses Trust NSW, 'NSW policewomen working in the Criminal Investigation Branch, Sydney, 1938 / photographer unknown', Justice and Police Museum, JP87/148, Record 46540, accessed online 12 December 2016 at <http://collection.hht.net.au/firsthhtpictures/fullRecordPicture.jsp?recnoListAttr=recnoList&recno=46540>.

Peg Fisher
Writer, *Razor*, pp. 242–246.

Women's Police in other Australian states
Tim Prenzler, *100 Years of Women Police in Australia*, Australian Academic
Press, Samford Valley, 2015, pp. 3–27; Leonie Stella, 'Policing Women:
Women's Police in Western Australia 1917–1943', Honours thesis,
Murdoch University, 1990, pp. 7, 22, 50, 58, 68–69, 120–122, 244–246,
251–252; Leigh Straw, *Drunks, Pests and Harlots: Criminal Women in
Perth and Fremantle, 1900–1938*, Humming Earth, Kilkerran, 2015.

Sun *article on Lillian*
'Now We Know What Policewomen Do', *Sun* (Sydney), p. 30.

Nettie Burnham
Kelly, *Rugged Angel*, pp. 70–75.

King's Medal
'Mittagong Police-Woman Makes History', *Southern Mail*, 28 March 1947, p. 3.

Retirement
'A Gallant Woman', *Truth*, 13 November 1949, p. 32; 'Policewoman Retires
After 34 Years' Duty', *Truth* (Sydney), 4 December 1949, p. 7; 'Woman
Police Officer Retires', *National Advocate*, 3 December 1949, p. 1;
'Gossip', *Townsville Daily Bulletin*, 6 December 1949, p. 6; 'Service
Gets Ill Reward', *Mail* (Adelaide), 8 November 1952, p. 16; 'Founder's
Pension', *The Canberra Times*, 12 August 1965, p. 13; 'Personal News
Flashes', *Western Herald* (Bourke), 30 July 1965, p. 1.

Nellie Cameron's death
'Nellie's Emotions', *Arrow* (Sydney), 4 December 1931, p. 1; 'Death of
Notorious Underworld Blonde', *Examiner* (Launceston), 10 November
1953, p. 4; 'Underworld Mourns Sydney "Queen"', *Advertiser* (Adelaide),
11 November 1953, p. 1; Blaikie, *Wild Women of Sydney*, pp. 181–82.

Kate Leigh's final years
'The Bloom Has Gone Off Sly Grog, Kate says', *Truth* (Sydney), 8 August
1954, p. 12; 'Kate Leigh in Form from Witness Box', *Cootamundra
Herald*, 15 October 1954, p. 1; Tanja Luckins, 'Pigs, hogs and Aussie
blokes: the emergence of the term "six o'clock swill"', *History Australia*,
vol. 4, no. 1, 2007, p. 12; 'Time Gents! . . . For a Word on Beer', *Truth*

(Sydney), 7 November 1954, p. 7; *Sydney Morning Herald*, 6 February 1964, p. 5; Bill Jenkings, *As Crime Goes By . . . The Life and Times of 'Bondi' Bill Jenkings*, Ironbark Press, Randwick, 1992, p. 132; *Sydney Morning Herald*, 6 February 1964, p. 5.

Lillian's death

Sydney Morning Herald, 27 August 1971, p. 2; Hazel King, 'Armfield, Lillian May (1884–1971)', *Australian Dictionary of Biography*, Australian National University, <http://adb.anu.edu.au/biography/armfield-lillian-may-5050>, accessed online 22 September 2016; Personal communication with Norm and Eva O'Brien, 13 December 2016.

Reflecting back on her career

'Sydney's Policewoman. The Sterling Work of Lillian Armfield', *Truth* (Sydney), 25 March 1928, p. 12; Kelly, *Rugged Angel*, pp. 10, 211–212.

Epilogue

100 years of women policing

Nicole Chettle, 'Women in police mark 100 years since entering the force parade through Sydney', *ABC News*, accessed online 7 December 2016, <http://www.abc.net.au/news/2015-09-03/parade-through-sydney-marks-100-years-since-women-joined-force/6747520>

Amy Millgate

Amy Taylor (nee Millgate) was included as part of the Justice and Police Museum's exhibition *The Force: 150 years of NSW Police*, curated by Anna Cossu. Amy was also interviewed by the press and Police Legacy about her work. See: Julia Ridulfo, 'Tailor made for policing', *Police Monthly*, June 2015, pp. 18–20, accessed online 2 April 2017, <http://www.police.nsw.gov.au/__data/assets/pdf_file/0006/353499/WIP-Millgate.pdf>; Steve Meacham, 'Pioneer Policewoman Whose Virtue was Vice', *Sydney Morning Herald*, 12 May 2012, accessed online March 2016, <http://www.smh.com.au/nsw/pioneer-policewoman-whose-virtue-was-vice-20120511-1yi2u.html>

US servicemen and World War II

Kate Darian-Smith, *On the Homefront: Melbourne in Wartime, 1939–45*, 2nd edn, Melbourne University Press, Carlton, 2009; John Hammond Moore, *Over-sexed, Over-paid and Over Here: Americans in Australia 1941–1945*, University of Queensland Press, St Lucia, 1981; Kelly, *Rugged Angel*, chapter 32.

Chief Margaret Jeffrey

'Chief of the Women Police. Grandma's New Job', *Sun-Herald* (Sydney),
14 March 1954, p. 7.

Irene Juergens

Geesche Jacobsen, 'Inspector legs it after 43 packed years', *Sydney Morning
Herald*, 12 December 2009, accessed online 24 March 2017,
<http://www.smh.com.au/national/inspector-legs-it-after-43-packed-years-
20091211-koke.html>

Christine Nixon

Christine Nixon and Jo Chandler, *Fair Cop*, Melbourne University Press,
Melbourne, 2011; Christine Nixon, 'The History of Women in
the Police Service', in Patricia Weiser Easteal and Sandra McKillip
(eds), *Women and the Law: proceedings of a conference held 24–26
September 1991*, Australian Institute of Criminology, Canberra, January
1993, pp. 225–228; Judith Smart and Shurlee Swain (eds), 'Nixon,
Christine', *The Encyclopedia of Women and Leadership in Twentieth-Century Australia*, Australian Women's Archives Project, accessed
online 2 February 2017, <http://www.womenaustralia.info/leaders/biogs/
WLE0714b.htm>

Deborah Wallace

'The Gang Buster', *Sydney Morning Herald*, 30 May 2010, accessed online
4 October 2016, <http://www.smh.com.au/nsw/the-gang-buster-
20100529-wmbk.html>; 'Don't try to Ms around with our top cop,
Detective Superintendent Debbie Wallace', *Daily Telegraph*, 14 February
2014, accessed online 4 October 2016, <http://www.dailytelegraph.
com.au/news/nsw/dont-try-to-ms-around-with-our-top-cop-detective-
superintendent-debbie-wallace/story-fni0cx12-1226826552301>; 'My
Life of Crime – A Luncheon with Deb Wallace', Southern Highlands
Business Women's Network, talk promotion details accessed online
4 October 2016, <http://www.bwnsh.com/events/my-life-of-crime-
a-luncheon-with-deb-wallace/> For other interesting and inspiring
stories see: NSW Government, NSW Police Force, 'Women of the
NSW Police Force', accessed online 24 March 2017, <http://www.
police.nsw.gov.au/about_us/100th_anniversary_of_women_in_policing/
women_of_the_nsw_police_force>

Bibliography

Newspapers

Advertiser (Adelaide)
Albury Banner and Wodonga Express
Armidale Chronicle
Arrow (Sydney)
Australian Women's Weekly
Barrier Miner (Broken Hill)
Bathurst Times
Braidwood Dispatch and Mining
    Journal
Canberra Times
Catholic Press
Catholic Weekly
Cootamundra Herald
Courier-Mail (Brisbane)
Daily Advertiser (Wagga Wagga)
Daily Examiner (Grafton)
Daily Herald (Adelaide)
Daily Telegraph (Sydney)
Dubbo Liberal and Macquarie
    Advocate
Evening News (Sydney)
Examiner (Launceston)
Freeman's Journal
Goulburn Evening Penny
Gundagai Independent
Lithgow Mercury
Mail (Adelaide)

Manilla Express
Mirror (Perth)
Narandera Argus and Riverina
    Advertiser
National Advocate
Newcastle Morning Herald and
    Miner's Advocate
Queensland Times
Riverina Herald (Echuca)
Scone Advocate
Southern Mail
Sun (Sydney)
Sun-Herald (Sydney)
Sunday Mail (Brisbane)
Sunday Times (Sydney)
Sydney Gazette and New South
    Wales Advertiser
Sydney Mail
Sydney Morning Herald
Townsville Daily Bulletin
Truth (Sydney)
Tweed Daily
West Australian
Western Herald (Bourke)
Western Mail
World's News (Sydney)

National Archives of Australia

National Archives of Australia: First Australian Imperial Force Personnel
    Dossiers 1914–1920, 'Armfield James: Service Number 2026', Statement
    of Service record, Series B2455, Item 3035188, accessed online
    21 December 2016, <http://recordsearch.naa.gov.au/SearchNRetrieve/
    Interface/ViewImage.aspx?B=3035188>

National Archives Australia: First Australian Imperial Force Personnel Dossiers 1914–1920, 'Chadban Henry: Service Number 2129', Statement of Service record, Series B2455, Item 3223612, accessed online 11 December 2016, <http://recordsearch.naa.gov.au/SearchNRetrieve/Interface/ViewImage.aspx?B=3223612>

Police Gazette Archives
New South Wales Police Gazettes, 1900–1940, 405, Archive CD Books Australia, digitised volumes.

Queensland State Archives
Circular from the Prime Minister's Office, 30 March 1917, Item 318941, Series 16855.

Registry of Births, Deaths and Marriages, New South Wales
New South Wales Government, Registry of Births, Deaths and Marriages, 'Armfield, Lillian May', 16195/1885, reproduced birth certificate in possession of the author.
New South Wales Government, Registry of Births, Deaths and Marriages, 'Armfield, George/Wright, Elizabeth', 3915/1882, reproduced marriage certificate in possession of the author.

State Records New South Wales
'Darlinghurst Gaol Photographic Description Books, November 1897–July 1914', NRS 2138, SR Reels 5102–5117.
'Registers of Police 1913–1924', NRS 10945, 7/6213, 8/3259.
NSW Legislative Assembly, 'Select committee into the condition of the working classes of the metropolis', *Votes and Proceedings*, vol. 4, 1854–60, p. 68.
State Penitentiary for Women, Long Bay, 'Photograph Description Book 1930–1970', 'Kate Leigh', NRS 2497, No. 155/92.
State Penitentiary for Women, Long Bay, 'Photograph Description Book 1930–1970', 'Kate Leigh', NRS 2497, No. 839, 14/3137.
State Penitentiary for Women, Long Bay, 'Photograph Description Book 1910–1930', 'Matilda Devine', NRS 2496, No. 659, 3/6007.
State Penitentiary for Women, Long Bay, 'Photograph Description Book 1930–1970', 'Nellie Cameron', NRS 2497, No. 792, 14/3137.

Interviews and transcripts
Some of the content in this book has been informed by my conversations over the years with locals in Darlinghurst and Surry Hills.

Baker, Hal, interview, 16 August 2013.

Baker, Jeannine, interview with her grandmother, Mary Baker, 18 April 1998, transcript given to the author.

Beahan, Mark, several conversations, June–December 2015.

City of Sydney Oral History Project, interview with Richard Mewjork, 12 September 2011, available online at <http://www.sydneyoralhistories.com.au/?s=surry+hills>, accessed 1 July 2015.

O'Brien, Norm and Eva, Personal communications, November 2016 – September 2017.

Writer, Larry, various conversations, July 2016 – September 2017.

Books

Allen, Judith A., *Sex and Secrets: Crimes Involving Australian Women Since 1880*, Oxford University Press, Oxford, 1990.

Anleu, Sharyn L., *Deviance, Conformity & Control*, Pearson, Frenchs Forest, 2006.

Barry, Kathleen, *Female Sexual Slavery*, Prentice Hall, New Jersey, 1979.

Bartley, Paula, *Prostitution: Prevention and Reform in England, 1860–1914*, Routledge, London, 2000.

Beaumont, Joan, *Broken Nation: Australians in the Great War*, Allen & Unwin, Sydney, 2013.

Bellanta, Melissa, *Larrikins: A History*, University of Queensland Press, St Lucia, 2012.

Bezzina, Charlie, *The Job: Fighting Crime from the Frontline*, Slattery Media Group, Docklands, 2010.

Blaikie, George, *Wild Women of Sydney*, Rigby, Adelaide, 1980.

Carlyon, Les, *The Great War*, Pan Macmillan, Sydney, 2006.

Daniels, Kay, *Convict Women*, Allen & Unwin, Crows Nest, 1998.

Darian-Smith, Kate, *On the Homefront: Melbourne in Wartime, 1939–45*, 2nd edn, Melbourne University Press, Carlton, 2009.

Doyle, Peter, *City of Shadows: Sydney Police Photographs, 1912–1948*, NSW Historic Houses Trust, Sydney, 2005.

——, *Crooks Like Us*, Historic Houses Trust, Sydney, c2009.

Dugan, Darcy with Michael Tatlow, *Bloodhouse*, HarperCollins, Sydney, 2012.

Ellis, Havelock, *The Criminal*, Walter Scott, London, 1890.

Evans, Richard, *The Pyjama Girl Mystery: A True Story of Murder, Obsession and Lies*, Scribe Publications, Melbourne, 2004.

Frances, Raelene, *Selling Sex: A Hidden History of Prostitution*, UNSW Press, Sydney, 2007.

Grabosky, Peter N., *Sydney in Ferment: Crime, Dissent and Official Reaction 1788–1973*, Australian National University Press, Canberra, 1977.

Green, Christina, *The Life of Riley*, Parramatta Female Factory Precinct Memory Project, North Parramatta, 2014.

Haebich, Anna, *Broken Circles: Fragmenting Indigenous Families, 1800–2000*, Fremantle Arts Centre Press, Fremantle, 2000.

Hughes, Robert, *The Fatal Shore*, New York, Vintage Books, 1987.

Jenkings, Bill, *As Crime Goes By . . . The Life and Times of 'Bondi' Bill Jenkings*, Ironbark Press, Randwick, 1992.

Karskens, Grace, *The Colony: A History of Early Sydney*, Allen & Unwin, Crows Nest, 2009.

——, *The Rocks: Life in Early Sydney*, Melbourne University Press, Carlton South, 1997 (1998 paperback edition).

Keating, Christopher, *Surry Hills: The City's Backyard*, Halstead Press, Ultimo, 2008.

Kelly, Vince, *Rugged Angel: The Amazing Career of Policewoman Lillian Armfield*, Angus & Robertson, Sydney, 1961.

——, *The Shadow: The Amazing Exploits of Frank Fahy*, Angus & Robertson, London, 1955.

Knightley, Phillip, *Australia: Biography of a Nation*, Jonathan Cape, London, 2000.

Kociumbas, Jan, *The Oxford History of Australia: Possessions 1770–1860*, Oxford University Press, South Melbourne, 1992 (reprinted 2004).

Kramer, Alan, *Dynamic of Destruction: Culture and Mass Killing in the First World War*, Oxford University Press, Oxford, 2007.

Macintyre, Stuart, *A Concise History of Australia*, Cambridge University Press, 2004.

Matthews, Jill Julius, *Good & Mad Women: The Historical Construction of Femininity in Twentieth-Century Australia*, Allen & Unwin, North Sydney, 1984 (1992 edition).

McCoy, Alfred W., *Drug Traffic: Narcotics and Organised Crime in Australia*, Harper & Row, Sydney, 1980.

Mellor, Doreen and Anna Haebich (eds), *Many Voices: Reflections on Experiences of Indigenous Child Separation*, National Library of Australia, Canberra, 2002.

Moore, John Hammond, *Over-sexed, Over-paid and Over Here: Americans in Australia 1941–1945*, University of Queensland Press, St Lucia, 1981.

Morton, James and Susanna Lobez, *Bent: Australia's Crooked Cops*, Melbourne University Press, Carlton, 2014.

Noble, Tom, *Walsh Street: The Cold-Blooded Killings That Shocked Australia*, Victory Books, Carlton, 1991 (2010 edition).

Noonan, David, *Those We Forget: Recounting Australian Casualties of the First World War*, Melbourne University Publishing, Carlton, 2014.

O'Brien, Anne, *Poverty's Prison: The Poor in New South Wales 1880–1918*, Melbourne University Press, Carlton, 1988.

Park, Ruth, *The Harp in the South*, Penguin Books, 1948 (reprinted 2009).

Prenzler, Tim, *100 Years of Women Police in Australia*, Australian Academic Press, Samford Valley, 2015.

Rees, Siân, *The Floating Brothel: The Extraordinary Story of the Lady Julian and Its Cargo of Female Convicts Bound for Botany Bay*, Hodder Headline Australia, Sydney, 2001.

Reynolds, Henry, *The Other Side of the Frontier: Aboriginal Resistance to the European Invasion of Australia*, University of New South Wales Press, Sydney, 1982 (2006 edition).

——, *Forgotten War*, NewSouth Publishing, Sydney, 2013.

Riis, Jacob, *The Battle with the Slum*, Montclair, New Jersey, 1902.

Robson, L.L., *The Convict Settlers of Australia*, Melbourne University Press, Carlton, 1994.

Saunders, Kay, *Notorious Australian Women*, HarperCollins, Sydney, 2011.

Smith, Babette, *Australia's Birthstain: The Startling Legacy of the Convict Era*, Allen & Unwin, Crows Nest, 2008 (2009 edition).

Smythe, Allan B., *Homicide Investigations: Criminal Justice, Law Enforcement and Corrections*, Nova Science Publishers, 2009.

Straw, Leigh, *Drunks, Pests and Harlots: Criminal Women in Perth and Fremantle, 1900–1938*, Humming Earth, Kilkerran, 2015.

——, *The Worst Woman in Sydney: The Life and Crimes of Kate Leigh*, NewSouth Books, Sydney, 2016.

Sturma, Michael, *Vice in a Vicious Society: Crime and Convicts in Mid-Nineteenth Century New South Wales*, University of Queensland Press, St Lucia, 1983.

Tarlington, George, *Street Kid: A Tale of Trouble and Survival Between the Wars*, Australian Military History Publications, Loftus, 2001.

Walkowitz, Judith, *Prostitution and Victorian Society: Women, Class and the State*, Cambridge University Press, Cambridge, 2001 (first published 1980).

Wright, Alan, *Organised Crime*, Routledge, London and New York, 2011 (first published 2006).

Writer, *Razor: Tilly Devine, Kate Leigh and the Razor Gangs*, Macmillan, Sydney, 2001 (2009 edition).

Journal articles

Auerbach, Nina, 'The rise of the fallen woman', *Nineteenth-Century Fiction*, vol. 35, no. 1, 1980, p. 34.

Bellanta, Melissa, 'The larrikin girl', *Journal of Australian Studies*, vol. 34, no. 4, 2010, pp. 499–512.

Bland, Lucy, '"Purifying" the public world: feminist vigilantes in late Victorian England', *Women's History Review*, vol. 1, no. 3, 1992, pp. 397–412.

Bodington, G.F., 'On the control and restraint of habitual drunkards', *The British Medical Journal*, 28 August 1875, pp. 255–256.

Doyle, Peter, 'Public eye, private eye: Sydney police mug shots, 1912–193', *Scan Journal*, vol. 2, no. 3, December 2005, accessed online 2 January 2017, <http://scan.net.au/scan/journal/display.php?journal_id=67>

Doyle, Sue, 'The pyjama girl', *Journal of Australian Studies*, vol. 24, no. 64, 2000, pp. 34–42.

Frances, Raelene, '"White slaves" and White Australia: prostitution and Australian society', *Australian Feminist Studies*, vol. 19, no. 44, July 2004, pp. 189–190.

Luckins, Tanja, '"Satan finds some mischief"?: drinkers' responses to the six o'clock closing of pubs in Australia, 1910s–1930s', *Journal of Australian Studies*, vol. 32, no. 3, 2008, pp. 295–307.

——, 'Pigs, hogs and Aussie blokes: the emergence of the term "six o'clock swill"', *History Australia*, vol. 4, no. 1, 2007, pp. 1–17.

McConville, Chris, 'The location of Melbourne's prostitutes', *Historical Studies*, vol. 19, no. 74, 1980, p. 90.

Nixon, Christine, 'The history of women in the police service', in Patricia Weiser Easteal and Sandra McKillip (eds), *Women and the Law: proceedings of a conference held 24–26 September 1991*, Australian Institute of Criminology, Canberra, January 1993.

Phillips, Walter, '"Six o'clock swill": the introduction of early closing of hotel bars in Australia', *Historical Studies*, vol. 19, no. 75, 1980, p. 261.

Piper, Alana, '"A growing vice": the *Truth* about Brisbane girls and drunkenness in the early twentieth century", *Journal of Australian Studies*, vol. 34, no. 4, 2010, pp. 485–497.

——'Women's work: the professionalisation and policing of fortune-telling in Australia', *Labour History*, no. 108, May 2015, pp. 37–52.

Smith, Norris, 'The shadow: an undercover pioneer', *Police Monthly*, April 2013.

Tennent, Margaret, '"Magdalens and moral imbeciles": Women's homes in nineteenth-century New Zealand', *Women's Studies International Forum*, vol. 9, no.s 5–6, 1986, pp. 491–502.

Williams, Marise, 'The gender politics of *Underbelly: Razor*', *Southerly*, vol. 17, no. 2, 2012, pp. 9–22.

Online Resources

Allen, Judith and Baiba Irving, 'Devine, Matilda Mary (Tilly)', *Australian Dictionary of Biography*, National Centre of Biography, Australian National University, accessed online 29 January 2017, <http://adb.anu. edu.au/biography/devine-matilda-mary-tilly-5970>

Australian Police, 'James Mitchell', accessed online 9 October 2016, <http://www.australianpolice.com.au/nsw-police-history-index/ police-commissioners-of-nsw/james-mitchell/>

Brookman, Fiona and Martin Innes, 'The problem of success: What is a "good" homicide investigation?', *Policing and Society*, 2013, DOI: 10.1080/10439463.2013.771538.

Cain, Frank, 'MacKay, William John (1885–1948)', *Australian Dictionary of Biography*, National Centre of Biography, Australian National University, published first in hardcopy 1986, accessed online 30 August 2015, <http://adb.anu.edu.au/biography/mackay-william-john-7381/text12829>

Charlwood, Sam, 'Inside a highway patrol car: The technology fitted to every NSW Police Force vehicle', *Drive*, 12 November 2015, accessed online 5 January 2017, <http://www.drive.com.au/motor-news/ inside-a-highway-patrol-car-the-technology-fitted-to-every-nsw-police- force-vehicle-20151111-gkwu1m.html>

Chettle, Nicole, 'Women in police mark 100 years since entering the force parade through Sydney', *ABC News*, accessed online 7 December 2016, <http://www.abc.net.au/news/2015-09-03/parade-through-sydney- marks-100-years-since-women-joined-force/6747520>

'Don't try to Ms around with our top cop, Detective Superintendent Debbie Wallace', *Daily Telegraph*, 14 February 2014, accessed online 4 October 2016, <http://www.dailytelegraph.com.au/news/nsw/dont-try-to-ms- around-with-our-top-cop-detective-superintendent-debbie-wallace/ story-fni0cx12-1226826552301>

Edwell, Penny, 'Lady Juliana', Dictionary of Sydney, accessed online 10 January 2016, <http://dictionaryofsydney.org/entry/ lady_juliana#page=all&ref=note4>

Fairfax Syndication Photos, 'Sydney crime figures and former rivals, Kate Leigh and Tilly Devine, photographed on 20 August 1948', accessed online 30 March 2017, <http://consumer.fairfaxsyndication.com/C. aspx?VP3=SearchResult&VBID=2ITP1GQBFSELM&SMLS=1&R- W=1440&RH=776>

Family History for James Ruse, Geni, accessed online 1 November 2016, <https://www.geni.com/people/James-Ruse/6000000002704496124>

Fletcher, B.H., 'Ruse, James (1759–1837), *Australian Dictionary of Biography*, National Centre of Biography, Australian National University, accessed online 25 January 2017, <http://adb.anu.edu.au/biography/ruse-james-2616>

Gilchrist, Catie, 'Tilly Devine', Dictionary of Sydney, accessed online 27 January 2017, <http://dictionaryofsydney.org/entry/tilly_devine>

Jacobsen, Geesche, 'Inspector legs it after 43 packed years', *Sydney Morning Herald*, 12 December 2009, accessed online 24 March 2017, <http://www.smh.com.au/national/inspector-legs-it-after-43-packed-years-20091211-koke.html>

King, Hazel, 'Armfield, Lillian May (1884–1971)', *Australian Dictionary of Biography*, Australian National University, accessed online 22 September 2016, <http://adb.anu.edu.au/biography/armfield-lillian-may-5050>

Historic Houses Trust NSW, 'NSW policewomen working in the Criminal Investigation Branch, Sydney, 1938 / photographer unknown', Justice and Police Museum, JP87/148, Record 46540, accessed online 12 December 2016 at <http://collection.hht.net.au/firsthhtpictures/fullRecordPicture.jsp?recnoListAttr=recnoList&recno=46540>

Mae Beer, Lucy, 'Chilling mugshots of the razor gang queens who ruled Sydney in the 1920s as they battled to control the criminal underworld – and their dirty deeds revealed in detail for the first time', *Daily Mail Australia* published online for Daily Mail UK, accessed 27 January 2017, <http://www.dailymail.co.uk/news/article-3607042/Photos-emerge-Tilly-Devine-Kate-Leigh-controlled-1920s-Razor-gangs-Sydney.html>

Meacham, Steve, 'Pioneer Policewoman whose virtue was vice', *Sydney Morning Herald*, 12 May 2012, accessed online March 2016, <http://www.smh.com.au/nsw/pioneer-policewoman-whose-virtue-was-vice-20120511-1yi2u.html>

'My Life of Crime – A Luncheon with Deb Wallace', Southern Highlands Business Women's Network, talk promotion details accessed online 4 October 2016, <http://www.bwnsh.com/events/my-life-of-crime-a-luncheon-with-deb-wallace/>

NSW Government, *Police Offences Amendment (Drugs) Act*, reproduced online, accessed 12 February 2017, <http://www.legislation.nsw.gov.au/acts/1927-7.pdf>

NSW Government, 'History of the NSW Police Force – Significant Dates', NSW Police Force, accessed online 1 February 2017, <http://www.police.nsw.gov.au/about_us/history>

NSW Government, NSW Police Force, 'Women of the NSW Police Force', accessed online 24 March 2017, <http://www.police. nsw.gov.au/about_us/100th_anniversary_of_women_in_policing/ women_of_the_nsw_police_force>

Perkins, Roberta, 'Control, regulation and legislation', chapter 2 in Roberta Perkins, *Working Girls: Prostitutes, Their Life and Social Control*, Australian Institute of Criminology, Canberra, 1991, <www.aic.gov.au/ publications/previous series/lcj/1-20/working/chapter 2 control regulation and legislation.html>

Petersen, Nick, 'Neighbourhood context and unsolved murders: the social ecology of homicide investigations', *Policing and Society: An International Journal of Research and Policy*, 2015, DOI: 10.1080/10439463.2015.1063629.

Ridulfo, Julia, 'Tailor Made for Policing', *Police Monthly*, June 2015, pp. 18–20, accessed online 2 April 2017, <http://www.police.nsw.gov. au/__data/assets/pdf_file/0006/353499/WIP-Millgate.pdf>

'Robert Mote's Family Tree', Ausigen.com, accessed online 15 January 2017, <http://www.ausigen.com/getperson. php?personID=I43298&tree=Ozigen>

Smart, Judith and Shurlee Swain (eds), 'Nixon, Christine', *The Encyclopedia of Women and Leadership in Twentieth-Century Australia*, Australian Women's Archives Project, accessed online 2 February 2017, <http://www. womenaustralia.info/leaders/biogs/WLE0714b.htm>

'The Gang Buster', *Sydney Morning Herald*, 30 May 2010, accessed online 4 October 2016, <http://www.smh.com.au/nsw/the-gang-buster- 20100529-wmbk.html>

van Krieken, Robert, 'State intervention, welfare and the social construction of girlhood in Australian history', TASA Sociology Conference, Flinders University, Adelaide, 10–13 December 1992, <ses.library.usyd.edu.au/ bitstream/2123/902/1/Girlhood.pdf>

Yarwood, A.T., 'Marsden, Samuel (1765–1838)', *Australian Dictionary of Biography*, National Centre of Biography, Australian National University, published first in hardcopy 1967, accessed online 11 January 2017, <http://adb.anu.edu.au/biography/marsden-samuel-2433>

Thesis

Stella, Leonie, 'Policing Women: Women's Police in Western Australia 1917– 1943', Honours thesis, Murdoch University, 1990.

Acknowledgements

THIS BOOK IS DEDICATED TO LARRY WRITER: INSPIRATION, friend and one of my favourite writers. Larry contacted me after I published my book on Kate Leigh and thanked me for bringing her to life. He then told me I was the best person to tell Lillian Armfield's story. From that first, exciting conversation in a café in Sydney, the Lillian project developed further and grew into a book. Larry's encouragement has truly made this book possible. Thank you, Larry.

The publication of this book would not have been possible without the support of Matthew Kelly, non-fiction publisher at Hachette Australia. Matthew appreciated the importance of Lillian's story and took it to his colleagues with an enthusiastic conviction that Lillian's unique place in Australian history deserves wider recognition. This book is a team effort and I have thoroughly enjoyed working with everyone at Hachette Australia. Many thanks to the copyeditor, Deonie Fiford, for really bringing out more of the stories. You edited with heart and soul and I appreciate it so much. Thanks also to Karen Ward, senior editor at Hachette Australia.

Lillian's nephew Norm O'Brien and his wife, Eva, provided me with Armfield family details and stories, all of which made me aware early on that while Lillian was a trailblazing member of the NSW Police Force, she was also a daughter, sister, cousin and aunt. A writer depends on being able to bring people to life in the stories that are being told on a page. Without the opportunity to meet Lillian Armfield, I am grateful to have had access to family photographs. Thank you, Norm and Eva. Your generosity in contributing to the telling of Lillian's story is much appreciated.

As with all my work, I am appreciative of the assistance given to me by archivists, library staff and curators who helped me to trace records relating to Lillian Armfield and Australian policing. I would like to thank staff at the State Records of New South Wales and the State Records Office of Western Australia for their help with requests for records and pointing me in the right direction to find related material. I am also thankful to the support of staff at the Justice and Police Museum in Sydney. A visit to the museum always reinvigorates my interest in crime in Sydney.

My thanks, as always, to the family and friends who support me through my writing, lecturing, parenting and general 'adulting'. It's getting easier – the adulting part – but I couldn't do it without your kindness, humour and understanding.

This isn't the first biography of Lillian Armfield and so I am also appreciative of the work of Vince Kelly. A journalist and author, Kelly sat down with Lillian Armfield and their conversations resulted in Kelly's 1961 book, *Rugged Angel: The Amazing Career of Policewoman Lillian Armfield*. It's time now for an updated account of Lillian's life. Vince Kelly's book is an important contribution to the telling of Lillian's story but it focuses on her policing career. I wanted to write a book that considered her whole life and included her family story, along with reflections on the legacy of her work in the many decades that have passed since her retirement and death. I think it's also important that a woman's perspective is offered in the writing of Lillian's story.

I wish I could have talked to Lillian – there are so many questions that I have for her – but I hope I have done her story justice. I expect she would be pleased I have gone from writing about Kate Leigh – clearly on the wrong side of the law – to now telling a police story about eastern Sydney crime. I feel very blessed to have been given the opportunity to write books on two powerful and unique Australian women.

Places can be just as important to the writing of a book as people so there are three locations I would like to single out and acknowledge for contributing the perfect space for me to write in. In Western Australia, Ned's Café in Nedlands is my favourite place to escape to when I've dropped the kids at day care and school and have a little time before work commitments. I have been coming to Ned's for the past eight years, sitting in the back corner typing and enjoying the welcoming atmosphere of the place. When I really need to escape and write I travel out to West Toodyay, an hour east of Perth. Surrounded by eucalypt trees and watching kangaroos and bobtail lizards explore the land around me, I appreciate the combination of family and writing time.

Every visit to Sydney is a reminder of the impact that living in Darlinghurst and Surry Hills has had on me, personally and professionally. I've always loved Australian history and have taught it at university for many years, but living in Sydney brought so many of my favourite stories to life. Of the many places that have shaped my creativity and writing in Sydney, Trinity Bar in Surry Hills is the closest to my heart. It was my date night spot with my husband before we had children and is the only place I've ever tasted chicken curry close to what my mum made while we were growing up. The upstairs part of the building is now a restaurant with old photographs depicting the Razor Wars and it is there I have sat writing some of Lillian's story.

My writing is sustained by the love and support of family life with three little boys and an understanding, devoted husband. I love you so much, Jack, Lawson and Riley, and thank you for the happy craziness of our daily lives. To Tony, I thank you for the balance you bring to my life amidst all the angst, self-doubting, creative obsessions and excitement that goes with being married to a writer. I love you.

Index